JOURNEY

Shikoku Pilgrimage

Craig McLachlan, Jessica Korteman

TAKAMATSU
START
P44
TOKUSHIMA

SHIKOKU PILGRIMAGE
KŌCHI
AMA
へんろ道
へんろ道

Join 1200 years of *henro* (pilgrims) who have walked around Japan's fourth-largest island in the footsteps of Kōbō Daishi, who, according to legend, achieved enlightenment on Shikoku. While most pilgrimages around the world have a specific site as their goal, the Shikoku pilgrimage is a circle – never-ending, just like the search for enlightenment. It's a mighty journey of 1200km and 88 temples – make that 89, as pilgrims walk back from Temple 88 to Temple 1 to complete the loop.

THE 88 TEMPLES

1. Ryōzen-ji (霊山寺)
2. Gokuraku-ji (極楽寺)
3. Konsen-ji (金泉寺)
4. Dainichi-ji (大日寺)
5. Jizō-ji (地蔵寺)
6. Anraku-ji (安楽寺)
7. Jūraku-ji (十楽寺)
8. Kumadani-ji (熊谷寺)
9. Hōrin-ji (法輪寺)
10. Kirihata-ji (切幡寺)
11. Fujii-dera (藤井寺)
12. Shōsan-ji (焼山寺)
13. Dainichi-ji (大日寺)
14. Jōraku-ji (常楽寺)
15. Awa Kokubun-ji (阿波国分寺)
16. Kannon-ji (観音寺)
17. Ido-ji (井戸寺)
18. Onzan-ji (恩山寺)
19. Tatsue-ji (立江寺)
20. Kakurin-ji (鶴林寺)
21. Tairyū-ji (太龍寺)
22. Byōdō-ji (平等寺)
23. Yakuō-ji (薬王寺)
24. Hotsumisaki-ji (最御崎寺)
25. Shinshō-ji (津照寺)
26. Kongōchō-ji (金剛頂寺)
27. Kōnomine-ji (神峯寺)
28. Dainichi-ji (大日寺)
29. Tosa Kokubun-ji (土佐国分寺)
30. Zenraku-ji (善楽寺)
31. Chikurin-ji (竹林寺)
32. Zenjibu-ji (禅師峰寺)
33. Sekkei-ji (雪蹊寺)
34. Tanema-ji (種間寺)
35. Kiyotaki-ji (清滝寺)
36. Shōryū-ji (青龍寺)
37. Iwamoto-ji (岩本寺)
38. Kongōfuku-ji (金剛福寺)
39. Enkō-ji (延光寺)
40. Kanjizai-ji (観自在寺)
41. Ryūkō-ji (龍光寺)
42. Butsumoku-ji (佛木寺)
43. Meiseki-ji (明石寺)
44. Daihō-ji (大寶寺)
45. Iwaya-ji (岩屋寺)
46. Jōruri-ji (浄瑠璃寺)
47. Yasaka-ji (八坂寺)
48. Sairin-ji (西林寺)
49. Jōdo-ji (浄土寺)
50. Hanta-ji (繁多寺)
51. Ishite-ji (石手寺)
52. Taisan-ji (太山寺)
53. Enmyō-ji (圓明寺)
54. Enmei-ji (延命寺)
55. Nankōbō (南光坊)
56. Taisan-ji (泰山寺)
57. Eifuku-ji (栄福寺)
58. Senyū-ji (仙遊寺)
59. Iyo Kokubun-ji (伊予国分寺)
60. Yokomine-ji (横峰寺)
61. Kōon-ji (香園寺)
62. Hōju-ji (宝寿寺)
63. Kichijō-ji (吉祥寺)
64. Maegami-ji (前神寺)
65. Sankaku-ji (三角寺)
66. Unpen-ji (雲辺寺)
67. Daikō-ji (大興寺)
68. Jinnein (神恵院)
69. Kannon-ji (観音寺)
70. Motoyama-ji (本山寺)
71. Iyadani-ji (弥谷寺)
72. Mandara-ji (曼荼羅寺)
73. Shusshaka-ji (出釈迦寺)
74. Kōyama-ji (甲山寺)
75. Zentsū-ji (善通寺)
76. Konzō-ji (金倉寺)
77. Dōryū-ji (道隆寺)
78. Gōshō-ji (郷照寺)
79. Tennō-ji (天皇寺)
80. Sanuki Kokubun-ji (讃岐国分寺)
81. Shiromine-ji (白峯寺)
82. Negoro-ji (根香寺)
83. Ichinomiya-ji (一宮寺)
84. Yashima-ji (屋島寺)
85. Yakuri-ji (八栗寺)
86. Shido-ji (志度寺)
87. Nagao-ji (長尾寺)
88. Ōkubo-ji (大窪寺)

Contents

Plan Your Trip

Go to p30 for the full route map

The Walk

Statue, Temple 9: Hōrin-ji (p54)

Toolkit

INSIGHT ESSAYS

Previous page:
Temple 75: Zentsū-ji (p203)

CRAIG MCLACHLAN/LONELY PLANET

SANGA PARK/SHUTTERSTOCK

My Shikoku Pilgrimage

Craig McLachlan @yuricraig

I was inspired by reading Oliver Statler's *Japanese Pilgrimage*, so set forth and walked the pilgrimage in 1995, two years after walking the length of Japan. It was just the experience I'd hoped for – an opportunity to contemplate life while my wife, Yuriko, and our sons spent time with her family in Osaka. I've driven the full pilgrimage twice since. I have always been happy with decisions made while on the pilgrimage, and I love these words attributed to Kōbō Daishi: 'Do not just walk in the footsteps of the men of old, seek what they sought.'

A Kiwi with wanderlust, Craig has been writing Japan guidebooks for Lonely Planet for over 25 years. He's covered Shikoku for six editions of Japan, *written a book on the pilgrimage, led tours to Shikoku, and is a regular there, with family living in Ehime.*

Craig at Temple 58: Senyū-ji (p179)

CRAIG MCLACHLAN/LONELY PLANET

MY BEST TEMPLES

Temple 66: Unpen-ji

The 500 mesmerising life-size *rakan* statues make this is one of my favourite places in Japan. p196

Temple 45: Iwaya-ji

Hanging cliffside above the valley, deep in the mountains; you can feel the deep spirituality. p143

Temple 38: Kongōfuku-ji

Remote and mystical at Shikoku's great southern cape of Ashizuri-misaki. p122

JESSICA KORTEMAN/LONELY PLANET

Jessica at Temple 23: Yakuō-ji (p76)

Jessica Korteman @jessicakorteman

If there's one thing I know for certain about the Shikoku pilgrimage, it's that no matter what you think your journey will look like, the pilgrimage has a grander plan for you. There's something very peaceful about surrendering to all the things you can't control (hello typhoons!) and simply taking each day one footstep and temple at a time. The pilgrimage for me is made even more memorable by the *osettai* (pilgrim hospitality) culture, the invisible island-wide safety net that spontaneously appears and guides you in some of the most unexpected ways.

Jessica is an Australian writer specialising in Japanese travel and culture. She's been exploring Shikoku, both on and off the pilgrim trail, for the better part of a decade. Jessica wrote the city guides and Toolkit.

MY BEST TEMPLES

Temple 37: Iwamoto-ji

Colourful murals make it unlike the others. Stay at the temple lodgings and participate in a morning *goma* fire ritual. p118

Temple 75: Zentsū-ji

Don't miss the Kaidan Meguri. p203

Kim Kahan @kimkaan

Kim moved to Japan for one year in 2017 and never left. She writes and translates, mainly on travel and culture, and currently lives between the city of Tokyo and the mountains in Nagano. Seeking out *hitou* (secret hot springs) is one of her favourite things to do.

Rie Miyoshi @trailmixr

Rie is a writer, photographer and videographer based in Yokohama, Japan. After living in Hawaii, she returned home and spent more than a decade working in adventure travel media. In her free time, you'll likely find her swimming, travelling with her husband and three energetic kids, or writing and illustrating children's books that introduce Japan's landscapes and culture to young English-speaking readers. Her Japan must-haves? A good onsen soak, tofu in all its forms, and deep winter powder.

Kathryn Wortley @japanadventurer

As a British, Japan-based travel writer with a passion for exploring and a curiosity for new places, I'm always on the lookout for my next adventure. I love to discover destinations by trying experiences, sampling regional cuisine, engaging with local people and learning about daily life. With Japan as my specialty, I've visited all of its 47 prefectures, from subarctic Hokkaidō to subtropical Okinawa, and continue to travel nationwide to uncover the best of what each place has to offer in each season.

James Gulliver Hancock @gulliverhancock

James is a well-travelled illustrator known for his playful illustration style. His obsession with drawing everything in the world has seen him work around the globe, with his work appearing on everything from train carriages to books, clothing, ceramics, boardgames, billboards and animations.

James drew the illustrated map at the start of this book.

Temple 47: Yasaka-ji (p162)
SHIKOKU 4K/SHUTTERSTOCK

Four Provinces

Shikoku is written 四国, meaning four provinces, and pilgrims will be walking through all four as they journey around Japan's fourth-largest island.

IN OLDEN DAYS, Shikoku was made up of the four provinces of Awa, Tosa, Iyo and Sanuki. With the Meiji Restoration of the emperor in 1868, however, a new system was introduced and Shikoku's four provinces became the four prefectures of Tokushima-ken, Kōchi-ken, Ehime-ken and Kagawa-ken (-*ken* means 'prefecture').

Old habits die hard though and *henro* (pilgrims) will still see the old provincial names in common use on Shikoku. Tokushima's famous dance festival is Awa-odori, Kōchi is home to the Tosa breed of dog, Ehime's regional bank is Iyo Ginkō and Kagawa's legendary udon noodles are *Sanuki-udon*.

Tokushima (Previously Awa)

In the east, Tokushima Prefecture is home to Temple 1: Ryōzen-ji, the first 23 temples of the pilgrimage, and in its far western corner, Temple 66: Unpen-ji. Its capital is Tokushima city (p34), with a population of 260,000, home of Awa-odori, the famous summer dance festival, for which the city is renowned all around Japan.

Tokushima received a major boost in 1998 with the completion of Akashi Kaikyō-Ōhashi, which, combined with the bridge Ōnaruto-kyō, created a road link via Awaji-shima to the Kansai metropolis, based around Osaka. This brought Tokushima much closer to the mainland, providing a much-needed economic stimulus. Of particular interest to pilgrims, Tokushima city is linked to Wakayama city by Nankai Ferry (two hours), good for visiting Kōya-san before or after the pilgrimage.

There's fertile agricultural land in the Yoshino-gawa valley, but the rest of the prefecture is extremely mountainous and inaccessible. In the west, the Iya Valley's growing fame is due to that inaccessibility.

Kōchi (Previously Tosa)

By far the largest in area of Shikoku's prefectures, Kōchi covers the south of the island, from well east of the great cape Muroto-misaki

SEAN PAVONE/SHUTTERSTOCK

Original Castles

Matsuyama-jō (p150)

This stunning castle sits high above the central city and can be clambered all over.

Kōchi-jō (p99)

Immaculately maintained castle and grounds in the middle of Kōchi city.

Uwajima-jō (p137)

This smaller castle in southwest Ehime is a beauty with coastal views.

Marugame-jō (p206)

Henro walk right past this castle featuring amazing stone walls in Kagawa.

Left: Matsuyama-jō (p150)
Right: Kōchi city (p96)

SEAN PAVONE/SHUTTERSTOCK

in the east to well west of the other great southern cape, Ashizuri-misaki, in the west. Over one-third of the pilgrimage distance is through Kōchi, yet it's home to only 16 of the 88 temples.

Long regarded as one of the wildest and most remote parts of Japan, Kōchi is cut off by the mountains from Shikoku's other three prefectures, facing the not very pacific Pacific Ocean to the south. This has historically produced a tough local populace of survivors, who, through the centuries, were not particularly encouraging to pilgrims passing through. Thi is not an issue these days though, and *henro* can expect a warm welcome in modern-day Kōchi Prefecture.

The capital is vibrant, bustling Kōchi city (p96), with a population of 330,000.

Ehime (Previously Iyo)

In the west, and second largest of Shikoku's prefectures, Ehime is home to the island's largest city, Matsuyama (population 510,000; p146) and 27 of the pilgrimage temples. Ehime sprawls around the western coast, remote and rugged in the southwest, populated and industrial in its northeast. The only large areas of flat land are around Matsuyama and along the prefecture's northern coastline.

Ehime's economy got a jump in 1999 with the opening of the third bridge system linking Shikoku to Honshū. The 70km-long Shimanami Kaidō links Imabari on Shikoku with Onomichi in Hiroshima Prefecture and features bridges connecting six Inland Sea islands along the way. The Shimanami Kaidō has become synonymous with cycling, with a designated cycle path

VINNIE HIROOKA/SHUTTERSTOCK

SHŌDOSHIMA 88 TEMPLE PILGRIMAGE

Officially part of Kagawa Prefecture and the second-largest island in the Inland Sea (Seto-nai-kai), Shōdoshima is home to a shorter version of the Shikoku pilgrimage. The 150km, seven- to 10-day walk claims links to Kōbō Daishi (p24), who is said to have stopped off here when travelling between Shikoku and Kyoto. Check out Shōdoshima Pilgrimage *(reijokai.com)* and the Facebook page 'Shōdoshima 88 temple walkers'.

USEFUL WEBSITES

shikoku-tourism.com
The official site of Shikoku Tourism has a lot of useful information on the 88 Temple Pilgrimage.

discovertokushima.net
Discover Tokushima; everything you need to know about Shikoku's eastern prefecture and plenty on the pilgrimage.

visitkochijapan.com
Kōchi Prefecture's excellent website has a page dedicated to the pilgrimage.

KAZU8/SHUTTERSTOCK

Seto Ōhashi bridge (p206)

making this the best-known cycling tourism destination in Japan.

Matsuyama is a joy to explore, especially its immaculately preserved feudal castle and Dōgo Onsen, one of the top hot springs resorts in Japan.

Kagawa (Previously Sanuki)

Shikoku's northern prefecture of Kagawa is not only the smallest of the four on Shikoku, but also the smallest of all Japan's 47 prefectures. Its warm weather is due to being protected by Shikoku's central mountains to the south and the mountains of western Honshū, across the Inland Sea, to the north. Kagawa is home to the last 22 of the pilgrimage temples and has the lively port city of Takamatsu (population 420,000; p210) as its capital. The 'art islands' in the Inland Sea are easily accessed from here.

Kagawa benefited immensely from the opening of the Seto Ōhashi bridge in 1988, Shikoku's first bridge to the mainland, which still provides the island's only rail link to Honshū. The bridge revolutionised life on Shikoku, allowing residents to not only take trains to Okayama city, but also to access to Honshū's shinkansen (bullet train) station there, bringing them much closer to the rest of Japan.

visitehimejapan.com
Visit Ehime Japan is Ehime Prefecture's inspiring official tourism website.

my-kagawa.jp
Kagawa Prefecture's official tourism website introduces the last 23 temples on the pilgrimage.

88shikokuhenro.jp
Website of Shikoku 88 Sacred Sites (Inc), operating since 1958; info on each of the 88 temples.

Temples Galore

There's a huge variety of temples on Shikoku. Some perch on mountaintops, some lie along the coast, some sit within valleys or urban areas, while others are found at remote weather-beaten capes.

WHILE THESE DAYS, the focus of the pilgrimage is very much on the 88 temples and collecting the temple stamps, in the days of old it was more about surviving and overcoming the adversities faced when walking between the temples.

The 88 Temples

Most of the temples on the pilgrimage were founded in the 7th and 8th centuries and were already there when Kōbō Daishi (774–835; also sometimes Kūkai), who is said to have established the pilgrimage, was active in the late 8th and early 9th century.

All of the temples have a basic layout. *Henro* enter through a main gate, in most cases a *niōmon*, with two fierce warriors called *Niō*, who are there to protect the temple. Inside the gate there is a wash basin, in which to cleanse hands and mouth, plus a bell tower where *henro* can ring the bell once to announce their arrival to Kōbō Daishi. The *hondō* (main hall) enshrines the statue of the main deity of the temple, while the Daishi-dō (Daishi Hall) holds a statue of Kōbō Daishi. The *nōkyō-jō* (temple office) is usually open 8am to 5pm and is where *henro* go to get their temple stamp after completing their *mairi* (the rituals of their visit).

Bigger and more prosperous temples have a lot more halls and buildings, a slew of statues in the gardens and possibly even a multistory pagoda.

Vulnerable Buildings

The buildings *henro* see today are highly unlikely to be the ones that were around in the Daishi's time. The bane of old wooden temple buildings has always been fire, whether lit accidentally or on purpose. That lovely pond full of carp, such as

Entrance, Temple 51: Ishite-ji (p165)
CRAIG MCLACHLAN/LONELY PLANET

at Temple 1: Ryōzen-ji (p48), may be aesthetically pleasing, but it also has a practical purpose as a water source for fighting fires. Temple buildings have burned down with great regularity over the last 13 centuries.

These fires haven't always been accidental. The Tosa (Kōchi) warlord Chōsokabe Motochika (1539–99), after wresting control of his own province, set about conquering the rest of Shikoku by using the intimidating tactic of burning down temples to subjugate the local lords and populace. After burning his way through Iyo, Sanuki and Awa he gained control in 1583, only to have it taken away two years later by Toyotomi Hideyoshi, who arrived in 1585 from Honshū with 113,000 men. During the campaign, Toyotomi's men burned temples too.

Another tough period for the temples was the early Meiji era from 1868, when Shintō was declared the national religion under the emperor and a policy of *shinbutsu-bunri* (p93) was instigated to separate Shintō and Buddhism. The two religions had been close ever since Buddhism came to Japan in the mid-6th century, but suddenly there was a wave of anti-Buddhist violence and numerous Buddhist temples were destroyed or damaged. Seven of Kōchi's 16 pilgrimage temples were abandoned at this time.

Rebuilt & Relocated

Many of the 88 temples have been relocated and rebuilt over the centuries. After being razed at the hands of Chōsokabe in 1582, Temple 9: Hōrin-ji (p54) moved out of the mountains to the plain and was rebuilt in its present location in the 1640s. Temple 56: Taisan-ji (p177)

RICHIE CHAN/SHUTTERSTOCK

PAGODAS

One of the most noticeable of temple buildings is the pagoda, especially the *gojū-no-tō* (five-tiered pagoda) representing the five elements: earth, water, fire, wind and space. These sacred towers also symbolise Buddha's enlightenment and the spiritual journey. *Henro* will see a number of pagodas on Shikoku. The most spectacular are at Temple 75: Zentsū-ji (p203), Temple 70: Motoyama-ji (p199) and Temple 31: Chikurin-ji (pictured above; p107).

HENRO HOMEWORK

Japanese Pilgrimage

Oliver Statler's 1983 book on the pilgrimage fills in the blanks on the history and meaning of the Shikoku pilgrimage in vivid detail.

Shikoku Japan 88 Route Guide

Updated annually, this small, light map and info guide, published by Buyodo Co. Ltd, is perfect for taking on the pilgrimage.

Henro Helper app

First released in 2024 and updated regularly, this app makes navigation easy while on the road; shows various route options between temples.

AMEHIME/SHUTTERSTOCK

Torii, Temple 41: Ryūkō-ji (p136)

SHINTŌ & BUDDHISM TOGETHER

When Buddhism arrived in Japan in the mid-6th century, it joined Shintō in a long syncretic relationship. The two complemented each other and saw advantages in coexistence and alliance; in the people's minds, they mingled and merged. The Meiji Restoration tried to 'cleanse' Shintō of Buddhism, but with no long-lasting success. *Henro* will see signs of the close relationship at many temples. The main gate at Temple 41: Ryūkō-ji (p136) is actually a *torii* (entrance gate to a Shintō shrine).

was relocated from its mountaintop home to the flatlands below, near Imabari city. Temple 62: Hōju-ji (p185) was moved 100m in 1921 to make way for new railway tracks. A number of other temples relocated looking to become more accessible to worshippers.

Other temples stayed up on the mountains and have used new technology to make it easier for worshippers to get to them. These days, Temple 21: Tairyū-ji (p73) and Temple 66: Unpen-ji (p196) can both be reached by aerial ropeway, while Temple 85: Yakuri-ji can be reached by a funicular cable car.

Every temple is different and each has its own story.

The Inner Sanctuaries

The 88 temples have *okunoin* (奥之院), an inner sanctuary that is usually detached from the main temple. Visiting them isn't required to complete the pilgrimage, but there are a few, in particular, that *henro* might consider. Kōbō Daishi wrote that, at age 19, he performed ascetic practice at what is now the *okunoin* of Temple 12: Shōsan-ji (p57), high above the main temple, and at Temple 21: Tairyū-ji, where the Sitting Kūkai statue (p75) is now located.

The *okunoin* at Temple 73: Shusshaka-ji, high on the mountain Gahaishi, is where legend says that the boy Mao threw himself off the mountain, crying 'If I am called to save the people,

Shikoku 88 Ohenro Pilgrimage

Facebook page with some 15,000 members sharing experiences and advice to potential pilgrims; up-to-date info from *henro* on the road.

88shikokuhenro.jp

Official website of the Shikoku 88 Temple Pilgrimage, introducing the pilgrimage, background information and each of the 88 sacred sites.

henrohouse.jp

Website of Henro House, with over 50 affordable lodgings around Shikoku that can be reserved online in English.

save me, O Buddha! If I am not, let me die!' A company of angels appeared, who caught the boy in their robes, carrying him to safety. This is now the *okunoin* for Temple 73, but was previously the temple itself, which was moved down to the valley to make it more accessible to worshippers.

Henro who travel to Kōya-san (p235) will visit the *okunoin* there, as this is the mausoleum where Kōbō Daishi is said to be resting.

Extra Temples: Bekkaku

There are many temples and sacred sites on Shikoku that are historically related to the pilgrimage, but are not listed in the 88 temples. They are known as *bangai*, meaning 'outside the number'. Twenty of the *bangai* organised themselves into an official group in the late 1960s and became known as the *Bekkaku (別格; bekkaku.com),* or extra distinguished sites. Adding 20 to 88, the result is 108, a significant number in Buddhism said to represent the 108 earthly desires, delusions or defilements humans must overcome to achieve enlightenment.

While visiting the *Bekkaku* is not required, some are on the pilgrim path. Bekkaku 8: Eitoku-ji is at the Sleeping Kūkai statue (p139), while Bekkaku 9: Monju-in (p162) is at the home of Emon Saburō, said to have been the first *henro*.

Others require a detour. Bekkaku 17: Kanno-ji (p203) is at Mannō-ike, the artificial reservoir 13km southeast of Temple 75: Zentsū-ji, where Kōbō Daishi is credited with excellent civil engineering skills by overseeing renovations in 821, after the banks ruptured due to flooding.

Most first-time walking pilgrims are happy with visiting the 88 sacred temples. The *Bekkaku* have become popular additions for those who go back to walk the pilgrimage a second time or more.

Stone bridge, Temple 75: Zentsū-ji (p203)

AMEHIME/SHUTTERSTOCK

FROM LEFT: CRAIG MCLACHLAN/LONELY PLANET, AMEHIME/
SHUTTERSTOCK, UNTERWEGS/SHUTTERSTOCK

❶ Temple 1: Ryōzen-ji, p48

The first of the pilgrimage temples holds great significance to *henro* as this is where the 1200km journey begins; pick up everything you need at the pilgrim shop.

❷ Temple 21: Tairyū-ji, p73

This mountaintop temple complex is simply stunning, complemented by the Sitting Kūkai statue at the place where Kōbō Daishi is said to have performed ascetic practice for 100 days.

❸ Muroto-misaki, p86

This first of Shikoku's great southern capes is where Kōbō Daishi is said to have achieved enlightenment at age 19; see the caves and visit Temple 24: Hotsumisaki-ji (pictured) high above.

FROM LEFT: CRAIG MCLACHLAN/LONELY PLANET, CRAIG MCLACHLAN/
LONELY PLANET, BRESTER IRINA/SHUTTERSTOCK

❹ Ashizuri-misaki, p124

The second of Kōchi's great southern capes, this is where the devout sailed forth, in search of Kannon's Pure Land in the South; Temple 38: Kongōfuku-ji (pictured) is captivating.

❺ Temple 66: Unpen-ji, p196

The Temple in the Clouds sits at 900m and is the highest on the pilgrimage; the 500 life-size *rakan* statues (the disciples of Buddha) are totally mesmerising and shouldn't be missed.

❻ Temple 88: Ōkubo-ji, p231

The last of the 88 temples sits high in the mountains of Kagawa Prefecture and is appropriately venerated; pilgrims stay focused to return to Temple 1 to close the circle of Shikoku.

Meet the Locals

The people of Shikoku are incredibly proud of their pilgrimage. There's only one requirement for *henro* in their eyes and that's to treat it with respect.

WHILE EVERYONE IS welcome on the Shikoku pilgrimage, regardless of religious affiliation, it's important to remember that this is a religious journey with a long history, not simply a long-distance hiking trail or stamp rally.

We Two, Pilgrims Together

Remember the words *Dōgyō Ninin* – We Two, Pilgrims Together – no-one walks alone, as Kōbō Daishi is always by their side. 同行二人 *(Dōgyō Ninin)* is written on pilgrims' sedge hats and on their *kongō-zue* (walking sticks), considered the physical embodiment of Kōbō Daishi's spirit. At times, *henro* may feel as if they are out there alone, but if they're walking in the spirit of the pilgrimage, then they're walking with the Daishi.

The Custom of Osettai

Unique to the Shikoku pilgrimage is *osettai*, the giving of gifts such as drinks, food and even money to assist a *henro* in achieving their goal. Giving *osettai* is seen as a way for the giver to participate in the *henro's* pilgrimage, of joining in what they perceive to be a meritorious endeavour. Remember, pilgrims are walking with the Daishi himself, so giving to *henro* also has a religious value to the giver.

The first time it happens, *henro* tend to be surprised and deeply moved. It may involve a can of ice coffee being handed out the window of a car, or an old woman crossing the road to press a coin into a *henro's* hand, or even a walking *henro* being stopped roadside and offered a place to sleep for the night. Often, it is the offer of a ride to the next temple.

In all cases – except the offer of a ride to a committed walking *henro* – the pilgrim should accept graciously. Traditionally, the giver says *'Osettai shimasu!'* and the *henro,* accepting the *osettai,* responds *'Arigatō gozaimasu!'.* Traditionally, *henro* pass over an *osamefuda* (name slip) with their details to everyone who helps them on their journey; this is not expected from foreign *henro* these days, but if you've got an *osamefuda* at hand, passing it over will be met with much appreciation.

Henro driving the pilgrimage seldom receive *osettai,* but walking pilgrims, especially if they are recognised as such from afar in their pilgrim gear, often find themselves receiving *osettai* from all sorts of people they meet.

Some pilgrims grow used to receiving *osettai* and their feelings of gratitude begin to fade – try not to be that *henro.*

CRAIG MCLACHLAN/LONELY PLANET

HENRO

A *henro* is a pilgrim and if you take part in the pilgrimage, you'll be a *henro,* too. You'll also see this word as *ohenro* and *ohenro-san.* The *o* and *san* are honorifics, used in the Japanese language when talking about someone else, never when talking about yourself. *Henro* is written 遍路 in kanji and へんろ in the phonetic hiragana script. You'll walk on *henro-michi* (pilgrim paths) and you may meet car or bus *henro* along the way.

Osettai, Temple 46: Jōruri-ji (p144)

Shikoku Cuisine

A mountainous island sliced by river valleys with fertile plains and surrounded by the sea, Shikoku has an abundance of sources for an astounding variety of cuisines.

JAPAN'S FOURTH-LARGEST ISLAND may be surrounded by the sea, but it's tucked into a pocket of the country, protected to the west by Kyūshū, to the north by mainland Honshū and to the east by Honshū's Kii Peninsula. Only the south is open and exposed to the wild Pacific Ocean.

Seafood is varied, due to differing conditions found between the wild Pacific Ocean and the protected Inland Sea, and the island's diverse geography allows for high-quality rice and vegetable production in the river valleys and on coastal plains, as well as game meat sourced in the mountains, and tasty fruits and nuts grown in valleys and along the coasts.

Shikoku's four prefectures have each developed their own culinary style thanks to local geographic and climatic characteristics, along with their unique traditions and histories.

Tokushima

Shikoku's eastern prefecture, bordered by the Inland Sea to the north and the Pacific Ocean to the south, has a mild climate with warm summers and cool winters. Quality rice is grown in the fertile Yoshino-gawa valley, while fresh seafood includes sea bream and abalone. *Sudachi* is a citrus fruit used for flavouring, while Naruto Kintoki are top-class sweet potatoes. Two popular dishes are *Tokushima ramen,* a noodle soup with rich pork-bone broth topped with a raw egg, and *handa somen,* a fine white noodle dish with a delicate texture and smoothness.

Kōchi

The island's southern prefecture, Kōchi, faces the Pacific and gets plenty of rainfall. Kōchi is celebrated for its lively culinary scene and the must-try here is *katsuo-tataki,* bonito lightly seared over burning rice straw, and seasoned with ponzu or salt and garlic. Premium crops include *yuzu,* a fragrant citrus used for flavouring, and ginger, known for its spicy,

MASAYUKI NAKAYA/LONELY PLANET

BEST EATS

Awaya, Tokushima city (p36)

Lively ramen restaurant and bar; try the signature in-house Awaya-soba served with *sudachi* (lime).

Hirome Ichiba, Kōchi city (p98)

Vibrant (often chaotic) market hall where locals and tourists converge for spirited banter, drinks and tasty local dishes.

Iyo Shokudō Otora, Matsuyama (p148)

Near Dōgo Onsen Station; traditional Japanese restaurant serving sea bream rice and other local specialities.

Uehara-ya, Takamatsu (p212)

Try the delectable *kake-udon* with lightly boiled noodles, and *dashi* broth derived from sardines and soy sauce.

Left: *Katsuo-tataki* (bonito with rice); Below: *Tokushima ramen* (noodle soup with pork-bone broth and egg)

SANAMOO/SHUTTERSTOCK

refreshing taste. Greenhouses grow vegetables such as tomatoes, peppers and cucumbers, and Kōchi is Japan's biggest *nasu* (eggplant) producer. Kōchi is also renowned for its crisp, refreshing sake, made in 18 breweries around the prefecture.

Ehime

Ehime, in the west, is focused on the seafood of the Inland Sea and Uwakai, the sea off the southwest of the island. The prefecture is Japan's leader in aquaculture and top sea bream, yellowtail and bluefin tuna are produced here. Ehime is also Japan's largest producer of citrus, generically known locally as *mikan,* although that covers a surprising variety of types. Don't miss trying *jakoten,* a type of deep-fried fish cake, and *taimeshi,* succulent sea bream atop a bed of steamed rice.

Kagawa

Bordering the Inland Sea, Kagawa may be *Udon-ken,* and *henro* are likely to be slurping noodles on a daily basis, but there's also a lot more happening on the culinary front. Chicken-on-the-bone, a spicy dish of baked crispy chicken thigh, is a speciality originating in Marugame that has taken Kagawa by storm. Offshore, Shōdoshima is the birthplace of olive cultivation in Japan; olive-fed *hamachi* (yellowtail) and beef are both flavourful and unique to Kagawa, while Shōdoshima's thin white *somen* noodles are also popular. *Sanuki-udon* is, however, the culinary icon of Kagawa.

SAID KARLSSON/LONELY PLANET

UDON-KEN

A prefecture has to be serious about udon (wheat flour noodles; pictured above) to have the nickname *udon-ken;* you can't walk down the street anywhere in Kagawa without stumbling upon a noodle shop. Look for the places with udon written in Japanese (うどん) or the restaurants with long lines out front. There are over 400 udon restaurants in Japan's smallest prefecture and they're proudly serving *Sanuki-udon,* using the old provincial name for the prefecture.

HENRO STAPLES

Noodles

Pilgrims tend to eat a lot of noodles, be they soba, udon or ramen; the best in fast, cheap eats on Shikoku.

Onigiri

Hard-to-beat riceballs for a *henro* on the go; tasty, cheap, filling and available at all convenience stores.

Pan

Yes, *pan* is Japanese for bread, and bakeries produce an astounding array of options, perfect for *henro* on the move.

Taimeshi (sea bream with steamed rice)

ATSUSHI HIRAO/SHUTTERSTOCK

A History of the Shikoku Pilgrimage

The origins of the pilgrimage are steeped in legend associated with the great Kōbō Daishi (774–835; also sometimes Kūkai), who, it is said, after achieving enlightenment on Shikoku, chose the 88 sacred places and established the pilgrimage. There is, however, no evidence to support this.

Early On

From the mid-6th century, when Buddhism arrived in Japan, it was thought that the entrance to heaven was in a wild, mystical southern land across the sea, and Shikoku, in those days, fit that description.

Before Kōbō Daishi, two religious zealots laid the groundwork for the pilgrimage. En no Gyōja (634–701) was the founder of Shugendō, a religion combining traditional Shintō and imported Buddhist beliefs, based on demanding ascetic practice in mountains and on the coasts. He trained in his mystical discipline on Shikoku and preached to the common people. Gyōki (665–749) also travelled the country, preaching Buddhism and helping the poor. He is said to have established 37 of the present pilgrimage's 88 temples.

Kōbō Daishi, born on Shikoku, was a charismatic figure who carried out ascetic practice on the island and, so the legend goes, achieved

MID-6TH CENTURY
Buddhism arrives in Japan from Korea

634–701
En no Gyōja establishes Shugendō

665–749
Wandering holy man Gyōki preaches to commoners

774
Kōbō Daishi is born as Mao, at what is now Temple 75: Zentsū-ji

enlightenment here. After studying in China, he returned to Japan, founded the Shingon (True Word) school of Buddhism, and established Shingon's mountaintop base at Kōya-san in present-day Wakayama Prefecture. He is also credited with creating the phonetic kana writing system that made it possible for common people to read and write, and with being an excellent civil engineer, calligrapher and poet.

The Legend Grows

When he died, Kōbō Daishi passed on his strong belief in ascetic practice and preaching to the common people, which was embraced by wandering holy men. They started making pilgrimages to Kōya-san to visit Kōbō Daishi's mausoleum, then to Shikoku, to sacred places that were important during his life. These included where he was born, at what is now Temple 75: Zentsū-ji; the mountain peaks at what are now Temple 12: Shōsan-ji and Temple 21: Tairyū-ji, where he wrote that he performed ascetic practice; and the caves at Muroto-misaki, where he became enlightened.

The legends of Kōbō Daishi were thereby enhanced by monks, who travelled the country, expounding their attractive brand of Shingon Buddhism to the common people.

Both the pilgrimage and legends associated with Kōbō Daishi had been developing for nearly

Pilgrim with *kongō-zue* (walking staff)

KŪKAI OR KŌBŌ DAISHI

Born in 774, as a child Kōbō Daishi's name was Saeki no Mao (佐伯 眞魚) and his childhood home was the present Temple 75: Zentsū-ji. It's said he took the name Kūkai (空海), meaning 'sky and sea', on achieving enlightenment at Muroto-misaki at age 19, as that was what he could see from the cave in which he was performing ascetic practices. During his adult life, until his death in 835, he was known as Kūkai. In 921, he was posthumously given the title Kōbō Daishi (弘法 大師), meaning 'Great Master', by Emperor Daigo.

793	804–6	819	835
Mao achieves enlightenment at Muroto-misaki and takes the name Kūkai	Kūkai travels to China and studies Chinese esoteric Buddhism	Kūkai's mountain retreat at Kōya-san is officially consecrated	Kūkai dies age 62 and is entombed on the eastern peak of Kōya-san

eight centuries by the time Japan's internal wars concluded in 1600 and the Tokugawa shogunate brought relative peace to the country during the Edo period (1600–1868).

The Commoners' Pilgrimage

Kōbō Daishi's Shingon sect differed from mainstream Buddhism by teaching that it was possible for everyone to attain enlightenment in this lifetime. Ever since Buddhism had entered Japan from Korea in the mid-6th century, it had been seen as a religion of the elite, who believed traditional teachings that only a select few could achieve Buddhahood and not in this lifetime. Shingon, however, taught that anyone could attain enlightenment through sincerity and practice, no matter their social status or gender, so it naturally appealed to and became the sect of the common folk.

In general, travel during the Edo period was prohibited, but if a commoner could show that pilgrimage was the reason for their travel, they could get papers that permitted them to go. With demand comes supply and the first guidebook appeared in 1687, *Shikoku Henro Michishirube (Guide to the Shikoku Pilgrimage),* published by a priest from Kōya-san named Shinnen. This is the first real record of the pilgrimage in the form that we know it today. Shinnen made over 20 pilgrimages to Shikoku and is credited with placing 200 stone marker posts around the island to help show *henro* (pilgrims) the way. He also built a chapel and shelter for *henro,* Shinnen-an (p119), at a particularly remote place on the way to the great southern cape, Ashizuri-misaki.

The people now had everything they needed to undertake a pilgrimage to Shikoku – in particular, a specific route that was spelt out in a guidebook – and the number of *henro* increased. Other factors were also involved: under the Tokugawa shogunate, farmers, merchants and artisans were more prosperous, so had the time and money required for a pilgrimage to Shikoku, and transportation, roads and lodging had improved thanks to the period of relative peace.

A Modern World

With the Meiji Restoration in 1868, the separation of Shintō and Buddhism was stipulated. The term *haibutsu-kishaku* was coined, meaning 'abolish Buddhism and destroy Buddha'. This had a devastating effect on the pilgrimage, especially in Kōchi, where seven of the 16 temples were abandoned. The Meiji government's stance eventually softened and its 1889 constitution granted freedom of religion, though the pilgrimage took decades to recover.

CRAIG MCLACHLAN/LONELY PLANET

Temple 46: Jōruri-ji (p144)

921	1600	1687	1868
Emperor Daigo posthumously gives Kūkai the title of Kōbō Daishi	Tokugawa Ieyasu wins the Battle of Sekigahara, beginning the Edo period	The priest Shinnen publishes the first pilgrimage guidebook	The Meiji Restoration stipulates the separation of Shintō and Buddhism

FROM LEFT: AMEHIME/SHUTTERSTOCK, AMEHIME/SHUTTERSTOCK, MASAYOSHI HIROSE/SHUTTERSTOCK,

Muroto-misaki, p86

This is where the young monk achieved enlightenment at age 19 and took the name Kūkai (空海) meaning 'sky and sea'.

Sitting Kūkai, p75

The young monk spent 100 days here performing ascetic practice, at what is now the *okunoin* (inner sanctuary) of Temple 21: Tairyū-ji.

Sleeping Kūkai, p139

Pilgrims refrain from tapping their staff on a bridge as Kōbō Daishi could well be sleeping underneath, as he did here.

The earliest reference to the pilgrimage by a non-Japanese is in the 1914 writings of Wenceslau de Moraes (1854–1929) of Portugal, who lived in Tokushima for his last 16 years of his life and wrote prolifically about his time in Japan. The first foreign *henro* to complete the pilgrimage is believed to be the celebrated Dr Frederick Starr (p169) from the University of Chicago, who travelled by foot, rickshaw and train in 1921.

As sealed roads and rail lines were built, *henro* started using other forms of transport. In 1921, Temple 62: Hōju-ji was relocated due to the construction of a new rail line. While WWII curbed enthusiasm for undertaking the pilgrimage, in 1953 the first *henro* bus tour was organised, successful to the point that bus tours remain popular into the 21st century.

Transport links to Shikoku were improving too. The four prefectural capitals all had civilian airports by 1960, but the real breakthrough came in 1988 with the opening of the Seto Ōhashi, the first bridge link between Shikoku and Honshū.

Two more bridge systems were opened before 2000. These advancements made it possible for Japanese *henro* from other parts of Japan to drive to Shikoku and complete a pilgrimage by car. The elderly and those physically incapable of completing a walking pilgrimage could easily get to Shikoku and visit the 88 temples.

Bring on the tourism boom times of the 2020s and the Japanese government's enthusiasm to attract 60 million international visitors per year by 2030, and the face of the pilgrimage is changing. Fewer Japanese can afford the costs of a pilgrimage, while more and more foreigners are keen to experience parts of Japan and its culture that are considered well off the beaten track.

In the distant past, *henro* setting out to complete a pilgrimage of Shikoku were seen to be taking a daring step towards heaven, one step short of death. In the 21st century, it may not be quite so dramatic as life and death, but it's still a mighty adventure.

1921	1953	1983	2024
Dr Frederick Starr is the first foreigner to complete the pilgrimage	Iyo Tetsu runs the first bus tour of the Shikoku pilgrimage	Oliver Statler's book *Japanese Pilgrimage* is published	The first version of the Henro Helper app is released

Ways to do the Shikoku Pilgrimage

Until the early 1900s, all *henro* (pilgrims) walked the 1200km pilgrimage. These days *henro* walk, ride bicycles or motorbikes, and take cars, buses and campervans. These are some of the best ways to build the trip of a lifetime.

1 On Foot

Time *40–60 days*

Best for *Wisdom-seekers with time, fitness and a love of adventure*

It is the essence of the pilgrimage to do it on foot, but you need to be physically fit, healthy and have the time and inclination. For over 80% of the journey you'll be walking on sealed roads; there are numerous *henro-michi* (pilgrim tracks), most outlined on the Henro Helper app that modern *henro* use for navigation. Walkers need to think ahead, especially when it comes to places to stay and eat in remote sections of the pilgrimage.

2 On Your Bike

Time *3 weeks*

Best for *Two-wheel adventurers wanting to explore*

Riding a bicycle around the pilgrimage is becoming popular. You can get to all the temples on sealed roads and cover a lot of ground quickly by bike. Being a bicycle *henro* used to be the realm of Japanese students on vacation, but these days the numbers of international bicycle *henro* is on the rise. Quite a few temples are up steep roads on mountains, so you may well pat yourself on the back if you splurge and ride an e-bike (p243).

3 With Motorised Wheels

Time *10–20 days*

Best for *Those with less time who want a central base*

It's easy to drive around Japan these days, thanks to multi-language car navigation systems. The big operators, such as Toyota Rent-a-Car, have English-language websites and outlets all over the country. As well as car *henro*, motorbike *henro* are not unusual and it's even possible to be a campervan *henro*. With wheels, you can pretty much do the pilgrimage in any season.

> **See p30 for the full route map**

AMEHIME/SHUTTERSTOCK

Pilgrims, Temple 19: Tatsue-ji (p71)

Pilgrim, Temple 6: Anraku-ji (p52)

TARO KARIBE/GETTY IMAGES

For essential trip tips, see p236

4 Use Public Transport

Time *3–4 weeks*
Best for *Non-walkers who prefer not to drive*

While it's possible to do the pilgrimage using public transport, be aware that in remote areas, bus and train departures can be few and far between. There are trains, but no lines around the southern capes of Muroto-misaki and Ashizuri-misaki and few through the mountainous interior. *Shikoku Japan 88 Route Guide,* updated yearly, includes bus timetables and is available at the Temple 1 Pilgrim Shop (p48). Public transport will get you close to most temples, but you'll be doing plenty of walking.

5 Take a Tour

Time *3 days–6 weeks*
Best for *Those who want to leave logistics to the professionals*

Along with Japan's great push to increase the number of international visitors have come opportunities for companies running both guided and self-guided tours of Shikoku and the pilgrimage. If you'd prefer to leave the planning to someone else, take a look at **Shikoku Tours** *(shikokutours.com)*, **Oku Japan** *(okujapan.com)*, **Walk Japan** *(walkjapan.com)* and **Japan Adventurer** *(japanadventurer. com)*, among others.

6 No Specified Order or Route

While most *henro* head to Temple 1: Ryōzen-ji and walk around Shikoku in numerical order (called *jun-uchi*), it's worth noting that some *henro* walk the pilgrimage *gyaku-uchi* (in reverse order), as this is what Emon Saburō did in order to meet Kōbō Daishi on the trail (p66). Others walk *kugiri-uchi,* splitting their pilgrimage into a number of timeframes, such as one prefecture a year over four years. There is no specified route between temples; options for walking on sealed roads and off-road trails are shown on the Henro Helper app.

WHEN TO GO

Mar–May

Spring is the busiest time for walking *henro* to set out; book accommodation early. Can be rainy early on.

Jun–Aug

The hot and humid rainy season and summer should be avoided by walkers; possible in an air-conditioned car.

Sep–Nov

Autumn is pleasant for everyone, cooling down later in the season; walkers should book accommodation early.

Dec–Feb

Winter can be cold for walkers, though fine if you're in a heated vehicle; easy to find places to stay. New Year is busy for everyone.

The Walk

A stage-by-stage, kilometre-by-kilometre account of the route. Your journey begins here.

KAGAWA PREFECTURE
Temple 65: Sankaku-ji to
Temple 79: Tennō-ji, p190
Temple 79: Tennō-ji to
Temple 1: Ryōzen-ji, p216
Temple 79: Tennō-ji
Takamatsu
Kagawa Prefecture
Awaji-shima
START/END
Temple 1: Ryōzen-ji
Tokushima
Temple 65: Sankaku-ji
Kii Channel
Temple 12: Shōsan-ji
SHIKOKU ISLAND
Tokushima Prefecture
Temple 23: Yakuō-ji
Kōchi
Temple 28: Dainichi-ji
TOKUSHIMA PREFECTURE
Temple 1: Ryōzen-ji to
Temple 12: Shōsan-ji, p44
Temple 12: Shōsan-ji to
Temple 23: Yakuō-ji, p62
Tosa Bay
NORTH PACIFIC OCEAN
KŌCHI PREFECTURE
Temple 23: Yakuō-ji to
Temple 28: Dainichi-ji, p80
Temple 28: Dainichi-ji to
Temple 36: Shōryū-ji, p102
Temple 36: Shōryū-ji to
Temple 39: Enkō-ji, p114

南無大師遍照金剛
相互供養
浄財

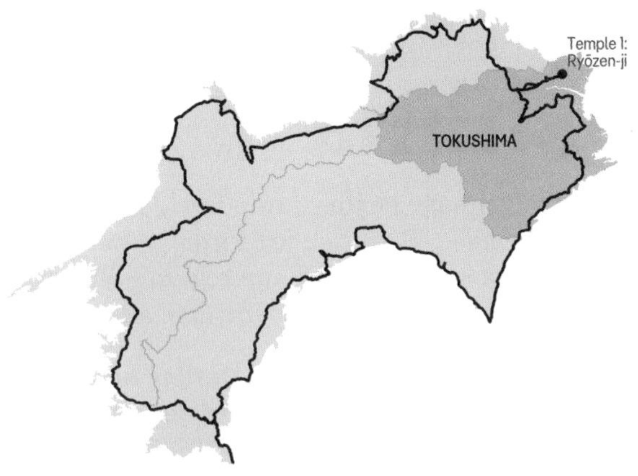

TOKUSHIMA PREFECTURE

Tokushima, known as the province of Awa in centuries past, is home to the first 23 temples, starting with Temple 1: Ryōzen-ji. Known as *Hosshin-no-dōjō* (the Place to Determine to Achieve Enlightenment), this is where pilgrims realise the magnitude of their task and begin the journey to complete their goal. It's a fairly gentle start, with the first 10 temples requiring less than 30km of walking, but then come the mountains, testing pilgrims' resolve and fortitude, both mentally and physically. Pilgrims eventually emerge from the interior to the prefecture's southern coastline, ready to carry on into Kōchi.

Temple 22: Byōdō-ji (p76)
CRAIG MCLACHLAN/LONELY PLANET

CITY GUIDE:

Tokushima

Before your Shikoku pilgrimage begins, jump into Japanese culture by getting to know Tokushima's (徳島) rich art forms. Whether it's a dance or puppet show, or crafting a souvenir from the region's illustrious indigo dye, Tokushima is a deserved starting point for the epic adventure to come.

WORDS BY
JESSICA KORTEMAN
Jessica is an Australian writer specialising in Japanese travel and culture.

 Arriving

See also p238.

By air Flights from Tokyo's Haneda Airport to Tokushima Awaodori Airport (TKS) take around 1¼ hours. It's approximately 30 minutes to Tokushima Station on the Airport Limousine Bus.

By rail There is no direct rail link to Tokushima from outside Shikoku; enter Shikoku via Okayama and the Seto Ōhashi bridge to Takamatsu, then board an onward train to Tokushima (1½ hours).

By bus Highway buses connect Kansai and Tokushima via Awaji-shima. An airport bus service runs from Osaka's Kansai International Airport (KIX) to Tokushima Station (three hours).

By car Cross the Akashi-Kaikyō and Ōnaruto bridges that connect Kansai and Shikoku via Awaji-shima (tolls apply).

HOW MUCH FOR A

Sudachi highball ¥700

Tokushima ramen ¥900

Awa-odori performance ¥1300–1600

Getting Around

Walking Central Tokushima is concentrated on an easily walkable gourd-shaped sandbar, known as Hyōtan-jima (Gourd Island), encircled by the Suketō-gawa and Shinmachi-gawa rivers.

Bus Local buses departing outside the station can get you further afield to destinations such as Awa Jūrōbē Yashiki Puppet Theatre (p39; 20 to 25 minutes). Visit Tokushima Welcome Center for timetables and help understanding the *seiri-ken* ticketing system (IC cards cannot be used on public transport in Tokushima).

Train For pilgrims starting their temple journey, a JR train service can transport you from Tokushima Station to Bandō Station in 20 minutes, from where it's a 10-minute walk to Temple 1: Ryōzen-ji.

Car A car is convenient for some outlying sights, but unless you're doing the pilgrimage by car and already have one, a combination of public transport, walking and supplemental taxi rides (if needed) will suffice.

For Kansai Airport Bus schedules, go to Kansai Airport Transportation Enterprise

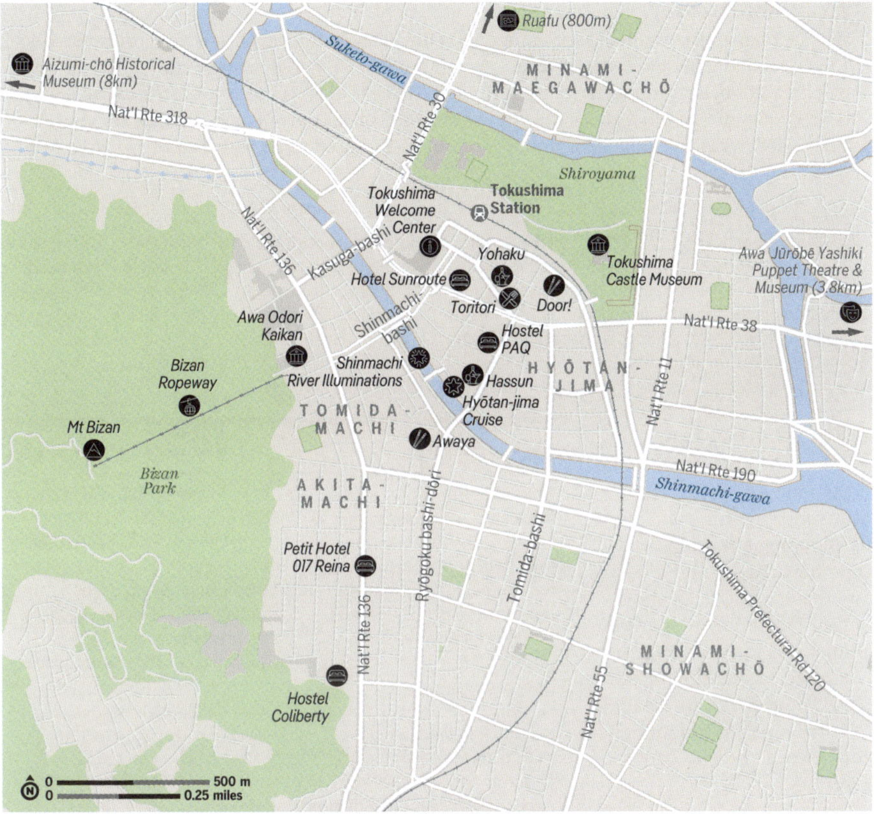

A DAY IN TOKUSHIMA

Start your day with a Japanese breakfast at **Door!** (p36). Take a walk through nearby Central Park to **Tokushima Castle Museum** and explore the former palatial garden. Proceed 15 minutes on foot to the banks of Shinmachi-gawa for a 25-minute ride on the river with **Hyōtan-jima Cruise**.

Grab a bowl of Tokushima ramen at **Awaya** (p36), then walk 10 minutes to the city's dance complex, **Awa Odori Kaikan** (p37). Take in a live performance at Awa Odori Hall, test your dance and percussion skills at Awa Odori Museum and take the **Bizan Ropeway** (p37) up adjacent **Mt Bizan** for fine city views.

At night, make the most of Tokushima's vibrant culinary scene on a guided **Tokushima Night Tour** (*tokushima-tour.jp*) of the city's *izakaya* (pub-eateries) and local food haunts. Afterwards, take a stroll along the **Shinmachi River Illuminations**. Before calling it a night, consider a nightcap at hidden cocktail bar **Yohaku**.

Where to Stay

In Tokushima, you'll find accommodation for all budgets from hostels to chain hotels. Check with your lodging about leaving a bag; a small number offer free luggage storage if you stay at least one night before and after your pilgrimage (Hostel PAQ has the largest storage capacity). If you find yourself in a bind, check out Tokushima Welcome Center's paid **storage service** (¥500 per bag per day) or the long-term storage options at **Fledged Ryūgaku** (*fledgedryugaku.com*).

BEST PLACES TO STAY

Hostel Coliberty ¥ By Mt Bizan, community-focused hostel with mixed dorms and private rooms. *hostelcoliberty.com*

Hostel PAQ ¥ Downtown hostel popular with pilgrims. Mixed and female dorms, plus private options. *hostelpaq.com*

Hotel Sunroute ¥¥ Comfortable three-star hotel with onsen (hot spring) opposite Tokushima Station. *sunroute-toku shima.com*

Petit Hotel 017 Reina ¥¥ Small apartment-style accommodation, good for those looking to self-cater. *017reina.com*

Where to Eat

Tokushima has a lively food and drink culture that makes restaurant- and bar-hopping a legitimate pastime here. You'll find a large and diverse range of culinary options, including a bunch of Tokushima specialities, concentrated in the Akita-machi (秋田町) and Tomida-machi (富田町) neighbourhoods, considered the city's foodie precincts.

TOKUSHIMA RAMEN & OTHER SPECIALITIES

Tokushima Prefecture enjoys three unique regional ramen varieties. The one from Tokushima city features a distinctive, brown-coloured soup made from a *shōyu* (soy sauce) and *tonkotsu* (pork bone) broth blend, and is topped with pork belly, green onions, fermented bamboo shoots and an optional raw egg (pictured below). A short distance north, the city of Naruto has a 'yellow' style of ramen, which uses chicken broth and a lighter soy sauce. Kōmatsushima city in the south has a 'white' variety that is closest to regular *tonkotsu* broth, and sometimes uses a white or clear soy sauce.

Other ingredients seen throughout Tokushima include the prefecture's branded Awa-odori chicken, local lime *sudachi* and Naruto Kintoki sweet potatoes, along with loads of fresh seafood and an emergent wild game scene. As for drinks, try the local fermented Awa Bancha tea (pictured left) and the wide variety of *sudachi*-flavoured sodas and highball cocktails.

FROM LEFT: STUDIOUP/SHUTTERSTOCK, JESSICA KORTEMAN/LONELY PLANET

BEST PLACES TO EAT & DRINK

Hassun ¥ Eclectic neighbourhood bar serving up home cooking and nostalgic vinyl tunes. *6-10pm Mon-Sat*

Door! ¥ Buildable Japanese-style breakfast: add salt-grilled fish, tofu and side dishes. *7.30am-3pm Mon-Sat*

Awaya ¥ Ramen restaurant. Try its Awaya-soba served with *sudachi* (lime). *11am-2pm & 7pm-late Tue-Sun*

Toritori ¥ Popular casual *yakitori* joint, famous for its *kimo* (chicken liver) skewers. *6pm-midnight Mon-Sat*

Learn Tokushima's Famed Dance

More than an annual dance festival, sample August festivities throughout the year at the city's five-storey Awa Odori Kaikan complex.

Getting here: A 10-minute walk from Tokushima Station

When to go: Year-round

Cost: Dance performance day/night ¥1300/1600; Awa Odori Museum ¥500; Mt Bizan Ropeway return ¥1500

Tip: A discounted ticket for all three attractions (same-day entry ¥2640) can be bought from the 1st-floor reception counter (applicable only to daytime shows).

More info: awaodori-kaikan.jp

The high-energy dance form associated with Tokushima's Awa-odori Matsuri (p39) is both graceful and wild. Visitors can get a taste of it any time of year at the city's dedicated dance hall, **Awa Odori Kaikan** (阿波おどり会館), located at the base of Mt Bizan.

You'll need a few hours to rotate through its three ticketed attractions. Plan your wanderings around the timings for the five daily dance performances. Live shows at the 250-seat capacity **Awa Odori Hall** (2nd floor) take place at 11am, 2pm, 3pm, 4pm (40 minutes) and 8pm (50 minutes), and include the opportunity to get on stage and try the steps for yourself – it's harder than it looks!

Upstairs, the **Awa Odori Museum** (*on the 3rd floor; 9am-5pm*) puts your dance and percussion skills to the test in two interactive gaming experiences, while a **cable car** departing from the Bizan Ropeway Station (5th floor) can transport you 290m to the summit of **Mt Bizan** (*return ¥1500; 9am-9pm Apr-Oct, to 5.30pm Nov-Mar*). Time the ropeway for sunset to enjoy fine city views in the changing light.

Performers, Awa-odori Matsuri (p39)

Get in a Spin

Northeast of Tokushima view the Naruto Whirlpools, a natural phenomenon that occurs due to a unique interaction of tidal currents and underwater topography along the narrow Naruto Strait.

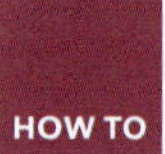

HOW TO

Getting here: Catch a bus from Tokushima Station to Naruto Park (1¼ hours), or a train to Naruto Station (40 minutes) and then a bus (20 minutes).

When to go: Timing is critical; check the tide table online for the most active daily viewing times.

Cost: Whirlpool boat tours: Uzushio Kisen ¥1600, Aqua Eddy ¥2400, Wonder Naruto standard/1st class ¥1800/2800.

More info: uzunomichi.jp; uzushio -kisen.com/en; uzusio.com/en

You may have already had a glimpse of the **Naruto Whirlpools** (鳴門の渦潮) in your ramen bowl; the distinctive pink fishcake swirl *Naruto-maki* that often tops noodle soups is named after, and symbolic of, the whirlpools here.

This is an attraction where timing is everything and could be the difference between seeing huge whirlpools up to 20m in diameter or nothing at all. Check the tide table (available online) to view when the whirlpools will be most active on the day of your visit and plan accordingly. It's even better if your schedule can align with one of the 'spring tides' days' (approximately every two weeks) when the whirlpools put on their biggest show.

The whirlpools can be viewed up-close by boat and from above via the 45m-high **Uzu-no-Michi Walkway** *(渦の道; ¥510)* on **Ōnaruto-kyō**, where you can observe the whirlpools via glass panels. It's best to visit the walkway during the height of the south current, which occurs right below the bridge. The northern current is about 300m to 400m away and so is best viewed by boat.

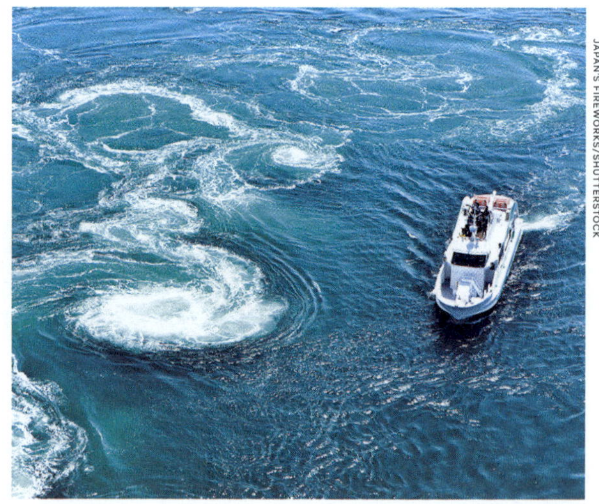

Naruto Whirlpools

MASAYUKI NAKAYA/LONELY PLANET

AWA-ODORI MATSURI

The Awa-odori Matsuri sees the city reach fever pitch when more than one million visitors come to witness this sizzling four-day summer dance spectacle. Held annually from 12 to 15 August, thousands of dancers in troupes known as *ren* perform the Awa-odori's synchronised dance steps to energetic lyrical melodies like the Awa-Yoshikono chant, the words translating to 'The dancers are fools, the watchers are fools, both are fools alike, so why not dance?' Perhaps the most iconic piece of dance attire is the semicircular straw hat worn by female dancers. Called *tori-oi-gasa* (bird scaring hat), it is best described as an inverted taco.

Theories about the origins of Awa-odori abound, including a spontaneous drunken street party after the completion of the city's castle, Tokushima-jō. What is more likely, according to the history books, is that the dance developed much more slowly, evolving from regional summer Bon dances inviting the ancestors back to the human world. Whichever theory you ascribe to, the consensus is that Awa-odori has been part of Tokushima's cultural landscape for over 400 years!

Ruafu dyeing workshop

Dye Japan's Signature Colour

The indigo hue dubbed 'Japan Blue' is one of Tokushima's most famous exports. The number-one indigo producer since the Edo period, Tokushima Prefecture produces 80% of the country's indigo dye and there are numerous opportunities to participate in *aizome* (indigo dyeing) workshops. **Aizumi-chō Historical Museum** (*Ai-no-Yakata;* 藍住町歴史館藍の館; *ainoyakata.jp; ¥300)* has excellent indigo exhibits and offers a walk-in *aizome* experience (30 to 40 minutes from ¥1000). A great option closer to town is **Ruafu** (藍染工房ルアフ; *@aizome_ruafu),* which accepts bookings up to the day before.

Attend the Puppet Theatre

Tokushima is the home and heartland of *ningyō jōruri* (人形浄瑠璃), a captivating form of puppet theatre with lyrical storytelling. Three performers operate one puppet simultaneously, skilfully synchronising their movements while completely cloaked in black sheaths. Experience it firsthand at **Awa Jūrōbē Yashiki Puppet Theatre & Museum** (徳島県立阿波十郎兵衛屋敷; *joruri.info/jurobe; ¥410).* The theatre holds two 30-minute performances daily (11am and 2pm, 11am only in January and February) of *Keisei Awa no Naruto,* depicting the compelling story of a young child in search of her long-lost parents.

The theatre is scheduled to temporarily close for restoration works from November 2026; check the website for updates.

Performers, Awa Jūrōbē Yashiki Puppet Theatre

DUNPHASIZER/WIKIMEDIA/CC BY-SA 2.0 DEED ®

Pilgrim Attire

THE WHITE ATTIRE worn by pilgrims signifies innocence and purity. As the traditional colour for Japanese funerals, in pre-modern times it also symbolised preparedness to die in one's spiritual quest, while the *kongō-zue* (wooden staff) could be used as a makeshift grave marker.

Even today, some pilgrims buy an extra white vest for stamp collecting that can one day be placed on themselves or a deceased family member before cremation. The staff's colourful fabric topper serves to conceal the upper 'grave marker' portion as well as pay respect to Kōbō Daishi, said to be embodied in the staff.

The white vest comes in long-sleeve (*hakui*) and sleeveless (*oizuru*) options (¥2000–3500). The neck sash (*wagesa*; ¥1500–3500) is an adapted version of the stoles worn by Buddhist priests. Conical or sedge hats (*sugegasa*; ¥1500–3000) protect pilgrims from the elements. Wear with the Sanskrit marking to the front. *Sugegasa* do not need to be removed when worshipping, whether inside or outside.

COURTESY OF SATOSHI ASANO AND SUMOTORIYA.

COURTESY OF SATOSHI ASANO AND SUMOTORIYA.

COURTESY OF SATOSHI ASANO AND SUMOTORIYA.

大師御宝号
同行二人
南無大師遍照金剛

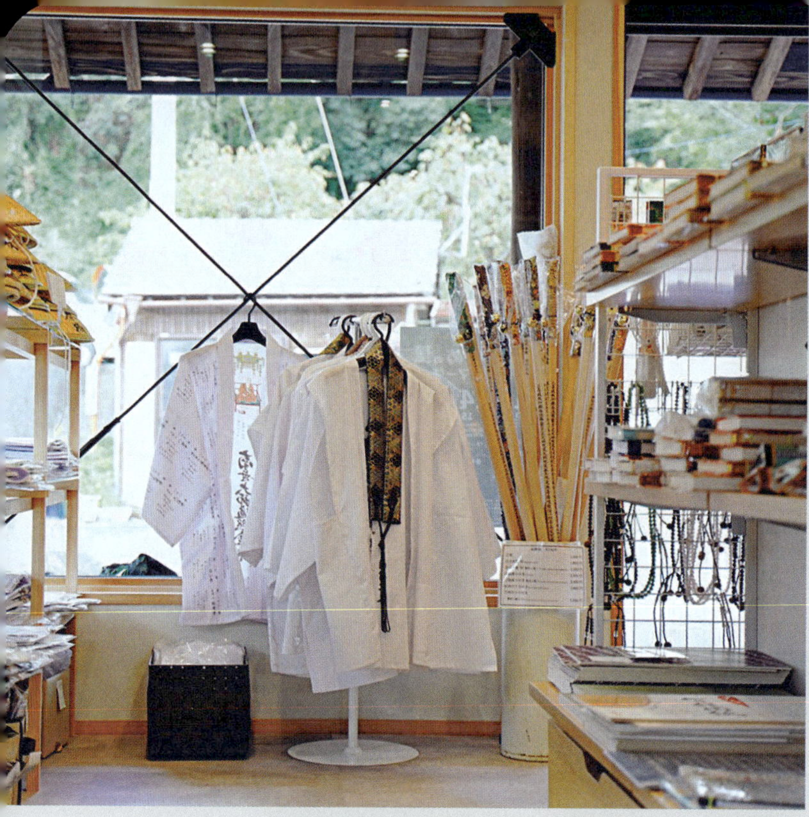

COURTESY OF SATOSHI ASANO AND SUMOTORIYA.

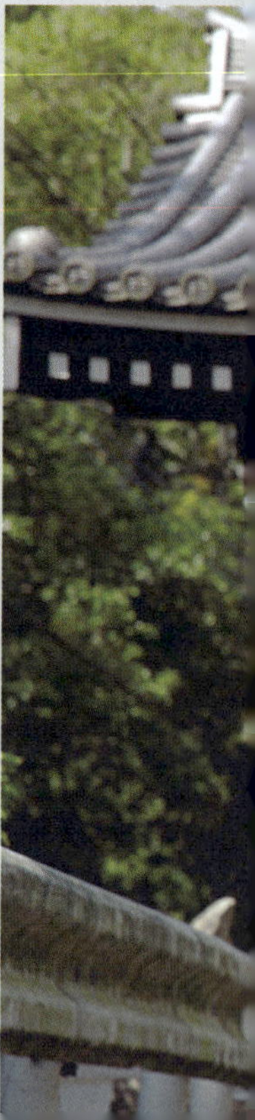

COURTESY OF SATOSHI ASANO AND SUMOTORIYA.

Many pilgrims wear a white cross-body bag (*zuda-bukuro*; ¥1500–3500) to carry their stamp book (*nōkyō-chō*; ¥2500–4000), candles, lighter, incense, name slips, written sutra offering papers, prayer beads and bell. Scrolls (p244) are supplied in a soft vinyl case.

COURTESY OF SATOSHI ASANO AND SUMOTORIYA.

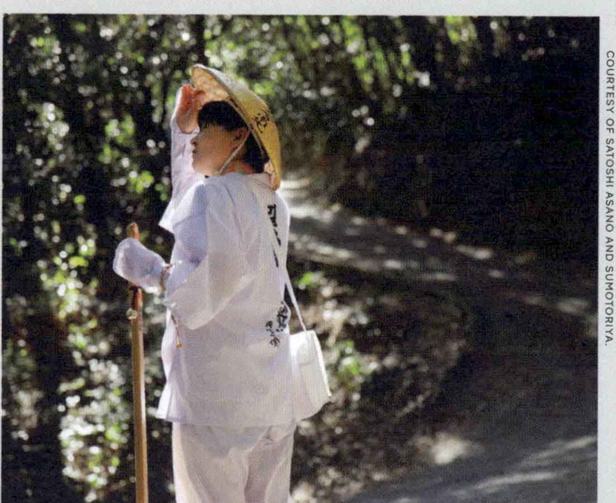

JESSICA KORTEMAN/LONELY PLANET

You'll need two name slips (*osame-fuda*; pack of 100 slips ¥150) per temple, plus extras to give in reciprocation for gifts (p19). The colour signifies the number of Shikoku 88 pilgrimages you have completed: use white for your first four pilgrimages. On it, write your name, address, the date and your wish. You can pre-fill them, minus the date (and wish, if it's likely to change), to save time.

Ryōzen-ji

TEMPLE 1

A nice, easy start for a 1200km pilgrimage, with the first nine
temples easily walked on the flat northern side of the Yoshino-
gawa river valley. You'll need to climb 333 steps to get up to
Temple 10: Kirihata-ji, but that's just a warm-up for the crossover
to the southern side of the river and the strenuous climb up to
Temple 12: Shōsan-ji, high in the mountains. Make it to Temple 12
and you're well on your way.

Craig McLachlan

Temple 10: Kirihata-ji (p55)
BRESTER IRINA/SHUTTERSTOCK

Shōsan-ji
TEMPLE 12

60KM
~3-4 DAYS' WALK

THIS LEG:

- Temple 1 Pilgrim Shop
- Temple 1: Ryōzen-ji
- Temple 2: Gokuraku-ji
- Temple 3: Konsen-ji
- Temple 4: Dainichi-ji
- Temple 5: Jizō-ji
- Temple 6: Anraku-ji
- Temple 7: Jūraku-ji
- Temple 8: Kumadani-ji
- Temple 9: Hōrin-ji
- Sumotoriya Asano Pilgrim Shop
- Temple 10: Kirihata-ji
- Crossing the Yoshino-gawa
- Temple 11: Fujii-dera
- Temple 12: Shōsan-ji

Walking Notes

Walkers will want to allow three to four days for this first section; while getting around the first 11 temples, located in the flat of the valley, is fairly easy, the climb from Temple 11 to Temple 12 has a reputation for being the toughest bit of the pilgrimage. You're unlikely to get complacent early; one look south at the mountains will tell you what's coming.

Breaking Your Journey

Plan ahead: spend your first night at Temple 6: Anraku-ji temple lodging (p52). The night before the climb to Temple 12, stay as close to Temple 11 as possible, so that you can get an early start. The night you hike up to Temple 12, stay as close as possible at Sudachi-an (p75).

Craig's Tips

BEST MEAL Dinner in the *shukubō* (temple lodgings) at Temple 6: Anraku-ji (p52).

FAVOURITE VIEW From Temple 10: Kirihata-ji, looking south over the Yoshino-gawa valley to the mountains (p55).

ESSENTIAL STOP Temple 1 Pilgrim Shop to purchase your *henro* (pilgrim) gear (p48).

TOP TIP Get your backpack delivered to Sudachi-an and walk with no gear up to Temple 12: Shōsan-ji (p59).

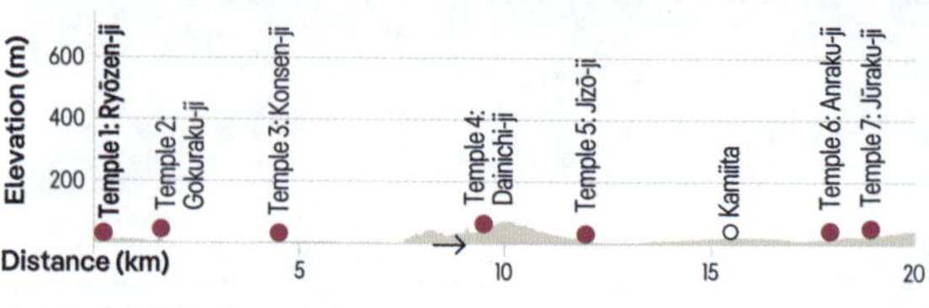

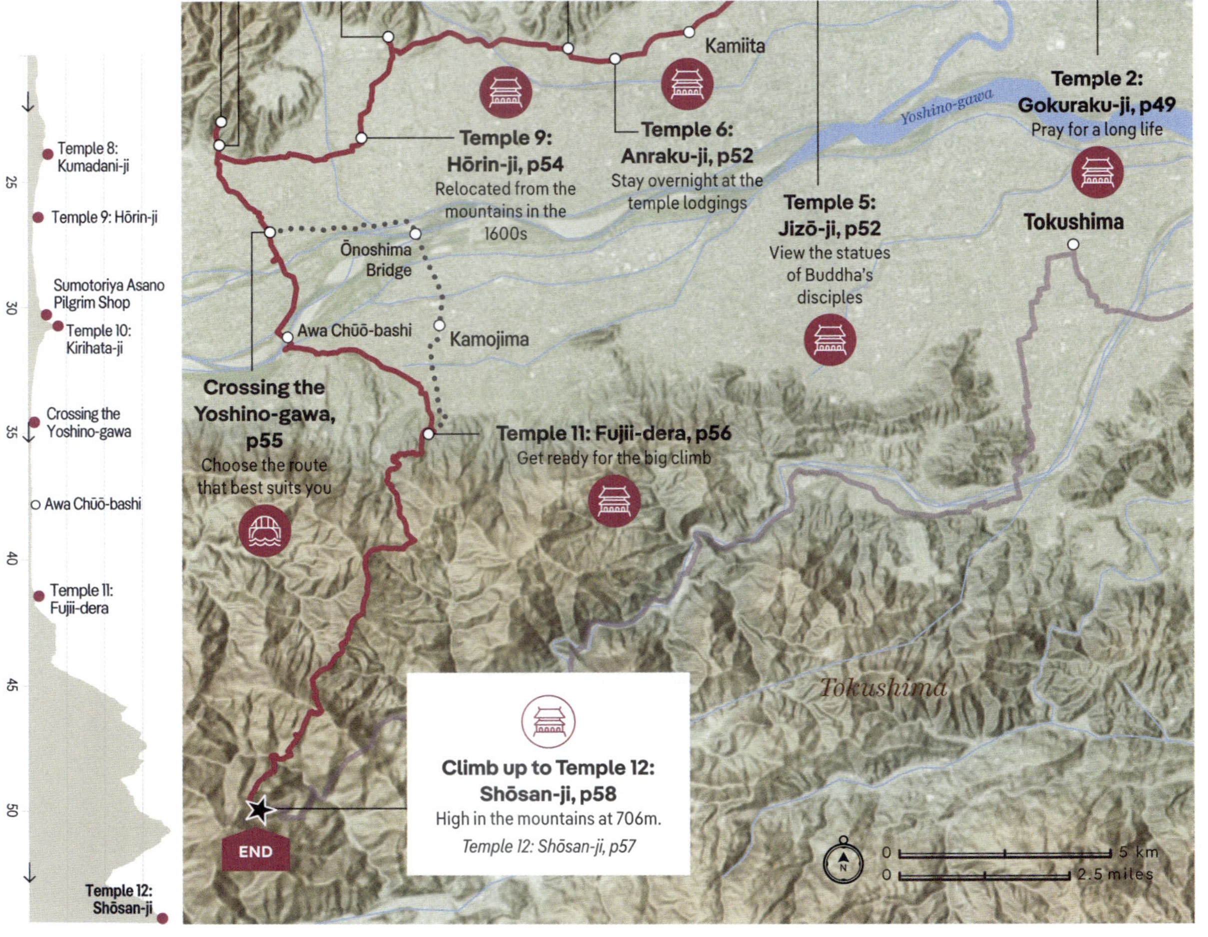

Kamiita
Temple 2:
Gokuraku-ji, p49
Pray for a long life
Yoshino-gawa
Temple 9:
Hōrin-ji, p54
Relocated from the
mountains in the
1600s
Temple 6:
Anraku-ji, p52
Stay overnight at the
temple lodgings
Temple 5:
Jizō-ji, p52
View the statues
of Buddha's
disciples
Tokushima
Ōnoshima
Bridge
Awa Chūō-bashi
Kamojima
Crossing the
Yoshino-gawa,
p55
Choose the route
that best suits you
Temple 11: Fujii-dera, p56
Get ready for the big climb
Tokushima
Climb up to Temple 12:
Shōsan-ji, p58
High in the mountains at 706m.
Temple 12: Shōsan-ji, p57
END
0   5 km
0   2.5 miles
N
Temple 8:
Kumadani-ji
25
Temple 9: Hōrin-ji
Sumotoriya Asano
Pilgrim Shop
30
Temple 10:
Kirihata-ji
35
Crossing the
Yoshino-gawa
Awa Chūō-bashi
40
Temple 11:
Fujii-dera
45
50
Temple 12:
Shōsan-ji

GETTING TO TEMPLE 1 Ryōzen-ji is Temple 1 as, through the centuries, it was the first temple pilgrims came to after arriving on Shikoku by boat at Muya port in Naruto city.

Most *henro* today will access Temple 1 (and the Shikoku pilgrimage route) from Tokushima city (p34). To get to Ryōzen-ji from Tokushima, catch a train (20 minutes; departures infrequent) on the JR Kotoku line from JR Tokushima Station to JR Bandō Station; it's just a 10-minute walk from the station to the temple. Alternatively, Ryōzen-ji is a 30-minute drive (16km) northwest of central Tokushima city.

To get an early start, stay near Temple 1. Visit the pilgrim shop and Ryōzen-ji the day that you arrive, so that you are prepared to begin your pilgrimage first thing in the morning.

Temple 1 Pilgrim Shop

When you arrive at Ryōzen-ji, head straight to the temple shop beside the car park to purchase your *henro* gear (see p40). There are no rules here: it's your pilgrimage, so buy what works for you. If you're walking, consider getting yourself something that will identify you as a pilgrim from afar. The good people of Shikoku have been helping walking pilgrims attain their goal for centuries, so it's helpful if people can see that you are a *henro*. Once you've picked up what you need, head to the temple grounds and perform your *mairi* (rituals; see p246).

The shop is also the *nōkyō-jo,* the place where the temple stamp is put in your *nōkyō-chō* (book of stamps). Before you hit the road, sign the Walker's Log: it's a simple notebook, nothing fancy, but it lets the temple know who is walking the pilgrimage and it feels great to log out when you come back on the completion of your journey.

If you forget to purchase something you need, you can get it at Sumotoriya Asano Pilgrim Shop (p55) below Temple 10: Kirihata-ji.

Temple 1: Ryōzen-ji

While **Ryōzen-ji** (霊山寺) is Temple 1, and nowadays the accepted starting point for the pilgrimage, it's worth noting that the earliest guidebooks suggested starting at Temple 75: Zentsū-ji (p203), Kōbō Daishi's birthplace. It doesn't matter where *henro* start their pilgrimage, as long as they make a determined effort and complete the circle. That *determined effort* may well involve wheels; it's accepted that not everyone is capable of walking 1200km around the island.

Unless you arrive at the same time as a couple of tour buses, Ryōzen-ji, founded around 700 CE by order of Emperor Shōmu, is a peaceful place. There's a beautiful pond with brightly coloured carp just inside the main gate that's useful on two fronts: for its ascetic beauty and for fighting fire, the bane of old wooden temple buildings. There's a lovely pagoda and a ceiling full of lit lanterns in the *hondō* (main hall). Get your thoughts together and prepare for your 1200km pilgrimage. There is no fanfare on a pilgrim's departure from Temple 1; they haven't achieved anything yet.

**Temple 1:
Ryōzen-ji**

1.2km

AMEHIME/SHUTTERSTOCK

Niōmon, Temple 2: Gokuraku-ji

Temple 2: Gokuraku-ji

It's a flat 1.2km walk west along the main road outside Temple 1's main gate to get to **Temple 2: Gokuraku-ji** (極楽寺; *ca.pikara.ne.jp/gokurakuji/*). Couldn't be easier. Bow before the red *niōmon* (temple gate) and admire the two fierce and intimidating guardian deities, who are there to make sure you are pure of intention, as well as to ward off evil spirits and protect the temple and its treasures.

The grounds and gardens here are immaculate. Gokuraku-ji is a popular, prosperous temple, where expectant parents (many of whom make handsome donations) come to pray for safe childbirth. There are countless

GRASSROOTS TEMPLES

If you've been to Kyoto and are expecting the pilgrimage temples to be grand affairs along the lines of the Kinkaku-ji, Ginkaku-ji or Kiyomizu-dera, think again. You're in grassroots temple territory here on Shikoku and the 88 temples are regular local temples serving their communities. Some are in Shikoku's big cities, others in small towns, some in rural areas and others at capes or on remote mountaintops.

As members of the 88, however, they are generally fairly prosperous when compared to the hundreds (possibly thousands) of other temples on Shikoku, some of which look on with envy.

Temple 2:
Gokuraku-ji

Don't miss the Longevity Cedar

BEST PLACES TO EAT

Gen, near Temple 1: Ryōzen-ji ¥¥
Great location for those overnighting near Temple 1; English menu and top meals of generous proportions. 元; 11am-9pm Wed-Sun, 11am-3pm Mon

Shukubō, Temple 6: Anraku-ji ¥¥
Excellent chance to try traditional local Tokushima set meals at the temple lodgings; book the 'with meals' option for dinner and breakfast. *shikoku6.or.jp*

Tanpopo, Kamojima ¥
Fill up on hearty *okonomiyaki* (savoury pancake) on your way to Temple 11: Fujii-dera. たんぽぽ; *tanpopo-yoshi-nogawa.com*; 11am-3pm & 5-9pm Wed-Mon

small statues of Jizō, deity of children, some wearing knitted red caps. The temple is also known for its **Longevity Cedar**, a gnarly old tree said to have been planted by Kōbō Daishi; *henro* touch it hoping to be granted a long life. Many have offered coins, pressing them into gaps in its tough bark, so that the lower levels of the cedar almost glitter.

Temple 3: Konsen-ji

The 2.6km walk from Temple 2 to **Temple 3: Konsen-ji** (金泉寺) presents a fine opportunity to test your navigation skills. From the car park, it starts with a short *henro-michi* (pilgrim track); look for the marker pointing the way. Alternatively, use that most modern piece of equipment, your phone; download the Henro Helper app to help you find your way.

Temple 3: Konsen-ji

Along the Way We Met...

MAREI & JONATHAN We've got lots of time, but we haven't got a big budget. A guy on the beach in the Philippines told us about the pilgrimage a few weeks ago. It sounded really interesting, so we did some research, started learning Japanese on Duolingo and began walking at Temple 1 this morning. We've got the Henro Helper app and it's already been very useful. We're a bit worried that we haven't done enough preparation though.

Marei (19) and Jonathan (20), from Germany, are on a gap year after high school.

MAREI & JONATHAN'S TIP: *Learn more about Japanese etiquette than we have. We're worried about doing something wrong, especially at temples.*

Konsen-ji's name means 'Temple of the Golden Spring' and it is said that Kōbō Daishi, upon finding the area had a shortage of good water, thrust his staff into the ground here and created a spring.

Don't leave without checking out **Benkei-no-chikaraishi**, a large stone said to have been lifted by 12th-century warrior Benkei to show his strength. Benkei visited Konsen-ji with his general, Minamoto Yoshitsune, while on the way to battle and they prayed for victory, which was achieved at the Battle of Yashima (p224). People have been praying for good luck at Temple 3 ever since. Benkei's name is in common use in modern Japanese, and while young people may not know the legends of Benkei, they all know his name. Benkei gave his name to the shin bone; it was supposedly the only place

Benkei could be hurt, and to this day, the shin is known as *Benkei-no-nakidokoro* (literally, 'Benkei's crying place').

Temple 4: Dainichi-ji

You're about to face something that the *henro* of old never encountered on the 5km walk to **Temple 4: Dainichi-ji** (大日寺; *dainichi ji-temple.com*). A tad disconcertingly, the route takes you under the E32 Tokushima Expressway, with cars racing overhead, east to the prefectural capital, and west, up the Yoshino-gawa valley. And you're going to have a slight climb, north up the Kurodani-gawa valley, with forested mountains on both sides.

The Dainichi-ji has had a much-needed facelift of late, with an upgraded car park, paved grounds and renovated buildings. The highlight here is a

JOHN S LANDER/GETTY IMAGES

Temple 2:
Gokuraku-ji

Temple 3:
Konsen-ji

Temple 4:
Dainichi-ji

2.6km

5km

Check out Benkei's large rock

Prepare for a slight climb

covered corridor connecting the *hondō* and the **Daishi-dō** (Daishi Hall) that features 33 statues of Kannon, deity of mercy and compassion.

 Temple 5: Jizō-ji

As you wander out of the valley on the 1.6km walk to **Temple 5: Jizō-ji** (地蔵寺), you can't help but feel confident. You've been to four of the 88 temples in only a few hours. Reality check yourself by looking ahead to what's coming – the mountains on the far side of the valley. And it could be raining. There are two ways of thinking about rain on the pilgrimage: it's seen as either the *henro's* torment or as part of a pilgrim's training, for which they should be grateful and thank Kōbō Daishi. Carrying an umbrella is not a bad option.

Jizō is best known as the compassionate deity of children and travellers, but at Temple 5 he is most unusually depicted as a warrior, in a figure said to have been carved by Kōbō Daishi when he founded the temple in 821 CE. There's an impressive 800-year-old gingko tree here that pilgrims pray to for an equally long life. On the hill behind the temple buildings is the **Rakan-dō**, built in 1775 and originally home to 500 *rakan* statues, each with a different facial expression. They represent Buddha's disciples. Unfortunately, many were lost in a fire in 1915 and only some 200 are left.

 Temple 6: Anraku-ji

It's a 5.2km walk along the flat valley to **Temple 6: Anraku-ji** (安楽寺; *shikoku6.or.jp*). If you're happy with a 16km, six-temple day to start your pilgrimage, then this is an excellent place to stay. Legend has it that Kōbō Daishi struck the ground with his staff here, creating a

hot spring with curative powers and building a healing bath for the locals. Anraku-ji is dedicated to the deity of healing, Yakushi, and many come to pray for a cure for illness.

This is your first chance to stay at a *shukubō*, with Japanese-style rooms, the opportunity to participate in evening and morning prayer sessions, plus dinner and breakfast included (if you wish). The onsen, with its curative waters, is open from 3pm to 9pm. Anraku-ji also has a donations-based *tsuyado* (space in the temple's bell tower), where up to two people can sleep. *Tsuyado* are provided as charity as a last resort for pilgrims in trouble and shouldn't be used as a free alternative by those who have the funds to pay for lodging.

 Temple 7: Jūraku-ji

There's nothing too remarkable at **Temple 7: Jūraku-ji** (十楽寺; *jyuurakuji.com*), only a 1.3km walk from Temple 6. What's likely to catch your eye here is the largest building on the temple grounds, the white **Hotel Kōmyō Kaikan**, which combines traditional pilgrim lodgings with modern facilities, private rooms and en-suite bathrooms. The result is a bit like a dated business hotel out in the countryside that somewhat dwarfs its temple next door. However, this place is another good option that can be pre-booked for the end of your first day of walking.

The temple specialises in eye ailments and many come to pray here for the cure of visual impairments.

 Temple 8: Kumadani-ji

Only a 4.2km walk from Temple 7, the name of **Temple 8: Kumadani-ji** (熊谷寺) translates to 'Bear Valley Temple', even though

Eye up the guardian deities with confidence

The onsen has curative powers

BRESTER IRINA/SHUTTERSTOCK

Temple 8: Kumadani-ji

it's not really in a valley. But if you're wondering, yes – there *are* still black bears on the island, though they are classed as 'critically endangered' and are facing extinction on Shikoku. The only population left is said to live around Tsurugi-san (p195), the island's second-highest mountain, in western Tokushima Prefecture.

Kumadani-ji is known for having the largest **temple gate** of all the 88. Built in 1688, the celebrated gate, through which cars can drive, has probably survived thanks to its distance from the main temple area, which has regularly been devastated by fire. A 1927 blaze razed the main hall. The temple has a middle gate, past the car park, then pilgrims walk up sets of stone steps

HENRO WITH WHEELS

- With a vehicle, *henro* can cover a lot of distance in a short time.
- Consider staying consecutive nights in Tokushima city and visiting the first 17 temples over three days (or more). There are plenty of excellent accommodation and eating options in the prefectural capital.
- Tokushima city to Temple 1: Ryōzen-ji is about 16km.
- Tokushima to Temple 10: Kirihata-ji is 31km.
- Tokushima city to Temple 12: Shōsan-ji is 36km.

**Temple 7:
Jūraku-ji**

1.3km

Don't miss the Rakan-do statues

4.2km

**Temple 8:
Kumadani-ji**

Be sure to walk through the huge gate

BRESTER IRINA/SHUTTERSTOCK

Temple 10: Kirihata-ji

BEST PLACES TO SLEEP

Temple 6: Anraku-ji
Temple Lodging ¥

Stay at an atmospheric *shukubō* with delicious meals for your first night on the pilgrimage. *shikoku6.or.jp*

Oyado Eleven ¥

In a great location, only 200m from Temple 11: Fujii-dera; get an early start the next morning for the big climb to Temple 12. *henrohouse.jp*

Hostel OE ¥

Stay at Hostel OE and book Sudachi-an (p75) for the next night, and they'll transfer your gear for free, so that you don't have to carry it up to Temple 12. *booking.com*

to get to the main temple buildings at what is probably the most picturesque of the temples visited to this point.

Temple 9: Hōrin-ji

It's a 2.4km walk to **Temple 9: Hōrin-ji** (法輪寺) in the middle of rice paddies and agricultural fields. Hōrin-ji was not always here though. Until the 1580s it was 4km north in the mountains, where it boasted a large temple complex. Like many of the temples visited so far, it was burnt by the forces of Chōsokabe Motochika, a warlord of Tosa (Kōchi), during the Sengoku-jidai (Warring States period), before

Temple 8:
Kumadani-ji

2.4km

Temple 9:
Hōrin-ji

Sumotoriya Asano
Pilgrim Shop

Pray for healthy feet here

Use the railings on the 333 steps

the unification of Japan. Chōsokabe sought to conquer, unify and rule all of Shikoku. One of his strategies to defeat resistance from locals was to destroy their temples, asserting his authority and control. He razed Hōrin-ji in 1582, along with Temple 7: Jūraku-ji and a number of other temples, eventually controlling and ruling the whole island. Chōsokabe's short-lived reign ended when Toyotomi Hideyoshi invaded the island in 1585.

The damage was done though, and many temples that had been burnt were relocated and rebuilt. Hōrin-ji was moved to its present location in the 1640s and started again. The temple is known for its **reclining Buddha image**, a rarity in Japanese temples. This is a temple at which to pray for those who have afflictions of the legs and feet. There is a legend of a pilgrim who could not walk without crutches being miraculously cured at Hōrin-ji; worshippers offer straw sandals as they pray for a cure for their lower leg issues.

Sumotoriya Asano Pilgrim Shop

Enjoy your last short walk for a while on the 4km hike to Temple 10: Kirihata-ji. The lane heading up, almost directly north from Rte 139, is lined with pilgrimage-related buildings. Many pilgrims used to stay at inns here after visiting Kirihata-ji, as they had to cross the Yoshino-gawa the following day. As you head up the lane, make sure you drop into the very inviting **Sumotoriya Asano Pilgrim Shop** (*sumotoriya.com),* on the right, just before the bend in the road. This place has been supplying pilgrims for over 130 years and is run by English-speaking Satoshi Asano (p60), a fountain of knowledge about

the pilgrimage. The shop has online sales and delivers overseas, so it's easy to get organised before coming to Shikoku. Asano-san is very accommodating; enjoy his company and knowledge, and leave your gear here while you climb up to Temple 10 and back.

Temple 10: Kirihata-ji

The first 10 temples have long been a short pilgrimage in their own right, with worshippers offering prayers for their ancestors at **Temple 10: Kirihata-ji** (切幡寺) as the goal. It's still known as 'ten *ri* ten temples', one *ri* being how far a person can walk in an hour at a reasonable pace (considered to be about 4km).

The 333 stone steps up to the temple make Kirihata-ji the pilgrim's first mountain temple. Though it only sits at 155m altitude, after all the flat walking it's likely to produce some groaning joints on both the way up and down.

Kirihata-ji means 'Cut-cloth Temple' and it's named for a young weaving girl who offered Kōbō Daishi cloth for a new robe. The Daishi was so moved that he granted her wish to be ordained as a nun, but as he did, the girl attained Buddhahood. This is very much a Shingon story, demonstrating the belief that anyone – of any social status or gender – can attain enlightenment in this lifetime. At the temple, gaze out over the Yoshino-gawa valley and marvel at the majestic pagoda.

Crossing the Yoshino-gawa

For walkers, life is about to change as they head south to the mountains on the far side of the valley. Stock up on supplies, ensuring you have plenty of refreshments for the trek

up to Temple 12, and book meals through your accommodation as, along the shortest walking route, there is nowhere to purchase food from Temple 11 until after Temple 16; see 'Keep Up With the Latest' (p67) for more.

Henro will have to cross the mighty Yoshino-gawa and there are only a couple of bridge options. The shortest route, via the **Ōnoshima** bridge and **Zennyūji Island**, is definitely the most picturesque, passing farmland producing rice, vegetables and flowers, but there are scant facilities and stores before getting to Temple 11. The alternative route, using the big **Awa Chūō-bashi** bridge on Rte 318, is less enjoyable, but will take walkers through the town of **Kamojima**, which has a supermarket and more.

Either way, pause to admire the second-longest river on Shikoku, the 194km-long **Yoshino-gawa**, the only river on the island gathering water from all four of Shikoku's prefectures. Nicknamed Shikoku Saburo, it is known as one of the three most powerful rivers in Japan and has been the cause of much death and destruction through flooding over the centuries. It's said that over 30,000 people perished in the great floods of 1866. Large-scale flood control projects and strong levees were built in the mid-1900s, making the river much more docile, especially out where it flows into the sea, just north of Tokushima city.

Temple 11: Fujii-dera

By the shortest route via Ōnoshima bridge, it's a 9.8km walk from Temple 10 to **Temple 11: Fujii-dera** (藤井寺). A lovely spot this, tucked into the foothills at the base of the

Along the Way We Met...

BEATRICE I love travel and walking. I did the Camino de Santiago by bicycle, but the Shikoku pilgrimage really captured my imagination. I'm not confident about walking the whole way, but I've committed to walking as far as Kōchi and have made accommodation bookings for my first 14 nights. I did a lot of preparation. There's a Facebook page on the pilgrimage with lots of information and advice. Plus, I'm using the Henro Helper app and Google Translate, as I don't speak Japanese.

Beatrice, from Montréal, Canada, is in her 75th year and dreamed of walking solo in Japan.

BEATRICE'S TIP: *My biggest issue is with the weight of my pack. Don't bring too much.*

Yoshino-gawa

Temple 11:
Fujii-dera

9.8km

Via Zennyuji Island is the enjoyable route – stock up on supplies now

mountains. *Fuji* means wisteria and it's said that Kōbō Daishi planted the original wisteria here. If you turn up in spring when the flowers are blooming, you may want to stick around.

Fujii-dera is the first of three Zen temples of the 88 on the pilgrimage. Destroyed during the Tensho period, it was revived during the Edo period and became a Zen temple in 1674.

One of the hazards of being close to forested mountains is that temples can be easily burnt by raging mountain fires and, over the years, Fujii-dera is said to have lost a number of important buildings on the temple grounds. While those who come by car are firmly focused on the temple itself, walkers tend to look to the left of the *hondō* at the notorious trail leading up the mountain to Temple 12: Shōsan-ji.

Temple 12: Shōsan-ji

The trek up may be arduous (see p58), but once you're there, **Temple 12: Shōsan-ji** (焼山寺), the first *real* mountain temple of the pilgrimage at 706m, is truly magnificent. It's surrounded by ancient cedars and boasts moss-coated statues, stone steps, a feeling of remote sacredness and views of the surrounding mountains. The *okunoin* (the temple's innermost sanctuary) is at the top of the 938m mountain, another hour or so of climbing, but most pilgrims are content with climbing as far as the main temple buildings, performing their *mairi* and getting their temple stamp there. The *okunoin* is, however, one of the places where Kōbō Daishi is said to have performed ascetic practices leading up to his enlightenment.

The **temple office** at Shōsan-ji closes at 4.30pm, meaning you've got a strict deadline

Temple 11: Fujii-dera

as you won't be able to get your temple stamp in your *nōkyō-chō* after that time. Make sure you arrive before it closes to avoid having to hike back up the hill the next day, when the office reopens at 8am.

Shōsan-ji used to have temple lodgings, but the *shukubō* closed in 2022. Sudachi-an (p75), 3km below Temple 12, is an option.

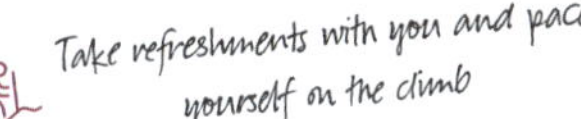

12.3km

**Temple 12:
Shōsan-ji**

Climbing to Temple 12: Shōsan-ji

The *henro* trail from Temple 11 to Temple 12 is notorious as the most difficult section of the pilgrimage for walkers; do some forward planning to make life easier.

HOW TO

Getting here: The trail begins at the left of the *hondō* at Temple 11. Stay somewhere close by, such as **Oyado Eleven** *(henrohouse. jp; ¥),* so that you do not have far to travel.

When to go: Set off early in the morning: the office at Temple 12: Shōsan-ji closes at 4.30pm and you cannot get your temple stamp after that time.

Tip: To ensure you get an early start, visit Temple 11: Fujii-dera before 5pm the day before to do your *mairi* and get your temple stamp.

More info: Take refreshments with you as there is nowhere to purchase them on the way up.

Everybody Is Different

Whether you find the climb from Temple 11 to Temple 12 difficult or not will come down to your age, experience and fitness level. Those who are young, fit and hike regularly may well find it a breeze and wonder what all the fuss is about. Those who are older, less fit or have joint issues are likely to find it tough going.

The trail is 12.3km, according to the somewhat gnarled *henro-michi* sign at the start of the trail at Temple 11 – allow four hours to Temple 12 if you're fit, and double that if you anticipate having issues. Be prepared, as there is nowhere to get supplies along the way. While you'll be walking with the Daishi, teaming up with another walker is not a bad idea.

Up & Down

The hike wouldn't be so much of an issue if the trail only climbed

up to Shōsan-ji, which, at 706m, is the second-highest temple on the pilgrimage. The problem is that the trail climbs up, then along a long ridge, then, horror of horrors, descends to a valley floor, crosses a river, then climbs up again.

A friendly sign then points out that you're on the steepest part of the pilgrimage. It's testing stuff and over the last 1.8km of track, you'll climb 270 vertical metres. This is the legendary *henro-korogashi* section, the 'pilgrims fall down' path. Here,

NO BAGS, MORE FUN

On the day you undertake the trek up to Temple 12, stay at **Sudachi-an** (p75), the closest accommodation, which is a 3km descent from Temple 12. Reserve the 'meals included' option.

Sudachi-an will transfer your baggage from some accommodation places around Temple 11 to Sudachi-an for free, if you stay at one of those places the night before your trek. This means you'll reap the benefits of walking from Temple 11 to Temple 12 without a backpack! Check up-to-date details at sudachian.com.

Left: Pilgrim climbing stairs to Temple 12: Shōsan-ji;
Below: Statue, forest near Temple 12: Shōsan-ji

in particular, you may well pat yourself on the back for investing in a *kongō-zue* (*henro* walking stick) when you made your purchases in the shop at Temple 1: Ryōzen-ji. And you're bound to be ecstatic if you're not carrying a heavy backpack.

Got Wheels?

Henro with wheels have a 35km drive from Temple 11 on winding mountain roads to get up to Temple 12. The drive takes about an hour and parking when you get there costs ¥300.

The Heart of Pilgrimage

The Shikoku pilgrimage is both a physical and spiritual journey. The motivations to follow the footsteps of monk Kōbō Daishi (Kūkai), the founder of the Shingon school of Buddhism, are diverse, but the outcomes can be transformative.

WORDS BY **KATHRYN WORTLEY**
A passionate explorer, I'm always looking for my next adventure.

WHILE TRAVELING IN Shikoku, I often pass by pilgrims. Frequently, they are dressed in traditional garb: a *hakui* (white cotton jacket with three-quarter-length sleeves), a *wakesa* (thin purple, orange or green scarf) and a *sugegasa* (conical hat made from sedge and bamboo). Others wear walking gear and merely carry a *kongō-zue*, the authentic walking stick typically inscribed with the Heart Sutra or the phrase *Dōgyō Ninin* (literally, 'as two, we walk together'), to symbolise that the pilgrim is always accompanied by Kōbō Daishi. Attached to the staff is a bell designed to pull the pilgrim's attention back to the present should their mind wander – even if you don't see pilgrims on your travels, you might hear them.

What unites all the pilgrims, though, are their expressions: awe as they gaze upon the temples, satisfaction after they've climbed hundreds of steep stone steps, gratitude as they accept small gifts from local people, wonder as they stroll mountain paths enveloped by unspoilt nature, joy as they chat with fellow pilgrims at teahouses along the way, and accomplishment as they reach the end of their journey.

For international pilgrims, in particular, this confidence is not always apparent at first. I recall, on several occasions, seeing small groups huddled together, nervously fixing backpack straps and checking maps at Ryōzen-ji, the first temple on the route. But unease among pilgrims as they depart is natural, says Satoshi Asano, the fifth-generation owner of Sumotoriya (p55), a store selling pilgrim goods near Temple 10: Kirihata-ji, and a passionate believer that people are at the heart of the Shikoku pilgrimage.

Satoshi Asano, owner of Sumotoriya Asano Pilgrim Shop (p55)

KATHRYN WORTLEY/LONELY PLANET

A Warm Welcome

Satoshi Asano meets hundreds of pilgrims at his store every year. Each of them has their own reason for walking, from paying tribute to their ancestors and making heartfelt wishes, to improving physical or emotional health and pursuing self-discovery. Many of the European visitors are familiar with the idea of a pilgrimage, having already travelled the Camino de Santiago, a network of ancient pilgrim routes stretching across Europe and coming together at the tomb of St James in Santiago de Compostela, Spain.

Still, most visitors are initially unsure of what to expect on the trail or even if it's appropriate for them to complete the Shikoku pilgrimage if they do not belong to the Shingon sect. Asano's goals are therefore to provide guidance and reassurance, as well as a place of rest and encouragement. Drawing on his background at the Tokyo and New York offices of the Japan National Tourism Organization, he has registered Sumotoriya as a tourist information centre, which provides as much information and advice in English as it does in Japanese.

'The Shikoku pilgrimage is rare as it's a circular loop with no fixed start or end point; one can keep walking indefinitely. And it's open to everyone,' he says. 'I try to welcome pilgrims with the spirit of *ichigo ichie* – cherishing each encounter as a once-in-a-lifetime moment – acting as a representative of the local community.'

A Shared Journey

Sumotoriya is a multifaceted business that also supplies Buddhist altar fittings and *kakejiku* (hanging scrolls), including those featuring pilgrim stamps from each temple, which Asano mounts onsite using techniques honed by artisans from generation to generation.

Asano fondly remembers the opportunities he has had to walk parts of the route, when he enjoyed deep self-reflection and connection to nature. Pilgrims today can expect similar experiences, as well as meaningful encounters, a spiritual reset and renewed feelings of purpose, fulfilment and well-being, he says.

Most life-changing, though, is often what walkers learn about themselves and others. Interacting with local people, whose care for pilgrims is embedded deeply in the way of life, can be transformative, giving once-hesitant visitors the self-assurance to make the most of their journey, regardless of its duration.

Residents' care includes *zenkonyado* (free or cheap lodgings) and *osettai* (small gifts or other acts of kindness), which are bestowed to pilgrims freely and without the expectation of anything in return. These customs are unique to Shikoku and are characterised by kindness and mutual respect, whereby local people view the pilgrimage as a shared, spiritual endeavour that they, too, are invested in. 'I offer *osettai* to those who visit Sumotoriya, with the feeling that they are walking the pilgrimage on my behalf,' explains Asano.

The community's warm embrace of pilgrims is one of the reasons the Shikoku pilgrimage is so special. When I next meet a pilgrim, I'll be sure to offer a snack or drink as *osettai* even though I'm not a resident of Shikoku. After all, we belong to the same global community of travellers.

Most life-changing, though, is often what walkers learn about themselves and others. Interacting with local people, whose care for pilgrims is embedded deeply in the way of life, can be transformative, giving once-hesitant visitors the self-assurance to make the most of their journey, regardless of its duration.

Shōsan-ji

TEMPLE 12

There's plenty of excitement at having survived the climb up to Temple 12, so it's easy to enjoy the descent and the walk through bustling Tokushima city. After an urban cluster west of the central city, the temples are further apart as pilgrims head south and into mountainous parts of the prefecture; two temples sit at high elevations, so there's more climbing to do, but then the trail heads out to the welcoming coastline.

Craig McLachlan

Temple 19: Tatsue-ji (p71)
AMEHIME/SHUTTERSTOCK

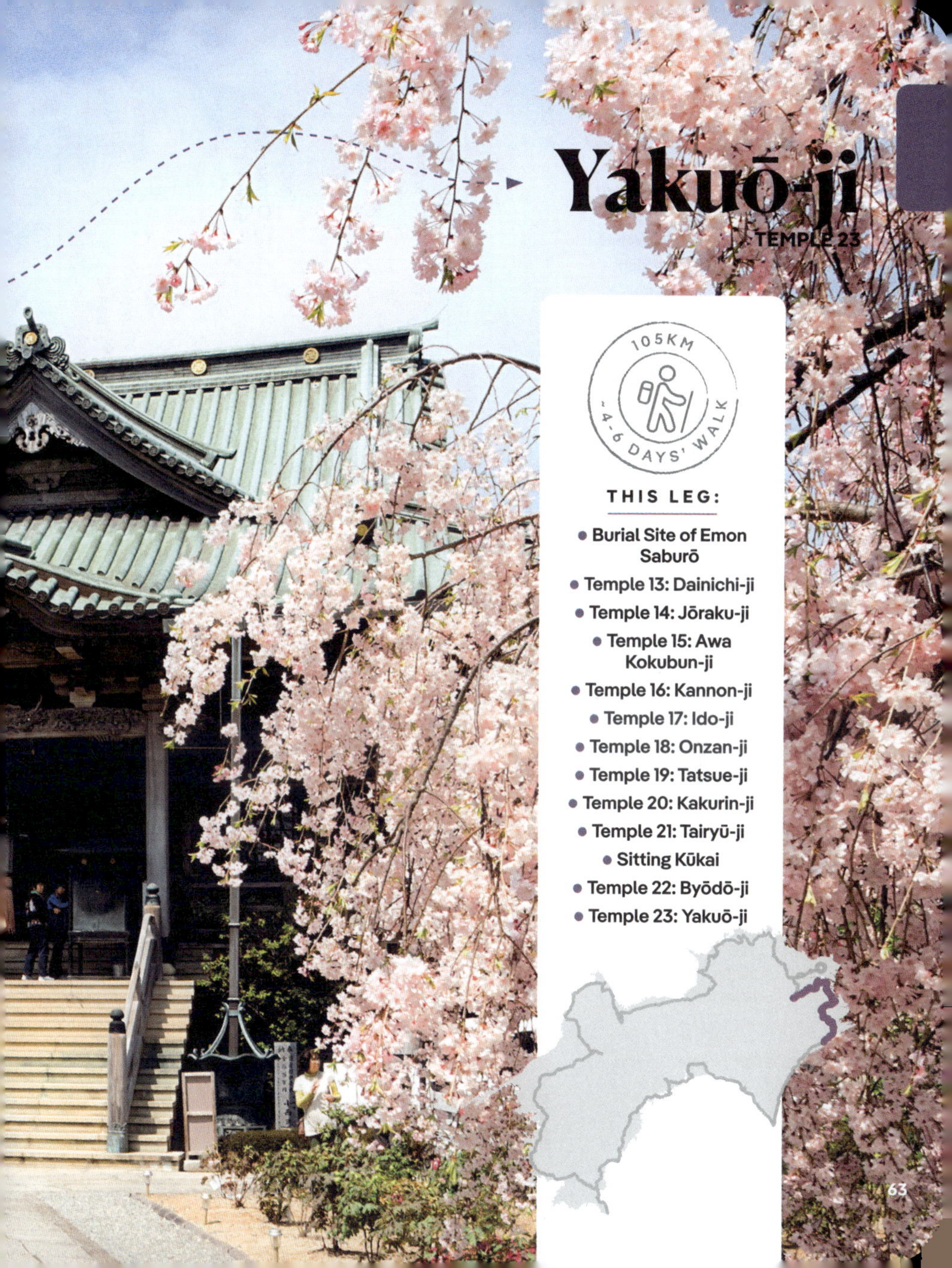
Yakuō-ji
TEMPLE 23

105KM
~4-6 DAYS' WALK

THIS LEG:

Burial Site of Emon Saburō
Temple 13: Dainichi-ji
Temple 14: Jōraku-ji
Temple 15: Awa Kokubun-ji
Temple 16: Kannon-ji
Temple 17: Ido-ji
Temple 18: Onzan-ji
Temple 19: Tatsue-ji
Temple 20: Kakurin-ji
Temple 21: Tairyū-ji
Sitting Kūkai
Temple 22: Byōdō-ji
Temple 23: Yakuō-ji

Walking Notes

Everything is fairly straightforward for walkers here until you turn inland from Temple 19 to head into the mountains, with tough climbs up to Temples 20 and 21, plus a knee-knocking descent between them. For *henro* (pilgrims) with wheels, there's another option for getting up to Temple 21, the Tairyū-ji Ropeway (p74).

Breaking Your Journey

Coming out of the mountains from Temple 12, there are lots of places to stay in and around Tokushima city (p34). Heading south, the *shukubō* (temple lodging) at Temple 19: Tatsue-ji is a good option; you'll want to do some careful planning as you head back into the mountains for Temples 20 and 21. Hiwasa township has good places around Temple 23.

Craig's Tips

MEALS Reserve meals where you stay around Temple 12 as there's nowhere to buy food.

FAVOURITE VIEW Unbelievable panorama from the Sitting Kūkai statue (p75).

ESSENTIAL STOP Temple 21: Tairyū-ji is simply stunning (p73).

TOP TIP Book early to get a spot to sleep at Sudachi-an below Temple 12 (p75).

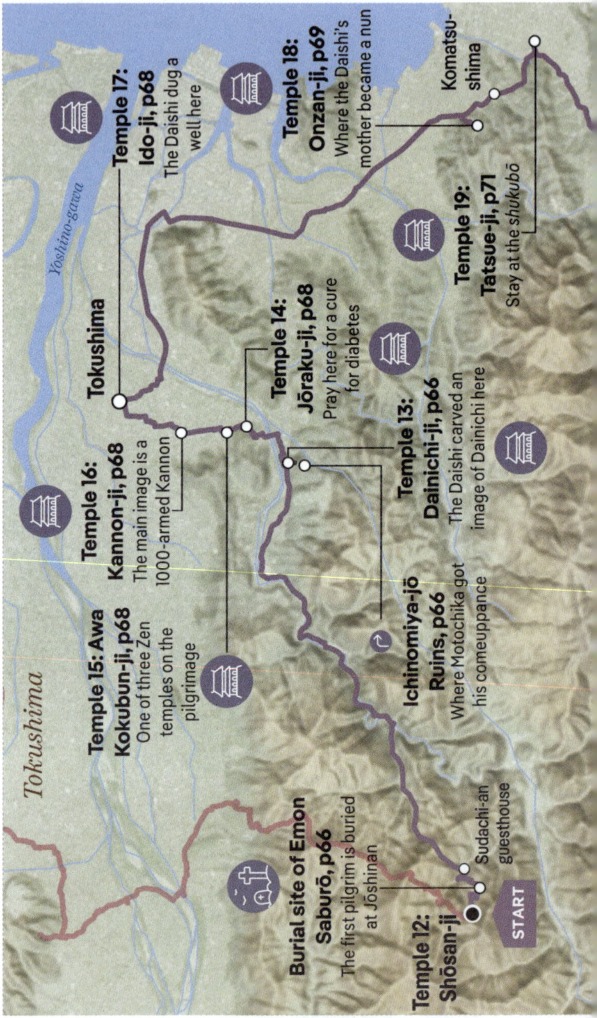

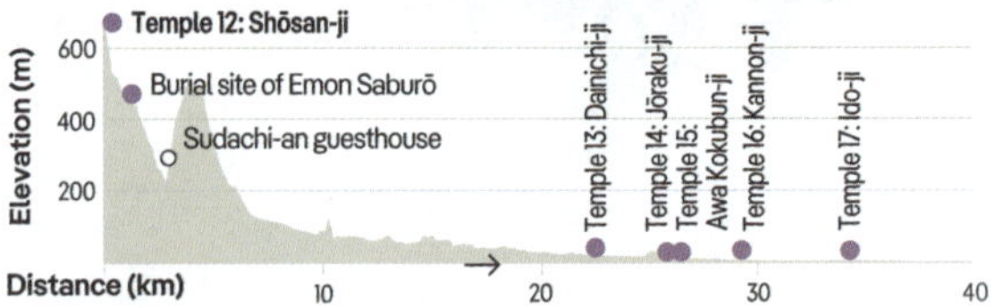

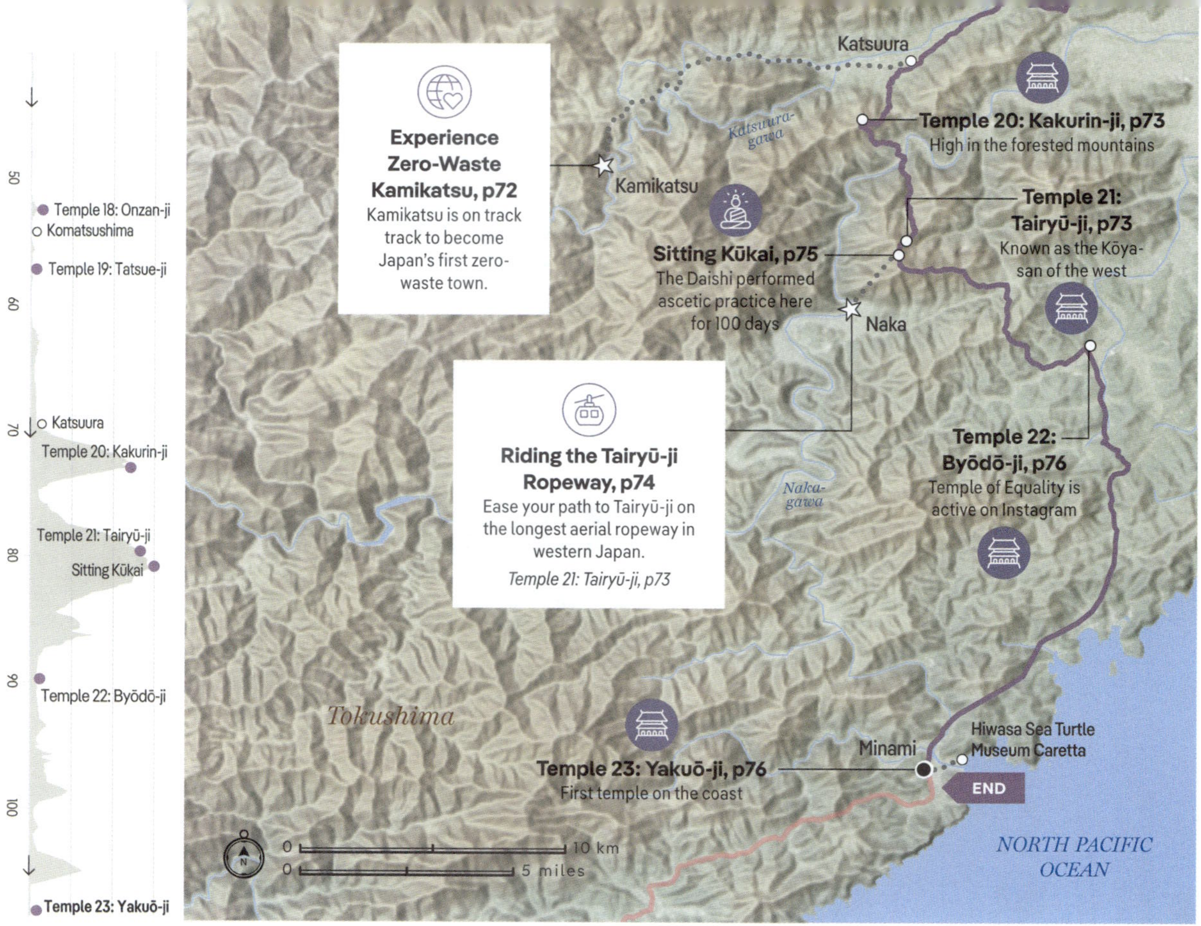

NORTH PACIFIC OCEAN

Temple 20: Kakurin-ji, p73
High in the forested mountains

Temple 21: Tairyū-ji, p73
Known as the Koya-san of the west

Temple 22: Byōdō-ji, p76
Temple of Equality is active on Instagram

Katsuura
Kamikatsu
Naka
Katsuura-gawa
Naka-gawa

Sitting Kūkai, p75
The Daishi performed ascetic practice here for 100 days

Experience Zero-Waste Kamikatsu, p72
Kamikatsu is on track to become Japan's first zero-waste town.

Riding the Tairyū-ji Ropeway, p74
Ease your path to Tairyū-ji on the longest aerial ropeway in western Japan.
Temple 21: Tairyū-ji, p73

Temple 23: Yakuō-ji, p76
First temple on the coast

Hiwasa Sea Turtle Museum Caretta
Minami
END

Tokushima

10 km
5 miles
0

N

Temple 18: Onzan-ji
Komatsushima
Temple 19: Tatsue-ji
Katsuura
Temple 20: Kakurin-ji
Temple 21: Tairyū-ji
Sitting Kūkai
Temple 22: Byōdō-ji
Temple 23: Yakuō-ji

50   60   70   80   90   100

BRESTER IRINA/SHUTTERSTOCK

PREVIOUS STOP From Temple 12: Shōsan-ji (p57), at 706m, you'll be heading down the hill on a well-used *henro-michi* (pilgrim track) into the valley below, probably to stay overnight. It's an easy walk after the strength-sapping climb up to Temple 12, with a pilgrimage highlight along the way.

Burial Site of Emon Saburō

A 1.3km amble down the hill from Temple 12: Shōsan-ji will bring you to the small roadside temple **Jōshinan** (杖杉庵), beside a statue of Kōbō Daishi and the man said to be the first pilgrim, Emon Saburō.

Saburō was a rich and greedy man who refused to help the Daishi when he appeared at his gate, but who, remorseful after tragedy struck his family, set out to find the Daishi and beg forgiveness. He circled Shikoku many times, before deciding to increase his chances of meeting Kōbō Daishi by going *gyaku-uchi* (around the other way). At this spot, struggling up the path and near death, Saburō finally met the Daishi, was given absolution, asked to be reborn to help others, and died. According to legend, Kōbō Daishi buried him and planted his staff by the grave, and that staff grew into the cedar that stands there today.

There's more to the story and, further along the trail, *henro* will hear of Emon Saburō again (p162). If you're planning to overnight at Sudachi-an, it's only another 1.5km ahead.

Temple 13: Dainichi-ji

You'll want to allow five to six hours to walk the 21km from Temple 12: Shōsan-ji to **Temple 13: Dainichi-ji** (大日寺; *dai13.jp*), which sits right next to the Akui-gawa.

Thought you'd already been to a Dainichi-ji? Yes, it's the same name as for Temple 4, and you'll see it again at Temple 28. In Shingon Buddhism, the Buddha Dainichi represents the universe and everything within it, making Dainichi-ji a popular name for temples. It's said that when Kōbō Daishi was performing a fire ceremony here, he had a vision of Dainichi, who told him he wanted a temple built on this spot; the Daishi carved an image of Dainichi and founded Dainichi-ji.

DETOUR: Ichinomiya-jō Ruins

Temple 13: Dainichi-ji is another temple that was razed at the hands of Chōsokabe Motochika in the early 1580s. All the buildings were burnt down and needed to be rebuilt. If you're up for an

REGGAEMAN/CC BY-SA 3.0/WIKIMEDIA COMMONS

Statue of Emon Saburō and Kōbō Daishi

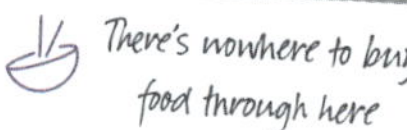

Temple 12: Shōsan-ji

Burial site of Emon Saburō

1.3km

Don't miss the significance of the Emon Saburo legend

There's nowhere to buy food through here

Ichinomiya Shrine

extra walk, just over the road from Dainichi-ji at **Ichinomiya Shrine**, a trail leads up the mountain to the castle ruins of **Ichinomiya-jō**, where Motochika got his comeuppance.

In 1585, when Toyotomi Hideyoshi invaded Shikoku with a force of over 100,000 men, a series of battles culminated in the siege of Ichinomiya-jō, which lasted for 26 days until the forces of Motochika surrendered. The castle was torn down in 1615 under the 'one domain, one castle' rule set down by the Tokugawa shogunate, but interesting stone walls, steps and ruins remain, plus tremendous views out north over the valley. Allow 30 minutes from the trailhead to get up to the ruins, which sit at 144m above sea level.

KEEP UP WITH THE LATEST

Konbini (convenience stores) are extremely convenient...until they're not. Unfortunately for walking *henro*, a 7-Eleven that was 500m west of Temple 13: Dainichi-ji closed in August 2025. This means that for pilgrims walking the shortest route, there is nowhere to purchase food from before Temple 11 until after Temple 16. Make sure to reserve meals with your accommodation and stock up accordingly. Up-to-date information such as this is regularly on the Henro Helper app and Facebook pages, so it's important to keep up with latest *henro* news, especially if you are walking.

**Temple 13:
Dainichi-ji**

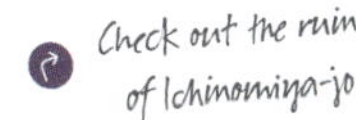

20km

You're now entering the cluster of temples in Tokushima city (p34)

Check out the ruins of Ichinomiya-jo

Temple 14: Jōraku-ji

Including Temple 13: Dainichi-ji, you're now into a cluster of five temples that may well feel like a little prize for having survived the climb to Temple 12. The five are all officially within the boundaries of Tokushima city, but sit well west of the central city and are often visited as a one-day mini-pilgrimage. From Temple 13, it's only 2.5km to **Temple 14: Jōraku-ji** (常楽寺).

Temple 14 has a couple of interesting specialities. It's said that the leaves of the tree to the right of the *hondō* (main hall), when ground up and drunk with water, are a cure for diabetes. A smiling statue of the Daishi can be seen high up among its branches. Many afflicted with diabetes come here to pray for a cure. Intriguingly, parents also come here to pray for an end to their child's bed-wetting and night-crying issues.

Temple 15: Awa Kokubun-ji

From Temple 14, it's a 1km walk to **Temple 15: Awa Kokubun-ji** (阿波国分寺). If you were surprised to find that three of the 88 temples are called Dainichi-ji, you'll probably be similarly surprised to hear that you'll be visiting four Kokubun-ji. The national temples were set up in each of Japan's provinces in 741 CE by Emperor Shōmu during the Nara period (710–94). A total of 68 Kokubun-ji were established across Japan, one in each of the 67 provinces, with Tōdai-ji in Nara serving as the head temple. The goal was to promote Buddhism as the state religion, strengthen imperial rule and foster a sense of national unity. It is surprising that Awa Kokubun-ji is one of three Zen temples on the pilgrimage, having been burnt down, rebuilt and changed to Zen in 1741.

Awa is the old provincial name for Tokushima and you'll still see it being used all over the place; Tokushima's big dance festival is the Awa-odori and the prefecture's home bank is Awa Ginkō.

A highlight at Awa Kokubun-ji is a dry pond garden and an artificial hill garden with stone arrangements on all four sides; it is a designated Place of Scenic Beauty (entry ¥300).

Temple 16: Kannon-ji

If the last couple of temples felt like they were on the verge of suburbia, **Temple 16: Kannon-ji** (観音寺), the first of two Kannon-ji on the pilgrimage, is best described as urban, being near the meeting of Rte 29 and National Rte 192. This is a very busy little temple, taking up minimal space on a busy street, but if you're driving, count yourself lucky as it has a good parking lot right next door that's free. Kannon-ji is a 2km walk north from Temple 15.

The temple's treasures include three images attributed to Kōbō Daishi, who is said to have carved them about 80 years after the temple was founded in 741. The main image is a **1000-armed Kannon**, goddess of mercy and compassion; 30 of the 88 temples are dedicated to Kannon and two of the temples are named for her. Parents pray to Jizō, guardian of children, here, for their offspring's health and growth.

Temple 17: Ido-ji

A 3km walk northeast from Temple 16 will bring you to **Temple 17: Ido-ji** (井戸寺). Although it was founded in 674 CE, you'll find new buildings here as the temple last burnt down in 1968. This is the Temple of the Well, and Kōbō Daishi is said to have solved the area's water problems by digging a well with his staff

---

Temple 14: Jōraku-ji

Temple 15: Awa Kokubun-ji

Temple 17: Ido-ji

Temple 18: Onzan-ji

2.5km   1km   2km   3km   20km

Temple 13: Dainichi-ji

First of the national temples built in 741 CE

Temple 16: Kannon-ji

Enjoy some time in central Tokushima city

to produce good drinking water in only one night. He then carved a nearly 2m tall statue of Kannon, goddess of mercy, out of a single piece of Japanese cypress, and it is this statue that is the temple's main treasure.

It's said that if you look into the legendary well dug by Kōbō Daishi and see a reflection of yourself, you will have good fortune and health. If not, you're up for misfortune within three years!

Temple 18: Onzan-ji

From Temple 17, it's a 20km walk, first east, then south, through Tokushima city on busy roads to get to **Temple 18: Onzan-ji** (恩山寺). There is a back route, but it involves climbing up and over hills. The good news is that there are lots of top places to stay and eat along the way.

Onzan-ji sits on its own forested hill, up a side road off Rte 136. If you've walked here on busy Tokushima and Komatsushima city roads, it feels like a quiet escape up in the hills.

Temple 19: Tatsue-ji Shukubō ¥¥
There are not many opportunities to stay and eat at temple lodgings these days, so book ahead with dinner and breakfast included. *tatsueji.com*

JA Yottene Market, Katsuura ¥
Stock up at this excellent roadside market before starting the climb up to Temple 20; a couple of big climbs coming up and no eateries. JA よって ネ市; *7am–5pm*

Michi-no-eki Hiwasa, Hiwasa ¥
Below Temple 23, fuel up at the Roadside Rest Area restaurant, get snacks for the road and soak your feet in the free *ashi-yu* (foot bath). 道の駅日和佐; *8am–5pm*

Temple 17: Ido-ji

AMEHIME/SHUTTERSTOCK

Temple 18: Onzan-ji

HENRO WITH WHEELS

- If you're driving, allow two to three days to visit Temples 12 to 23.
- Base yourself in Tokushima city to visit Temples 12 to 17; Temple 12: Shōsan-ji is 36km from Tokushima city and Temples 13 to 17 are within 10km of the central city.
- The day you head south, get an early start, use the Tairyū-ji Ropeway (p74) to get to Temple 21 and aim to be at Temple 23 on the coast by late afternoon.
- The beach and surf towns of Shishi-kui, Shirahama or Ikumi make for fun places to stay.
- If you drive as far as Ikumi Beach (p84) from Tokushima city, you'll have driven less than 120km for the day.

The story goes that when Kōbō Daishi was here for ascetic training, his mother came to visit him, but was turned away at the gate for being a woman. Females were not admitted to sacred sites in those times, but the Daishi took exception to this rule, staging a lengthy ritual and performing a ceremony for the liberation of women. His mother was admitted, cut her own hair and became a nun. This story is said to show the Daishi's regard for women and his assertion that they, as well as men, could achieve Buddhahood. The pilgrimage is an egalitarian one, seen throughout modern history as a pilgrimage

Temple 18:
Onzan-ji

Takes you up in the forested foothills

4.5km

for the common people, based on the Shingon belief that anyone can achieve enlightenment in this lifetime.

Temple 19: Tatsue-ji

It's a 4.5km walk from Temple 18 to **Temple 19: Tatsue-ji** (立江寺; *tatsueji.com*), relocated and rebuilt in 1659 after being burnt by the forces of Chōsokabe Motochika. Tatsue-ji is a colourful, busy urban temple near the Tatsue-gawa, surrounded by its township.

While the *henro* of old faced political barriers at provincial boundaries, showing a 'passport' issued by their home authorities that authorised them to be out on the pilgrimage, they were also met with religious barriers: famously, Tatsue-ji is one of four encountered by *henro* on the pilgrimage. At a temple barrier, *henro* face a spiritual test – if they are pure of intention, are able to worship and continue on their way without mishap, then they have passed the test. If, however, they have not lived up to their obligations as a pilgrim, not maintained their vows or are confronted with trouble, then tradition says that they should return to Temple 1: Ryōzen-ji and start again!

Here you will find a **statue of Binzuru**, a physician who was the first among the 16 disciples of Buddha. The statue has been made shiny by pilgrims rubbing him, then pressing the part of their own body that hurts in an effort to relieve pain. Don't linger though, or you may have to return to Temple 1 to restart your pilgrimage.

Tatsue-ji also runs a *shukubō;* to stay at the temple lodgings, call ahead at least one day in advance.

Continues on page 73

Along the Way We Met...

MIKE I'm a practising Buddhist. I'm interested in learning about the various sects and have travelled to Thailand to study, too. The people here are amazing. I walked with an 83-year-old Japanese man for three days. He couldn't speak English and I can't speak much Japanese, but we had a blast. This is Type 2 fun. Some of it might not feel like fun at the time, but it's incredibly rewarding and you'll appreciate it later.

Mike, from Colorado, has just retired and is now on his 'voyage of self-discovery'.

MIKE'S TIP: *Wearing pilgrim gear is great for meeting locals as everybody will know what you are doing.*

Temple 19:
Tatsue-ji

Head west into the mountains

Experience Zero-Waste Kamikatsu

How does a small town not only survive but thrive in rural Shikoku? By aiming to be Japan's first zero-waste town and seizing all opportunities.

HOW TO

Nearest stop: Temple 20: Kakurin-ji

Getting here: From Temple 20, drive west on Rte 16 from Katsuura, at the foot of the temple access road, for 15km. From Tokushima city, it's one hour from JR Tokushima Station by car or two hours (with one transfer) by public bus.

Tip: Stay overnight at WHY. Reserve rooms in English on the website.

More info: tourism-kamikatsu.jp

It can't be easy convincing everyone in a town of 1400 that all household waste should be separated into 45 categories and sent to be recycled, but **Kamikatsu town** (上勝町) is doing just that. Some 80% of waste produced in the town is recycled, compared with a 20% average throughout the rest of Japan.

Things have been pumping since the opening of **Kamikatsu Zero Waste Center WHY** (*why-kamikatsu.jp; ¥¥*) in 2020, predominantly built using waste materials such as old windows and frames, designed in the shape of a question mark, and winner of an award from the Architectural Institute of Japan.

Why build a hotel next to a garbage station? So that visitors can come, stay in rooms made from local cedar, learn about Kamikatsu's zero-waste endeavours, and enjoy both local cuisine and the starry skies out here in the mountains.

The kanji characters for the town's name 上勝 can translate to Rise and Win and that's been taken on by the excellent **RISE & WIN Brewing Co** (*kamikatz.jp*), based in its stunning barbecue and general store.

THE WASHINGTON POST/GETTY IMAGES

Kamikatsu Zero Waste Center WHY

Continued from page 71

Temple 20: Kakurin-ji

While the path since descending from Temple 12: Shōsan-ji has been easy going on the flats around Tokushima city, it's time to return to the mountains. That means turning west into the Katsuura-gawa valley. Plan where to stay as, once you make the climb up to Temple 20, you're committed to a long walk. Roadside **JA Yottene Market** in Katsuura is a good place to stock up on food, while **Henro Yado Sora** (*henroyadosora@gmail.com*) is an excellent place to stay near the start of the climb.

It may be only a 13km journey from Temple 19 to **Temple 20: Kakurin-ji** (鶴林寺), but over the last 2.8km you'll be climbing steeply up to the temple at 486m, high into the forested mountains, mostly on a *henro* trail. It's a lot easier than the hike up to Temple 12, but still a breathtaking climb. Drivers will be facing a particularly winding road to get up close to the temple.

As with most mountain temples, the grounds are gorgeous, with ancient trees, plenty of moss and lots of stone steps connecting different parts of the complex. Kakurin-ji means Crane Forest Temple and Kōbō Daishi is said to have founded it and named it after a pair of white cranes that he saw protecting a statue of Jizō at the foot of a tall cedar. Statues of elegant cranes sit around the grounds.

Temple 21: Tairyū-ji

Walkers really only have one knee-knocking option to get from Temple 20 to **Temple 21: Tairyū-ji** (太龍寺), which sits at 490m on a 600m-high mountain to the south, on the far side of the Naka-gawa valley from

Temple 20: Kakurin-ji

Temple 20. As on the route to Temple 12, this is *henro-korogashi* (pilgrims fall down) territory as you tumble down a *henro* trail from Temple 20 at 470m to the road and river bridge in the valley at around 50m, then climb 440m up to Temple 21 at 490m, all in about 6km of trail. Tairyū-ji is known as a *nansho* for walkers – one of the most difficult places to get to on the pilgrimage, a test of the *henro's* dedication and stamina. It is, however, not at all difficult for those who are driving, thanks to the Tairyū-ji Ropeway (p74).

However you get there, you'll marvel at this sacred place with its sky-reaching cedars, time-honoured temple buildings and perfectly planned gardens, known as 'the Kōya-san of the west'. It's easy to see why it has been made so accessible by ropeway; everyone should have the opportunity to visit such a life-encouraging place.

Continues on page 75

**Temple 19:
Tatsue-ji**

13km

A big climb up to
Crane Forest Temple

**Temple 20:
Kakurin-ji**

6km

Temple 21: Tairyū-ji

Henro with wheels can
explore Kamikatsu

Riding the Tairyū-ji Ropeway

Temple 21: Tairyū-ji, one of the most difficult temples for pilgrims to reach on foot, is easy for those with wheels to get to thanks to the longest aerial ropeway in western Japan.

HOW TO

Nearest stop: Temple 21: Tairyū-ji

Getting here: It's 12km by car from Temple 20: Kakurin-ji to the ropeway's bottom station, Washi-no-sato Michi-no-eki (roadside rest stop), in Naka Town.

When to go: Runs every 20 minutes from 8am to 4.40pm daily

Cost: Adult/child return ¥2600/1300

More info: shikoku-cable.co.jp

Nearly everyone was a winner when the **Tairyū-ji Ropeway** opened in 1992. Temple 21: Tairyū-ji was happy, as dwindling numbers of pilgrims who could walk up to the notoriously difficult-to-reach temple were suddenly complemented by a surge of visitors who were whisked up in 10 minutes. The local townspeople were ecstatic, with jobs brought to their little corner of rural Shikoku. And, of course, those who couldn't walk up, but wanted to go there, were over the moon.

The only grumpy group were the purists who believe that a physical effort should be required as part of the pilgrimage. Nevertheless, the ropeway assured prosperity for the temple, with pilgrims arriving in batches of 100 per car every 20 minutes.

And this is one stunning ride, not only gaining altitude, but horizontal distance too, passing over the Naka-gawa, then climbing over a ridge to deposit you at the upper station, more or less right at the temple. At 2.775km in length, it's the longest aerial ropeway not only on Shikoku, but in western Japan.

Tairyū-ji Ropeway

FROM LEFT: ARAIYASUSHIGE/CC BY-SA 4.0/WIKIMEDIA COMMONS, CRAIG MCLACHLAN/LONELY PLANET

Stairs from Tairyū-ji Ropeway to Temple 21: Tairyū-ji (p73)

Continued from page 73

Sitting Kūkai

Although there are other options, an excellent way for walking *henro* to carry on to Temple 22: Byōdō-ji is via **Sitting Kūkai**, a large statue of Kōbō Daishi high on the mountain, with superb views out over the valley, at Shashinga-take, a 15-minute walk from Temple 21: Tairyū-ji. Clearly visible to those riding the ropeway, this is the spot where legend has it that the Daishi engaged in 100 days of ascetic practice, reciting the mantra of Kokuzo one million times, leading up to his enlightenment at Muroto-misaki.

Also here, you'll find **Yama Sakimori**, a sculpture in the Sakimori series by Masayuki Nagare;

BEST PLACES TO SLEEP

Sudachi-an ¥
Book early with meals for a spot at this rural guesthouse, 3km below Temple 12. *sudachian.com*

Temple 19: Tatsue-ji Temple Lodging ¥
Only six of the 88 temples have a *shukubō* for solo *henro* these days; call to book at least one day ahead. *tatsueji.com*

Oyado Hiwasa ¥
Classic Japanese rooms in a renovated fisher's house in Hiwasa, close to Temple 23: Yakuō-ji. *oyadohiwasa.com*

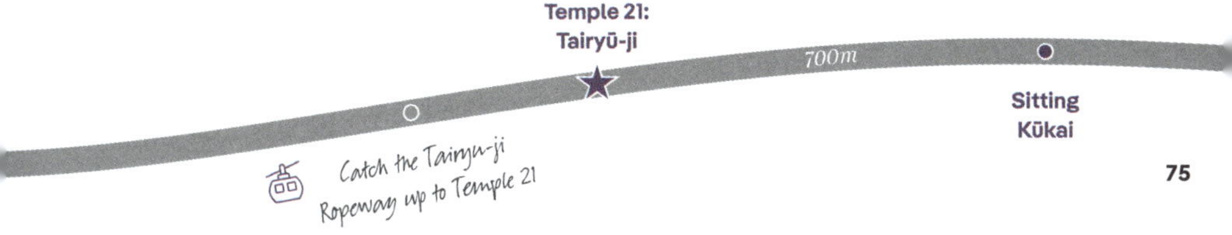

Temple 21:
Tairyū-ji

700m

Sitting Kūkai

the statue depicts a mountain sentinel, a protector of nature. The Sakimori series of abstract humanoid sculptures is characterised by a large hole in the chest, representing the removal of organs and desires.

When ready, *henro* can descend on the *henro-michi* to the valley in the east on their way to Temple 22: Byōdō-ji.

Temple 22: Byōdō-ji

Descending via the Sitting Kūkai statue, **Temple 22: Byōdō-ji** (平等寺; *byodoji.jp*) is an 11km walk from Temple 21. With a name meaning 'Temple of Equality', it's in the foothills of the small township of **Aratano**, close to the Kuwano-gawa.

Kōbō Daishi believed that all people should be equal in terms of having good health, so he dug a well here and purified his body in its clear, holy waters. Worshippers visit Byōdō-ji to drink the water, which is said to cure disease, and to pray for good health. With Yakushi, the Buddha of medicine, as its central deity, this modern-thinking temple has embraced the internet and has a 24-hour live stream of the goings-on in the *hondō*. The temple is also active on Instagram @byodoji.

If you're counting by temple numbers, you've now officially been to one-quarter of the temples.

JESSICA KORTEMAN/LONELY PLANET

Temple 23: Yakuō-ji

It's hard not to feel excited as you walk the 23km out to **Temple 23: Yakuō-ji** (薬王寺; *yakuouji.net*) as this is the last temple in Tokushima Prefecture and the first that is out on the coast. In the small town of **Hiwasa**, Yakuō-ji sits on a hillside overlooking the port town and the hilly entrance to its harbour. It is a very popular temple, well known as a *yakuyoke-dera* (temple visited to ward off

Along the Way We Met...

EIJI I wasn't very religious, but my wife was. She had a very good influence on me. We prayed at home regularly, but I lost her to cancer. So exactly a year later, I started walking the Shikoku pilgrimage. I wanted to come to terms with her death and think about the rest of my life. The people on Shikoku are so passionate and proud of their pilgrimage. I feel like it is a great privilege for me to walk around the 88 temples.

Eiji (57) was born and brought up in Japan, but has been living in New Zealand for 27 years.

EIJI'S TIP: *Appreciate the support of locals on Shikoku and the fellowship of other pilgrims.*

Steps at Temple 23: Yakuō-ji

ill fortune and evil spirits), especially during 'unlucky years'.

The unluckiest year for women is age 33, while for men it is age 42. Sixty-one is an unlucky age for both men and women. After crossing the *yakuyoke-bashi* bridge at Yakuō-ji, there are 33 stone steps leading up to the main hall for women to use, called the *onna-zaka* (women's slope); 42 steep stone steps are the *otoko-zaka* for men to climb. There are then 61 steps for both men and women to use. It is believed that climbing these steps and dropping a coin on each step along the way will cleanse pilgrims of their bad luck. At busy times, the steps can be covered in coins.

TURTLE TERRITORY

When you hit the coast in Hiwasa, you're in turtle territory and **Hiwasa Sea Turtle Museum Caretta** (*caretta. town.minami.lg.jp; adult/child ¥1000/500*), dedicated to the study and conservation of sea turtles, is a 30-minute walk from Temple 23: Yakuō-ji, out at **Ōhama Beach**. Recently refurbished, there's an indoor museum and large outdoor pools where you can view turtles up close. Ōhama Beach is known as a nesting site with loggerhead turtles returning annually between mid-May and mid-August to lay their eggs. The Hiwasa community has been actively involved in their protection for over 50 years.

Temple 23:
Yakuō-ji

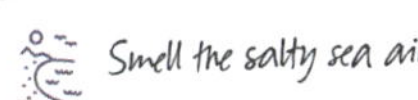

奉納 南無大日如来
奉納 南無大日如来
奉納 南無大師遍照金剛
奉納 南無大師遍照金剛
奉納 南無大師遍照金剛
京表装・各宗数珠・肌着
師小売

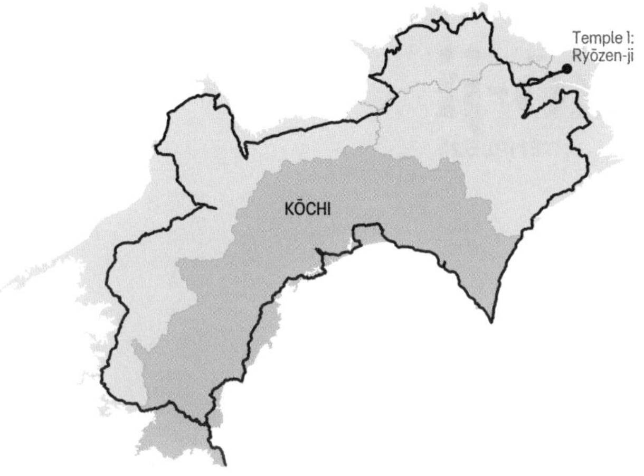

KŌCHI PREFECTURE

———

Formerly known as the province of Tosa, Kōchi is *Shugyō-no-dōjō* (the place of practice), the pilgrims' testing ground. The trail through Kōchi makes up more than a third of the pilgrimage's total distance, but has only 16 of its 88 temples. Kōchi, regarded as one of the wildest and most remote parts of Japan, faces the Pacific Ocean. It's a long haul around the coast between the two great southern capes, Muroto-misaki and Ashizuri-misaki. *Henro* (pilgrims) have always breathed a sigh of relief on getting through Kōchi, for the hardest part of the pilgrimage has been completed.

Temple 28: Dainichi-ji (p91)
AMEHIME/SHUTTERSTOCK

Yakuō-ji

TEMPLE 23

THIS LEG:

- Shishikui
- Kōchi Prefectural Border
- Shirahama
- Ikumi Beach
- Temple 24: Hotsumisaki-ji
- Temple 25: Shinshō-ji
- Temple 26: Kongōchō-ji
- Kiragawa
- Temple 27: Kōnomine-ji
- Aki
- Temple 28: Dainichi-ji

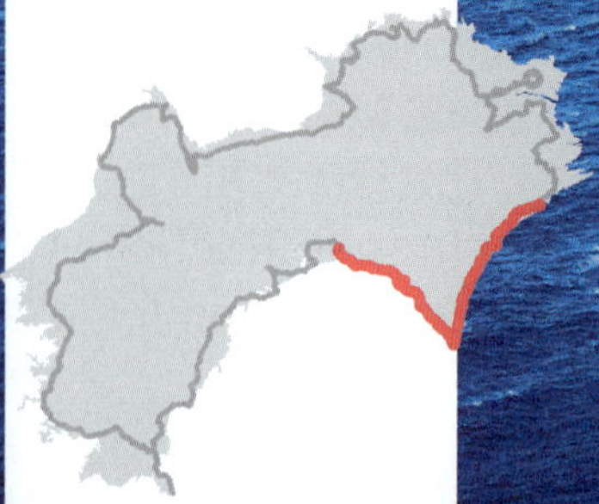

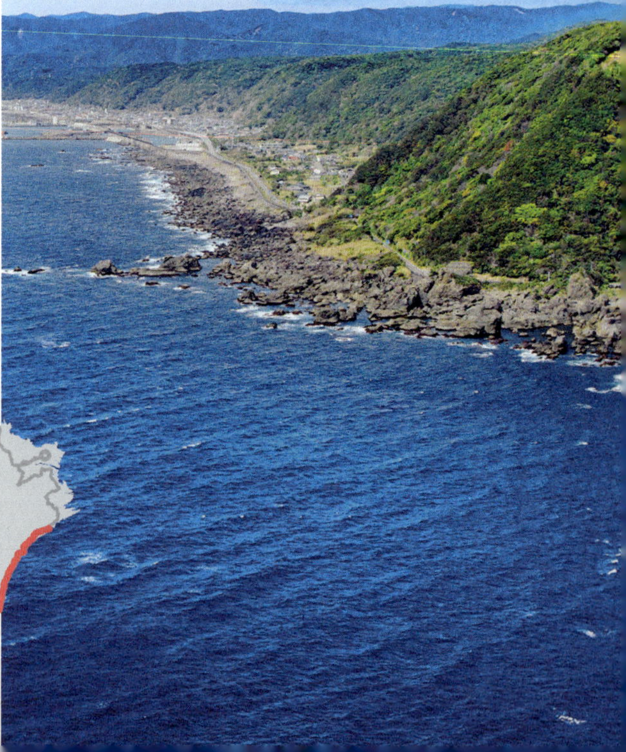

Dainichi-ji

TEMPLE 28

A long walk southwest down the Pacific coast leads to one of Shikoku's two great southern capes, remote Muroto-misaki, said to be where Kōbō Daishi achieved enlightenment at the age of 19. Will you become enlightened too? Once you've visited weather-battered Temple 24: Hotsumisaki-ji and are around the cape, you're still on the coast, though heading northwest now, up the other side towards the prefectural capital of Kōchi city (p96).

Craig McLachlan

Muroto-misaki (p86)
RYU_JP/SHUTTERSTOCK

Walking Notes

It's hard to avoid sealed roads until you get down near Muroto-misaki, except by climbing over mountain passes on the occasional *henro-michi* (pilgrim tracks), but they tend to make the journey longer. Temple 27: Kōnomine-ji is the tough climb here; avoid carrying your gear if you're going up and down the same route.

Breaking Your Journey

There are some fun places to stay along the surf coast, such as in Shishikui, Shirahama or Ikumi Beach. There are good places to overnight at Muroto-misaki and around Temple 25: Shinshō-ji. Heading northwest up the coast towards Temple 28: Dainichi-ji, there are lots of options: Kiragawa, Nahari, Tōnohama and Aki are all good spots to spend the night.

Craig's Tips

BEST MEAL Drop in to the stylish road-side cafe Hikōsen, in Shishikui (p89).

FAVOURITE VIEW From the coastal walking trails around Muroto-misaki (p86).

ESSENTIAL STOP Stop off for refreshments at Ikumi Beach to watch the surfers (p84).

TIP Stay at Minshuku Tōnohama before tackling the trail to Temple 27: you can leave you gear and pick it up on the way back (p90).

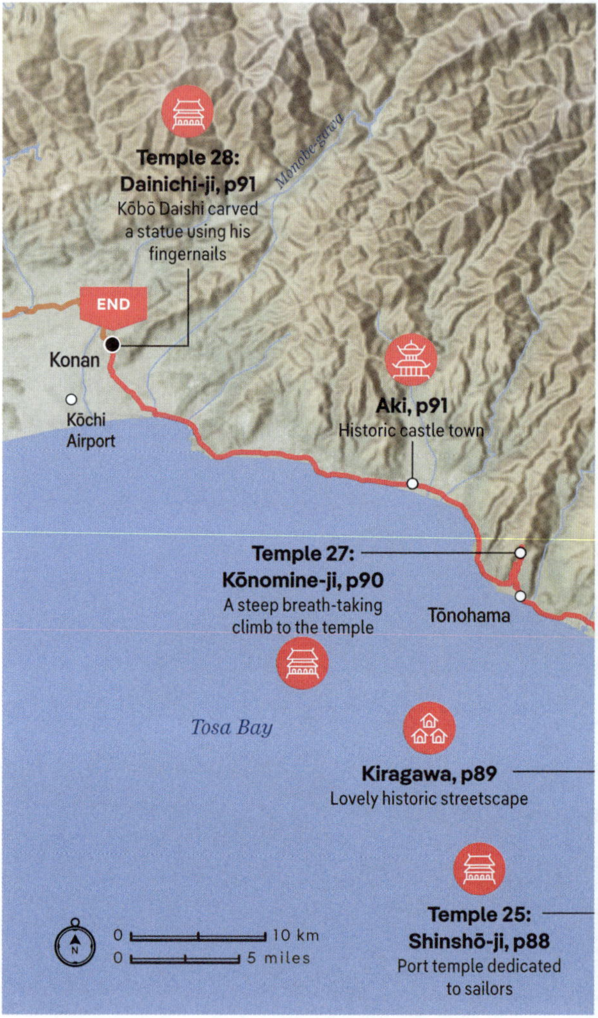

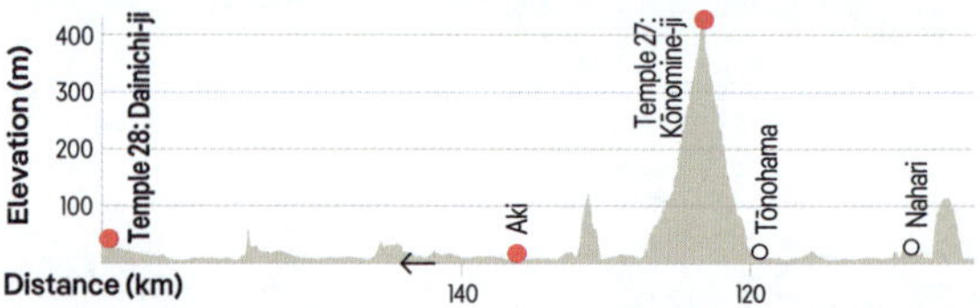

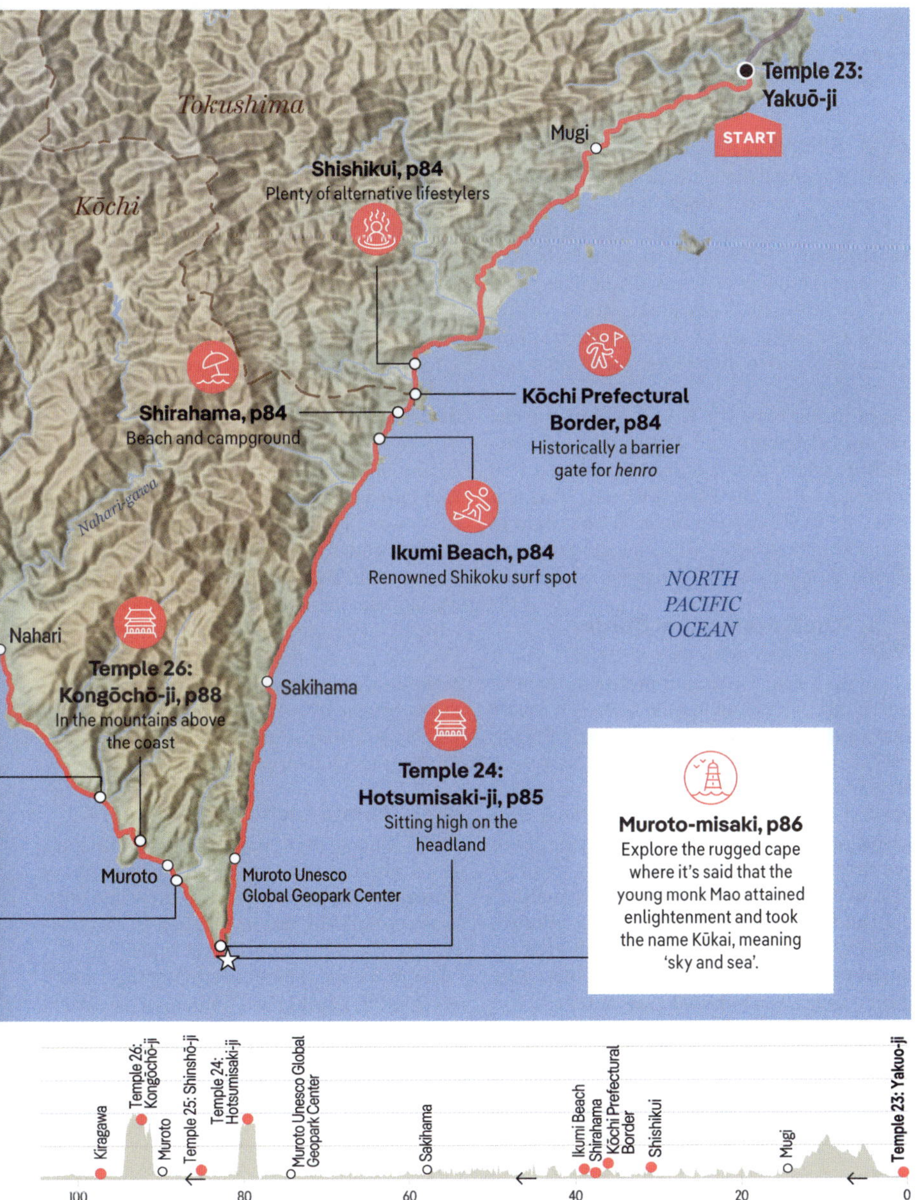

Tokushima
Kōchi
Temple 23:
Yakuō-ji
START
Mugi
Shishikui, p84
Plenty of alternative lifestylers
Shirahama, p84
Beach and campground
Nahari-gawa
Kōchi Prefectural
Border, p84
Historically a barrier
gate for henro
Ikumi Beach, p84
Renowned Shikoku surf spot
NORTH
PACIFIC
OCEAN
Nahari
Temple 26:
Kongōchō-ji, p88
In the mountains above
the coast
Sakihama
Temple 24:
Hotsumisaki-ji, p85
Sitting high on the
headland
Muroto
Muroto Unesco
Global Geopark Center
Muroto-misaki, p86
Explore the rugged cape
where it's said that the
young monk Mao attained
enlightenment and took
the name Kūkai, meaning
'sky and sea'.

Kiragawa
Temple 26:
Kongōchō-ji
Muroto
Temple 25: Shinshō-ji
Temple 24:
Hotsumisaki-ji
Muroto Unesco Global
Geopark Center
Sakihama
Ikumi Beach
Shirahama
Kōchi Prefectural
Border
Shishikui
Mugi
Temple 23: Yakuo-ji
100
80
60
40
20
0

LUCY.C/SHUTTERSTOCK

PREVIOUS STOP From Temple 23: Yakuō-ji (p76), the pilgrim path heads southwest towards the great southern cape, Muroto-misaki.

Shishikui

Walking 34km southwest, initially inland as far as the town of **Mugi** (16km), then along the coast, will bring *henro* to the small town of **Shishikui**, not far before the prefectural border. There are a number of places to overnight along the way. Shishikui is a popular surfing, diving and sea kayaking area, home to some real Japanese alternative lifestylers, good cafes and places to stay.

Beside the road you'll find **Michi-no-eki Shishikui Onsen** and **Hotel Riviera Shishikui** (*hotel-riviera.co.jp; ¥¥),* looking like something from the French Riviera. This is a great splurge, boasting **natural hot springs** (*adult/child ¥800/400)* with views out over the Pacific. Stop for a bath, even if you don't stay.

Kōchi Prefectural Border

Only 1km or so past Shishikui, you'll pass into Kōchi, the second prefecture of your pilgrimage, with absolutely no fanfare. It wasn't that easy for the *henro* of old though, for the province of Tosa was not welcoming. *Henro* were strictly examined at the barrier gate, needed to present a valid permit and were treated with suspicion of being spies. If allowed in, they were restricted to a prescribed *henro* path, given 30 days to pass through, and treated with indifference and even contempt by the strong-minded, practical populace. These days Kōchi Prefecture is most welcoming. Count yourself lucky you didn't come a few hundred years earlier.

Shirahama

A short distance into Kōchi, *henro* come down a hill and blink their eyes in amazement, for white-sand beach **Shirahama** is calling. There's an attractive campground, **Tōyō Shirahama Resort Hotel** (*toyoshirahama-hotel. com; ¥¥)* and enticing **Aunt Diner** (*¥)* with a good menu in English. No, it's not all a mirage.

You may be brought back to reality with a thud by the massive five-level **tsunami evacuation building** just back from the beach. Kōchi Prefecture is getting prepared for 'the big one' with a mind-boggling 126 tsunami evacuation towers that have been constructed around the prefecture's coast. The vertical evacuation shelters are for residents who mightn't have time to get to high ground if the anticipated Nankai Trough megaquake hits offshore. Japan has been on edge following the 2011 Tōhoku earthquake and tsunami, plus regular film, television and anime remakes of shows based on the 1973 novel *Japan Sinks,* by Sakyō Komatsu. The towers, many of which are eyesores, are a critical part of Kōchi Prefecture's disaster preparedness strategy.

Ikumi Beach

Only a few kilometres past Shirahama, you'll pop out of a tunnel to find yourself at **Ikumi Beach**, arguably the most popular surfing beach on Shikoku. Take a break here to watch the surfers who come from all over Japan.

Henro are spoilt for choice along this stretch of coastline. **Ikumi** has a number of *minshuku*

Temple 24: Hotsumisaki-ji

(guesthouses), cafes and the beachside **Ikumi White Beach Hotel** (*Hotel Nalu; hotelnalu.jp; ¥¥*). **Cafe Nalu** (*¥*) looks out over the beach, and is a good spot for checking out the action. It's 35km from Ikumi to Temple 24: Hotsumisaki-ji.

Temple 24: Hotsumisaki-ji

The 77km walk from Temple 23: Yakuō-ji, the last temple in Tokushima, to **Temple 24: Hotsumisaki-ji** (最御崎寺), the first temple in Kōchi, takes most *henro* three to five days. Before there were roads, pilgrims walked along the dangerous seashore, known as the *gorogoro-ishi* route, named for the rumbling sound of

Continues on page 88

PROOF OF PASSAGE

It's thought that the tradition of *nōkyō* (temple stamps) probably came about due to restrictions on travel during the Edo period, when the movement of commoners was tightly regulated by a system of guard posts on major roads. Commoners could travel for pilgrimage, but they had to obtain travel permits from their home province, follow a certain route, and pass through the guard posts within a tight time limit. Tosa was particularly strict on *henro* passing through. The *nōkyō-chō* (temple stamps book) represented proof of passage and was effectively the equivalent of a modern-day passport.

Exploring Muroto-misaki

This great southern cape, poking south into the Pacific Ocean, is where Kūkai is said to have achieved enlightenment. Many come here to see the 'sky and sea' and try to do the same.

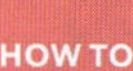

HOW TO

Nearest stop: Temple 24: Hotsumisaki-ji

Getting there: Muroto-misaki is 75km southwest along the coast from Temple 23: Yakuō-ji.

Tip: Leave your backpack at the bottom of the trail up to Temple 24 while you head right out to the cape.

More info: The excellent **Muroto Unesco Global Geopark Center** (*muroto-geo.jp*) is 6km northeast of the cape on Rte 55.

Muroto-misaki is famous in Japanese history and literature as one of the wildest parts of the country, the doorway to the land of the dead. Pummelled by waves from the Pacific, there is little in the way of sand here – just a battered, rough, rocky coastline. It's said that Muroto is like a hook, catching trouble. Many of the typhoons that hit Japan are drawn in, smashing the cape and Temple 24: Hotsumisaki-ji, high above it.

Getting Close

You'll know you're close to the cape when you see the large white statue of young Kōbō Daishi against a background of forested hills on the inland side of Rte 55, which you've been following down the coast. It's in the **Raiei Temple complex**, protected by two fierce orange guardians at the gate, easily approached if you want to take a closer look.

Shortly, on the left of the road, you'll see a **walking track**, more or less right beside the sea, that can be followed the rest of the way to the cape. At times it's concrete, sometimes paved, occasionally boardwalk, but whatever its state, it's easy to follow. There are lots of information boards (including in English) as this is all part of the **Muroto Unesco Global Geopark**, known for its dramatic rock formations.

Site of Enlightenment

Cross the road to visit **Mikurodō Cave**. This is where the young monk, known as Mao, aged 19 at the time, is said to have lived and trained, to the sound

EXPERIENCE ★

STRANGLER FIGS

There may be some amazing rock formations along the coastal walk at Muroto-misaki, but you're also likely to be amazed by the *akō* trees at the cape. They are a species of *ficus superba,* sometimes known as strangler figs. At the cape, this wild subtropical tree, used to living with strong winds and wild weather, simply grabs on to the rocks with countless roots to produce such a spectacular tangled root system that the *akō* here have been designated a National Treasure.

Left: Mikurodō Cave
Below: Muroto-misaki lighthouse

of crashing waves and roaring winds, attaining enlightenment in the cave Shinmeikutsu next door. He took the name Kūkai (空海) here, meaning 'sky and sea', exactly what he could see from the southeast-facing caves. Later, posthumously, he became known as Kōbō Daishi.

Back over the road, the trail continues to the cape, passing the *henro-michi* that climbs steeply up to the headland to Temple 24: Hotsumisaki-ji. Look up to see the white **lighthouse** high on the point.

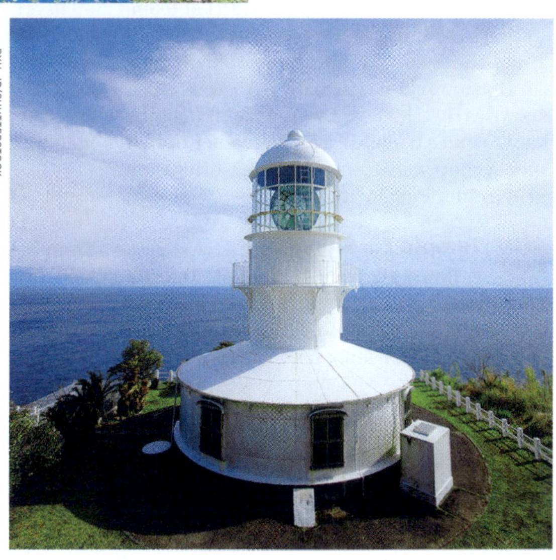

Along the Way We Met...

CHANG I quit my high-pressure job and decided to restart my life, so am walking the pilgrimage. I don't speak much Japanese, but everyone has been so kind to me. An old woman stopped her car to hand out a can of tea; one night it was raining so hard that my tent was leaking – the staff at a 24-hour convenience store let me sit in their seating area all night!

Chang, from Taiwan, is thinking about his life, hoping to become a tour guide in Taiwan in the future.

CHANG'S TIP: *Stay flexible. I made a 45-day plan to walk from Temple 1 to 88, but it became irrelevant after about three days!*

Continued from page 85

rocks being pushed across the rocky shore by the waves. Nowadays it's a long walk southeast on Rte 55 to Muroto-misaki, but there's palpable excitement heading to the place where Kōbō Daishi is said to have achieved enlightenment. At the cape, climb for 20 minutes on a *henro-michi* up to the headland to reach Temple 24 at 165m.

Known as Muroto-sanzan, Temples 24, 25 and 26 are said to be at Muroto, though only Temple 24: Hotsumisaki-ji is actually at the cape. Also known as Higashi-dera (East Temple), it would be hard to find a temple in a more weather-beaten spot. A short walk towards the cape brings you to Muroto-misaki lighthouse.

Temple 25: Shinshō-ji

A 7km walk from Temple 24, **Temple 25: Shinshō-ji** (津照寺) is also known as Port Temple and sits on top of a hill overlooking Murotsu port and its fishing fleet. This is a temple

dedicated to saving sailors and, since the town has always made a living from fishing, fishers pray here for prosperity and safety at sea. In their absence, wives and mothers have prayed for their return from the unforgiving waters around Muroto-misaki. Everyone knows that it's always hardest for the ones left at home.

There's a steep set of stairs up to the main hall, from where there are good views out to sea. Kōbō Daishi carved a Jizō image here in 807 CE, known as *Kajitori Jizō* (Helmsman Jizō) and in the main hall are donated images of Jizō holding a ship's steering wheel.

Temple 26: Kongōchō-ji

The third of the Muroto temples is **Temple 26: Kongōchō-ji** (金剛頂寺), a 4km walk, initially up the coast, then up into the mountains from Temple 25. Also known as Nishi-dera (West Temple), its supporters claim that it was on the rocky point on the coast below

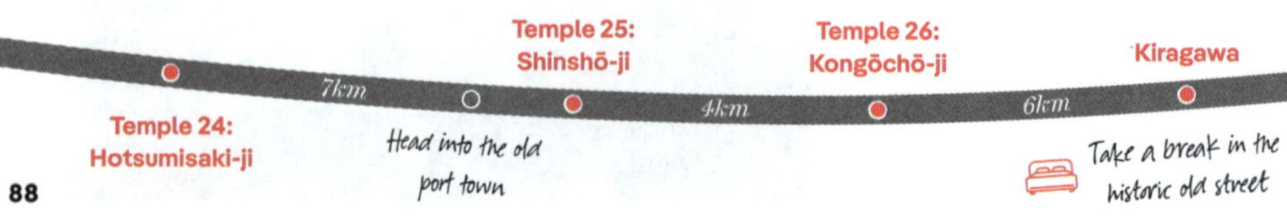

Temple 26 that Kōbō Daishi actually did his ascetic training and achieved enlightenment, not at Muroto-misaki. The buildings were almost all burnt in 1899 and later rebuilt. Only the **Daishi-dō** (Daishi Hall), dating from 1486, survived.

The Confucian precept of *nyonin-kinsei* (no women allowed) was adopted by the Tokugawa shogunate during the Edo era and women were not allowed to visit this temple until 1872, when the Meiji government announced that temples and shrines would no longer be able to ban women, as such discrimination was not helpful for a nation trying to modernise, and compete with and impress foreign powers.

Take the *henro-michi* over the headland down to the coast; don't go down the way you came up.

Kiragawa

Right on the pilgrim trail, the small town of **Kiragawa** (吉良川) is only 6km up the coast from Temple 26: Kongōchō-ji. The old street of town, which parallels Rte 55, is a designated

Hikōsen, Shishikui ¥

The *henro* route goes right past this stylish, friendly little cafe in Shishikui; stop off for a meal or a drinks break. ひこうせん; *@hikosentanimie;* 8.30am-5pm Thu-Mon

Mon Mart Muroto, Sakihama ¥

On the long 50km walk from Shishikui through to near Temple 25, there are no regular convenience stores, just a few small local shops and Mon Mart Muroto. *7am-8pm Fri-Wed*

Tonpuku-tei, Nahari ¥¥

Filling *tonkatsu* (fried pork) meals right by Nahari station at the end of the Gomen-Nahari line. 豚福帝; *tonpukutei.com; 11am-2pm & 5-8pm Sat-Mon, Wed & Thu*

Temple 25: Shinshō-ji

JESSICA KORTEMAN/LONELY PLANET

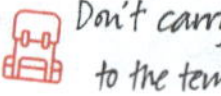

Gardens, Temple 27: Kōnomine-ji

BEST PLACES TO SLEEP

Pavilion Surf & Lodge, Shishikui ¥
A great spot for surfers and pilgrims alike, a day's walk from Temple 23; very reasonable with good facilities and eateries nearby. *pavilion-surf.com*

Minshuku Muroto-sō, Muroto-misaki ¥
Right at the cape, this simple place has decent rooms, meals and can be booked online. *travel.rakuten.com*

Minshuku Tōnohama, Tōnohama ¥
Stay at this converted wedding venue and leave your gear here while you hike up to Temple 27: Kōnomine-ji and back. *m-tounohama.com*

National Preservation Area for its traditional white-walled homes and *kura* (storehouses) built during the Meiji (1868–1912) and Taisho (1912–26) periods. The town is often pummelled by typhoons, so the buildings have features to protect them from fierce wind and rain, such as water-draining roof tiles and walls coated in a waterproof material known as Tosa plaster. Stay overnight to enjoy the small-town scenery.

Temple 27: Kōnomine-ji

It's a 28km walk from Temple 26 to **Temple 27: Kōnomine-ji** (神峯寺), mostly along the coast, but then with a rather vicious

Kiragawa

Temple 27: Kōnomine-ji

22km

10km

Don't carry your gear up to the temple and back

AMEHIME/SHUTTERSTOCK

3km climb inland, up to the temple at 443m. Take the *henro-michi* when you can, as the road curls all over the place and cars heading up spit out very unfriendly fumes. Just as Temple 19: Tatsue-ji was the barrier temple in Tokushima Prefecture, this is Kōchi's equivalent; remember, if you're unworthy, not pure of practice and intention, you're supposed to head back to Temple 1 and start again. This is also one of the *henro-korogashi* (pilgrims fall down) trails, so watch your step.

The temple has immaculate gardens and lovely views of the surrounding mountains, the coastal plain, and waves crashing on the shore in the distance. The revered **Ishi-mizu** is a spring behind the bell tower, celebrated for its Kōnomine water, believed to have the power to cure all illnesses.

To access Kōnomine-ji, you'll go up and down the same steep trail; if you stay at **Minshuku Tōnohama** (left), leave your bag there and pick it up when you're done. Alternatively, hide your gear at the turnoff and pick it up on your return.

Aki

The historic town of **Aki**, 10km up the coast from the Temple 27: Kōnomine-ji turnoff, is worth a stop to explore the **old castle ruins**, inland on the Aki-gawa, and the neighbouring well-preserved samurai district known as **Doi Kachū**. You can also visit the thatched-roof childhood **home of Iwasaki Yatarō**, founder of Mitsubishi. The company's iconic three-diamond logo was a blend of the Iwasaki family crest and that of the Yamauchi clan, the former rulers of Tosa. Aki is one of Japan's top *nasu* (aubergine) producing areas; try a roasted eggplant-flavoured ice cream. From Aki, it's a 24km walk to Temple 28: Dainichi-ji.

HENRO WITH WHEELS

- The 77km walk from Temple 23: Yakuō-ji to Temple 24: Hotsumisaki-ji may be extremely challenging for walkers, but for *henro* travelling by car, it will only take 1½ hours or so.
- Up the western side of the cape, it's only 70km to Temple 28: Dainichi-ji, also taking about 1½ hours.
- Even with visiting all the temples, it's quite feasible for car *henro* to complete this leg in a day.
- Consider driving to Kōchi city (p96) and basing yourself there for the next few days.

Temple 28: Dainichi-ji

Yes, this is the third temple with the same name on your pilgrimage so far, **Temple 28: Dainichi-ji** (大日寺; *dainichiji28.org*). It's a 38km walk from Temple 27, tucked into foothills, some 8km inland from the coast and not far from Kōchi Airport. If you hear an unexpected roar, it's unlikely to be an angry deity, and more likely to be a jet taking off at the airport.

While this Dainichi-ji is proud of its central **image of Dainichi**, deity of the universe, there is also a **statue of Yakushi**, the deity of healing, which it is said Kōbō Daishi carved out of a camphor tree using only his fingernails, an act of extreme asceticism. People come from all over to pray to Fingernail Yakushi for the cure of various illnesses, particularly those above the neck.

Aki

28km

There's much of interest in the historic town of Aki

Temple 28: Dainichi-ji

Hand-washing basin, Temple 62: Hōju-ji (p185)

CRAIG MCLACHLAN/LONELY PLANET

Sacred Steps: The Shikoku 88

Step into a journey that's part adventure, part meditation: the Shikoku pilgrimage winds 1200km across Japan's smallest main island, linking ancient Buddhist temples. Hike misty mountains, stroll coastal villages and experience the kindness of locals – this is Japan at a pace that awakens the senses.

WORDS BY RIE MIYOSHI
Rie is a travel writer and producer based in Japan

The Pilgrimage

The Shikoku pilgrimage is deeply connected to Kōbō Daishi (774–835; also sometimes Kūkai), the 9th-century monk who founded the Shingon school of Buddhism. Born in Shikoku, he travelled to China to study esoteric Buddhism before returning to become one of Japan's most influential religious figures. Legend holds that Kōbō Daishi trained, prayed or performed miracles at each of the 88 temples on the pilgrimage, and pilgrims believe that by following his path, they walk alongside him in spirit.

The practice likely began in the Heian period (8th to 12th centuries), when devotees visited a few of his sacred sites. Over time, the route expanded and was codified into 88 temples. The number 88 is significant, symbolising the purification of the 88 worldly desires and representing a spiritual journey towards enlightenment. Completing the circuit was believed to bring enlightenment, purification and good fortune.

History & Survival

The Shikoku pilgrimage has not always been so serene, however: for centuries, Shintoism, Japan's indigenous faith, and Buddhism blended in a process called *shinbutsu-shūgō* (syncretism). Shrines and temples often shared grounds, and deities were interpreted as manifestations of the same universal truths.

The Meiji era brought dramatic change. As Japan modernised in the late 19th century, the government enforced *shinbutsu-bunri*, separating Buddhism from Shinto to strengthen state Shintoism. Temples lost shrines, images were destroyed and some sites fell into decline. Pilgrimages were discouraged, and their followers dismissed as vagrants.

Yet the Shikoku pilgrimage endured. Deep devotion to Kōbō Daishi and the support of local communities kept the tradition alive. By the late Meiji years, guidebooks and improved transport encouraged revival. After WWII, state Shintoism was dismantled, religious freedom was restored and Japanese people returned to a more personal, flexible approach. The *henro* (pilgrim) spirit survived, reshaped but not erased.

Becoming a Henro

Today, many Japanese call themselves 'non-religious', yet spiritual customs – New Year shrine visits, O-Bon ancestor rituals and *matsuri* (festivals) – remain part of everyday life.

> The number 88 is significant, symbolising the purification of the 88 worldly desires and representing a spiritual journey towards enlightenment.

You don't need to be religious to set out on the Shikoku pilgrimage. Many walkers are drawn by the allure of adventure, culture and reflection along one of Japan's great long-distance routes.

Traditionally, *henro* travelled on foot in white clothing and straw hats, carrying walking sticks representing Kōbō Daishi's presence. Bowing at temple gates, ringing the bronze bell and collecting a vermilion stamp in your *nōkyō-chō* (stamp book) are rituals accessible to all. Along the way, locals offer *osettai* –gifts of food, drink or lodging – a tradition of generosity that continues today. *Osettai* reflects the deep-rooted Buddhist spirit of generosity and connection.

Accommodation ranges from *shukubō* (temple lodgings, sometimes with vegetarian Buddhist meals and morning prayers) to family-run *minshuku* (guesthouses) and *ryokan* (traditional inns) with tatami rooms and home-cooked dinners. In larger towns you'll find business hotels. Completing the full circuit takes six to eight weeks on foot, though many travellers tackle shorter sections. Modern *henro* also use buses, cars or bicycles.

Spiritual Encounters

Perched on the slopes of Godai-san in Kōchi Prefecture, Temple 31: Chikurin-ji has long been a place of reflection for pilgrims. Its head priest, Washu Ebizuka, was born and raised in Kōchi and today, at 67, continues a family legacy as the temple's third-generation caretaker. Beyond rituals, he helps maintain the pilgrimage paths themselves.

Ebizuka recalls how the pilgrimage has shifted throughout his lifetime. Fifty years ago, some pilgrims were intimidating men seeking redemption after brushes with the law. Local children, including himself, were often sent out to offer *osettai,* nervously handing over the gifts before scurrying away. In the Showa era, busloads of *dantai henro* (group pilgrims) crowded the temples. Later, older Japanese walkers sought solace and purpose in retirement. Today, around 5000 pilgrims walk the route each year – nearly half of them are foreigner visitors. What touches people most, he says, are heartfelt encounters with locals, the essence of the Shikoku experience.

For Ebizuka, the pilgrimage has also brought personal moments of wonder. Once, while ill and resting, he noticed a ladybug beside him gazing at the vast sky. 'It made me feel like I was the ladybug,' he recalls. 'We rush through life, but the pilgrimage changes our heart's channel, like switching a radio.'

Another time, he walked behind a silent pilgrim in black. No matter how fast he went, he couldn't catch up. Yet, when he reached the mountaintop temple, he was told he was the only pilgrim to arrive that day. 'Who was it?' he muses. 'Perhaps Kōbō Daishi himself, walking with me.'

A Local's Perspective

Masako Vierstraete has walked the Shikoku pilgrimage twice, first in 2015 when she spent 60 days combining temple visits with sightseeing. 'It's close to civilisation and not too hardcore,' she explains. 'The paths are clearly marked and cared for by locals. You rarely feel lost or cut off.' Above all, she emphasises the human side: 'Osettai isn't just snacks or tea – it's conversation, connection and encouragement.'

That sense of care left a deep impression. After completing the route, Vierstraete relocated to Tokushima and began volunteering in rural revitalisation programs, helping maintain trails with locals. 'You realise the pilgrimage exists thanks to invisible people constantly repairing, clearing and marking the path,' she says.

For beginners, Vierstraete suggests starting at Temple 1: Ryōzen-ji in Tokushima. The first 11 temples wind gently through countryside villages before the tougher climb to Temple 12: Shōsan-ji. Her favourite stretch is between Temple 20: Kakurin-ji and Temple 21: Tairyū-ji, where the route follows one of the oldest trails. 'No one ever complains about Temple 21,' she laughs. 'It's the longest mountain stretch, but also the most rewarding.'

The pilgrimage is changing. Family-run inns – often managed by elderly owners – are closing as rural populations shrink, and walk-in lodging is no longer guaranteed. Wild camping, once tolerated, is discouraged. 'Don't rely on advice from 10 years ago,' she cautions. 'Book ahead, and remember even the smallest *minshuku* requires preparation from hosts.'

Whether you walk a week or the full loop, the Shikoku pilgrimage offers more than a hike. It's a rhythm of walking, ritual and kindness that leaves even non-believers with a sense of quiet transformation.

> *Osettai* isn't just snacks or tea – it's conversation, connection and encouragement.

JOYCE YPP/SHUTTERSTOCK

Statue of Kōbō Daishi, Temple 12: Shōsan-ji (p57)

四国第十二番霊場焼山
森本寿堂

Kōchi

An old castle town by the coast with a distinctive food market culture, Kōchi's (高知) palm-tree-lined streets are primed for relaxed strolls and good eating. Grab a seat at lively food hall Hirome Ichiba, where the easy-going nature of Kōchi-ites is on display every day and night of the week.

WORDS BY
JESSICA KORTEMAN
Jessica is an Australian writer specialising in Japanese travel and culture.

Arriving

By foot If you're walking the pilgrimage and visiting the temples in numerical order, you'll approach Kōchi City from Temple 30: Zenraku-ji, around 5km from downtown Kōchi.

By bus Ichinomiya-jinja-mae (一宮神社前) bus stop, three minutes' walk from Temple 30, can get you to Kōchi Station Bus Terminal in around 15 minutes. Inter-city highway buses connect Kōchi with other prefectures.

By car Driving pilgrims can take any local road convenient to their destination in Kōchi. Be sure to check the parking situation with your accommodation.

By air From Kōchi Ryōma Airport (KCZ), an airport limousine bus can connect you to central Kōchi in 25 minutes.

HOW MUCH FOR A

Glass of Tosa sake
¥850

Katsuo-no-tataki (seared bonito)
¥1600

Entry to Kōchi-jō
¥500

Getting Around

Walking Kōchi's city centre has numerous undercover pedestrian-only shopping arcades for easy wandering, even on rainy days.

Tram Rest your legs and travel between points of interest in central Kōchi city on the Tosaden Streetcar (tram), with a convenient terminus at Kōchi Station's south exit. A flat-fare zone (¥230; cash only) operates in the city-centre area, which can get you within a block of Hirome Ichiba and Kōchi-jō. All lines converge at the Harimaya-bashi intersection. If transferring to another line, pay and request a transfer ticket (乗換券, *norikae-ken*) from the driver. This allows you to continue within the flat-fare zone at no extra cost.

Bus For Mt Godai/Makino Botanical Garden and Katsura-hama, take the MY-YU bus from Kōchi Station. The MY-YU daily bus pass (¥900 to ¥1300) also covers tram use in the city centre flat-fare zone, and provides admission discounts. Buy it at either of the Kōchi Tourism Information Centres.

For information and trip planning, go to MY-YU Bus:

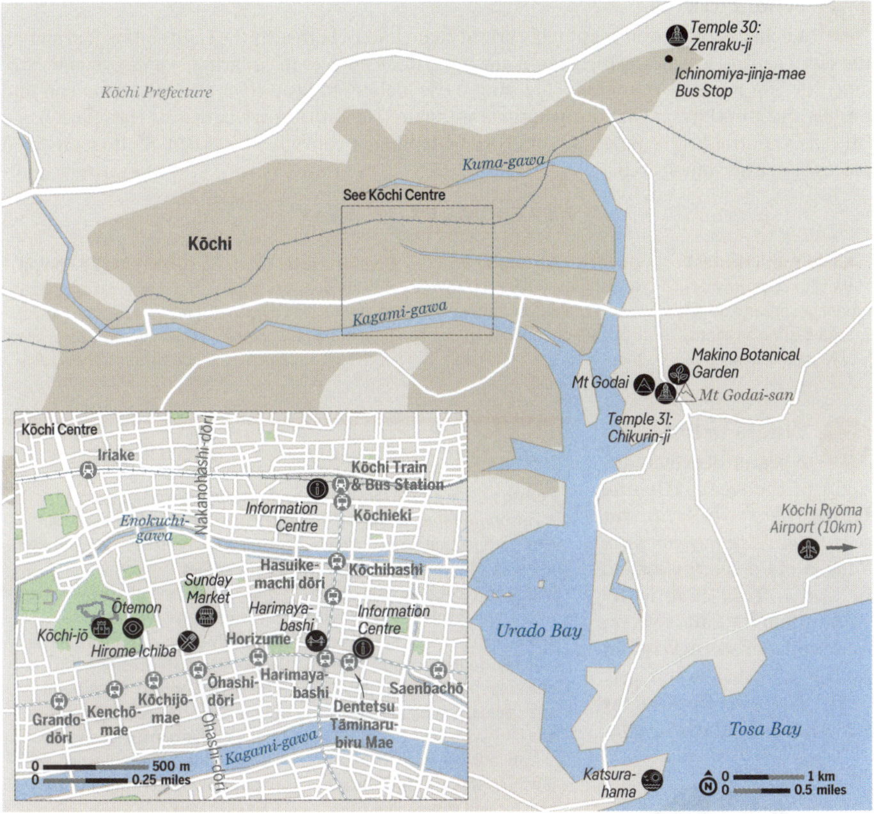

A DAY IN KŌCHI

Time your visit with the city's weekly **Sunday Market** (p101). After eating your fill of local specialities, enter Kōchi Park to visit magnificent **Kōchi-jō** (p99), one of Japan's 12 only remaining original castle keeps, and take in the city from above via the citadel's open-air balcony.

Take a bus to **Makino Botanical Garden** (p100) to learn more about Japan's esteemed 'father of botany' and visit the spectacular three-level conservatory. If you want to combine a visit to **Temple 31: Chikurin-ji** (p107), it's right next door. Round out your afternoon at **Katsurahama** (p105) with a casual beach stroll.

At night, it's all about food and drink, and plenty of it. Venture into lively food hall **Hirome Ichiba** (p98) to sit side-by-side with locals on shared tables as you taste local specialities like *katsuo-no-tataki* and experience Kōchi's vibrant and welcoming dining culture.

Where to Stay

Kōchi has numerous reasonably priced chain hotels, both near the train station and among the city's central arcades, which can make a welcome change for pilgrims wanting some extra amenities for a couple of nights. That said, those looking to keep costs to a minimum can find hostels and guesthouses with dorm options and shared facilities. Anywhere near Harimaya-bashi (the city's central bridge junction) and Hirome Ichiba, or convenient to Kōchi Station, are good places to centre your search.

BEST PLACES TO STAY

Kōchi Youth Hostel ¥ West of town, private-room hostel with on-site sake-tasting sessions. *kyh-sakenokuni.com*

Guest House Bonito ¥¥ Near Hirome Ichiba, mixed and female-only dorms, private options, and a thoughtful host. *booking. com*

Comfort Hotel ¥¥ Good-value business hotel by the station with a notably good breakfast. *choice -hotels.jp/hotel/kochi*

Dormy Inn ¥¥ Central hotel with hot spring and complimentary late-night ramen. *dormy-hotels.com/ dormyinn/hotels/kochi*

Where to Eat

A beacon of activity any night of the week, **Hirome Ichiba** (ひろめ市場; *hirome. co.jp; 10am-11pm, from 9am Sun*) is *the* place for a meal in Kōchi. This chaotically vibrant market hall is where locals and tourists converge for lively banter, drinks and tasty local dishes. Also check out the weekly Sunday Market (p101).

KŌCHI'S CULINARY FAVOURITES

Perhaps Kōchi's most famous dish is *katsuo-no-tataki*, or seared bonito (pictured below left). Cooked using a flash-grill method, the bonito is enjoyed sashimi-style with a hint of smokiness from the seared exterior. It's usually served with raw garlic and green onions, and dipped in salt or a special *tare* (sauce) combining soy sauce and citrusy *yuzu*.

Also look out for *inaka-zushi* (Kōchi's version of sushi, made with pickled vegetables, fried tofu pockets and *yuzu*-flavoured rice; pictured right), spicy ginger drinks made from locally grown Tosa ginger, and *aisukurin*, Kōchi's unique dairy-based treat, somewhere between an ice cream and a sorbet.

Although generally easy-going, one thing local residents are intensely proud of is their sake, where it's often considered Kōchi (Tosa) sake or bust. Consistently at the top of the rankings for highest sake consumption per capita in the country, the people of Kōchi Prefecture undeniably love their liquor.

FROM LEFT: FUNNY FACE/SHUTTERSTOCK, MIXA/GETTY IMAGES

BEST PLACES TO EAT & DRINK (NON-MARKET PICKS)

Manshū Janmen ¥ Try Kōchi *janmen*, a thick Cantonese-style noodle soup with eggs and chives. *11am-2.45pm & 5-9pm Thu-Tue*

Hiromatsu ¥ *Izakaya* near Harimaya-bashi specialising in Tosa chicken. *11am-3pm & 5-9pm Thu-Tue, to 10pm Fri & Sat*

Hidamari-Kōji ¥ By Hirome Ichiba, this Japanese cafe serves lunch sets and tasty desserts. *11am-4.30pm Thu-Tue*

Obiya Kansuke ¥¥ Kōchi cuisine in an opulent *izakaya* setting without the steep price tag. *Hours vary Tue-Sun*

Ascend Kōchi-jō

At Kōchi's most iconic landmark, step back to the Edo era in a self-guided tour of one of Japan's last remaining original castle keeps.

Getting here: The castle is a three-minute walk from Kōchi-jō-mae tram stop.

When to go: Open year-round. The surrounding park gets busy during cherry blossom season.

Cost: Adult/child ¥500/free

Tip: Get a ¥100 discount by showing a valid MY-YU daily bus pass.

More info: kochipark.jp/kochijyo

Even among Japan's 12 original castle keeps, **Kōchi-jō** (高知城) is unique. It's the only one still in possession of its Lord's Reception Suite, as well as retaining all its original Edo-era architecture in the main citadel.

The most direct approach to the castle tower entrance is a series of steps and landings that will take you around 10 minutes.

Unlike some of Shikoku's smaller castles, Kōchi-jō has a rather long interior route over six levels. If you're interested in delving into specifics, the ample signboards do an excellent job of explaining the architectural features and history of the castle, along with some interesting exhibits about life during the Tosa domain.

The highlight of the tour is the *mawari-en,* a thrilling open-air balcony in the castle's *bōrō* style that encircles the entire top level of the main citadel, allowing for unobstructed views from all sides. Other important castle features include the ornate roof gables and the 'ninja spikes' on the wall of the northeast corner that mitigated against attack.

MUSASHI2001/SHUTTERSTOCK

Kōchi-jō

Stroll Makino Botanical Garden

Right by Temple 31: Chikurin-ji, visit this fascinating garden during your pilgrimage or set aside a few hours on a rest day.

Getting here: It's a 30-minute MY-YU bus ride from Kōchi Station Bus Terminal to the garden's main gate.

When to go: Different varieties of plants mean there is something new to see in all seasons.

Cost: Adult/child ¥850/free

Tip: Get a ¥100 discount by showing a valid MY-YU daily bus pass.

More info: makino.or.jp

The 8-hectare **Makino Botanical Garden** (高知県立牧野植物園) is a green space on Mt Godai dedicated to Kōchi-born botanist Dr Tomitarō Makino. Dubbed Japan's 'father of botany', he collected upwards of 400,000 specimens and named over 1500 new plant species in his lifetime.

Gain an appreciation for his formidable body of work at the **Makino Museum of Plants & People Exhibition Hall** in the **North Garden**, where you can peruse detailed exhibits and watch a 13-minute film with English subtitles at the on-site **theatre** (*every 30min 9.30-11.30am & 1-4pm*). Scan QR codes throughout the gardens for multilingual explanations and audio guidance.

The garden grounds showcase more than 3000 species related to Dr Makino's work. Plan on spending two to four hours here, depending on your interest level in plants. The large **Conservatory** by the South Gate, an ethereal greenhouse with cascading flora and towering palms, streaming waterfalls and huge *Victoria amazonica* water lilies over three fascinating levels, is a must-see. Take the winding staircase or use the in-greenhouse elevator for various vantage points.

Makino Museum of Plants & People Exhibition Hall

JOHN S LANDER/GETTY IMAGES

YOSAKOI MATSURI

Kōchi city's lively summer dance festival, the **Yosakoi Matsuri**, began in 1954 as a means to revive the main shopping arcade after WWII. Long story short, the street dance party worked, drawing residents back to the city's central business district. Now held annually from 9 to 12 August (with the main event on the 10th and 11th), the relative freedom of dance troupes in attire, music and dance steps is a defining and exciting feature of the festival. In fact, there are only three rules: firstly, dancers may only move forward and must be holding a *naruko*, a wooden clacking instrument traditionally used in farming to scare away birds, in both hands. Secondly, at some point, music arrangements need to include the melody to the traditional song *Yosakoi-Naruko-Odori*. And finally, a decorated band truck called *jikata-sha* must lead each dance group. Anything else goes! Every year, onlookers await with great anticipation to see the unique routines each *ren* (dance troupe) come up with. Often incorporating a range of dance styles, previous festivals have seen influences from samba, hip-hop and hula.

Performers, Yosakoi Matsuri

Dance to Kōchi's Beat

Get a taste of Kōchi's famed dance festival, the Yosakoi Matsuri, any time of year at the **Yosakoi Information Exchange Center** *(高知よさこい情報交流館; honke-yosakoi.jp; entry free)*. Peruse multilingual exhibits and watch an informative 15-minute video with English subtitles detailing the festival's evolution. In the Experience Corner, don the festival attire, learn dance steps and play the festival's distinctive *naruko* as you follow an interactive video. For a fee, you can make a pair of *naruko* to take home (plain/coloured ¥1500/2000). The centre is closed on Wednesdays.

Wander the Sunday Market

On Sundays, Ōte-suji, the main road leading to the castle, becomes the setting for Kōchi's weekly **Sunday Market** (日曜市). From Kōchi-jō's Ōtemon gate, the market stretches 1.3km east and features more than 400 stalls, with food the main attraction for visitors. Don't walk past the sizzling fryers of the Imo-ten stall, easily identified by its constant, fast-moving lines. These bite-sized pieces of fluffy sweet potato tempura are so popular they have become synonymous with a trip to the market itself. Most stalls are open from around 8am to 2pm – aim to arrive early before things sell out.

Stallholder, Sunday Market

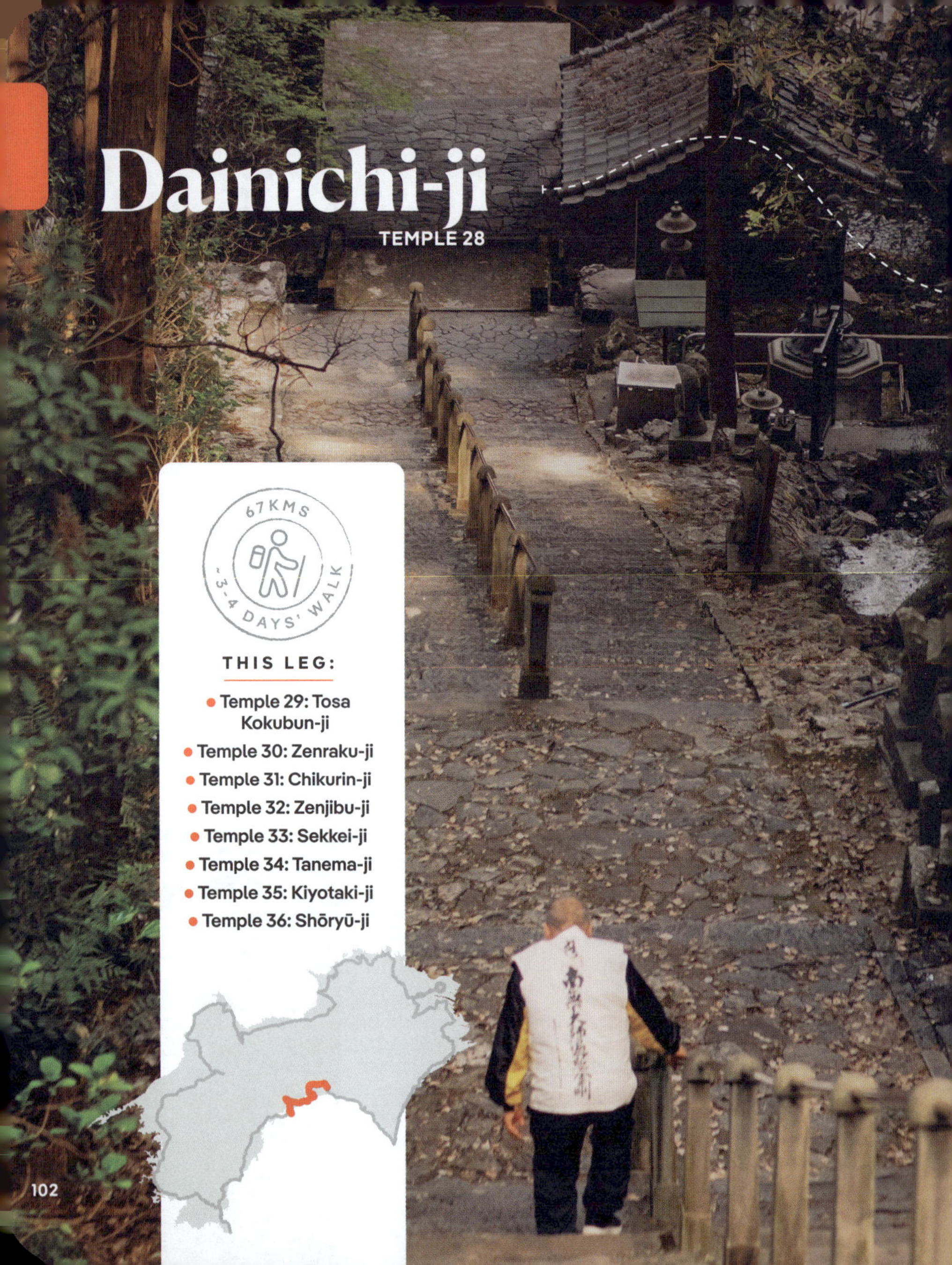

Dainichi-ji

TEMPLE 28

67KMS
~3-4 DAYS' WALK

THIS LEG:

- Temple 29: Tosa Kokubun-ji
- Temple 30: Zenraku-ji
- Temple 31: Chikurin-ji
- Temple 32: Zenjibu-ji
- Temple 33: Sekkei-ji
- Temple 34: Tanema-ji
- Temple 35: Kiyotaki-ji
- Temple 36: Shōryū-ji

Shōryū-ji

TEMPLE 36

After the long walk around Muroto-misaki, it's exciting to be faced with nine temples in and around the prefectural capital of Kōchi city (p96). Here you'll find shorter distances between temples and plenty of places to stay and eat. Kōchi is a vibrant, modern city with a big history, so take some time to check it out, because there are big distances to another remote cape on the horizon.

Craig McLachlan

Temple 36: Shōryū-ji (p113)
BRESTER IRINA/SHUTTERSTOCK

Walking Notes

It's pleasant walking around Kōchi city and its nearby agricultural areas, though there are a surprising number of small, nobbly hills breaking up the landscape. There are a few climbs up to temples, the hardest being to Temple 35: Kiyotaki-ji, but it's only at 150m in elevation. *Henro* (pilgrims) with wheels might base themselves in Kōchi's city centre.

Breaking Your Journey

Plenty of sleeping and eating options exist in and around the prefectural capital. There's a lot to see in central Kōchi city, so walkers could consider taking a break here to mentally prepare for what is coming up after this leg: three temples in 200km.

Craig's Tips

BEST TEA Enjoy a matcha green tea at the cafe at Temple 29: Tosa Kokubun-ji (p106).

FAVOURITE VIEW From up high at Temple 35: Kiyotaki-ji (p113).

ESSENTIAL STOP Don't miss the traditional scenic garden at Temple 31: Chikurin-ji (p107).

TOP TIP The ladles that hold no water at Temple 34: Tanema-ji (p112).

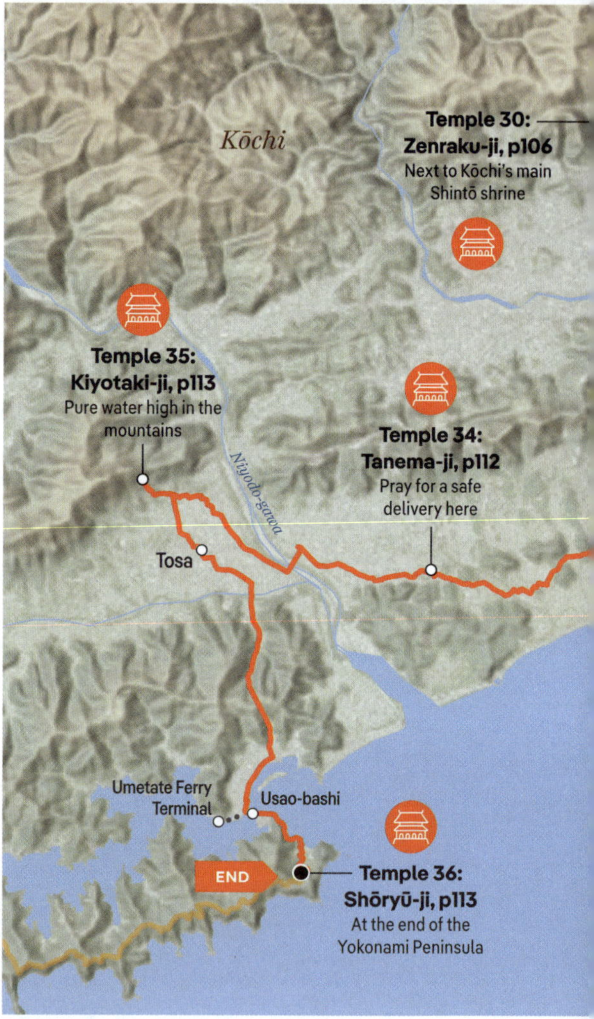

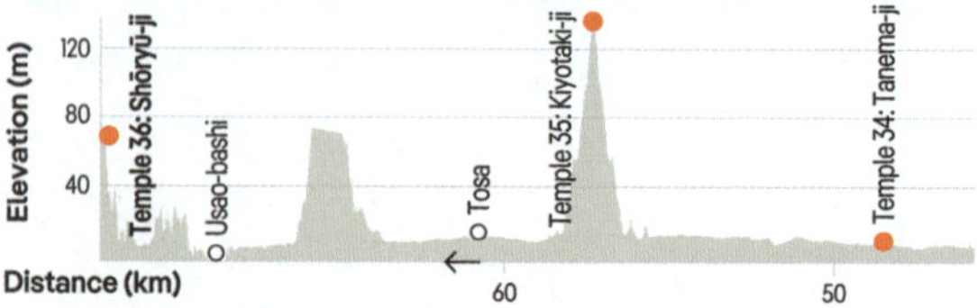

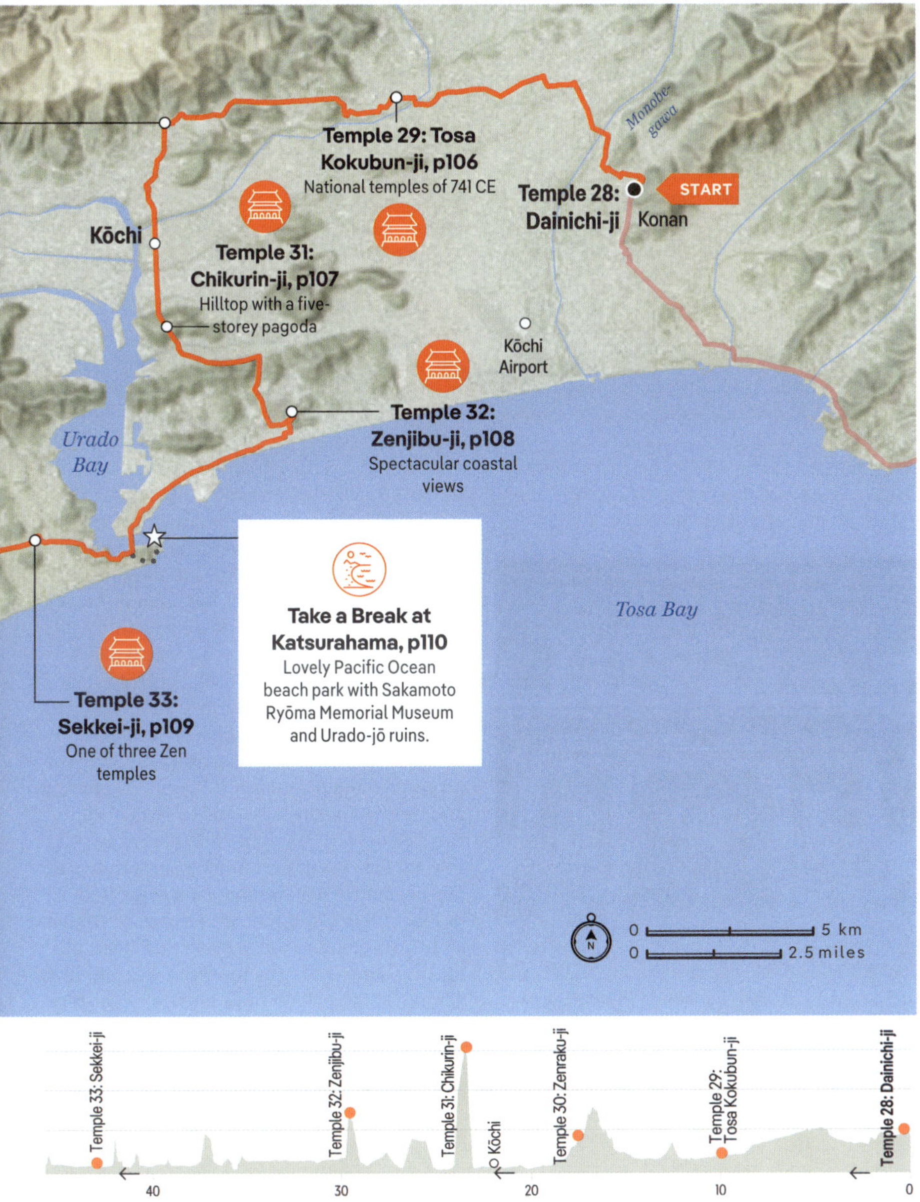
Monobe-gawa
Temple 29: Tosa
Kokubun-ji, p106
National temples of 741 CE
Temple 28:
Dainichi-ji
Konan
START
Kōchi
Temple 31:
Chikurin-ji, p107
Hilltop with a five-
storey pagoda
Kōchi
Airport
Temple 32:
Zenjibu-ji, p108
Spectacular coastal
views
Urado
Bay
Tosa Bay
Take a Break at
Katsurahama, p110
Lovely Pacific Ocean
beach park with Sakamoto
Ryōma Memorial Museum
and Urado-jō ruins.
Temple 33:
Sekkei-ji, p109
One of three Zen
temples
0   5 km
0   2.5 miles
N
Temple 33: Sekkei-ji
Temple 32: Zenjibu-ji
Temple 31: Chikurin-ji
Kōchi
Temple 30: Zenraku-ji
Temple 29:
Tosa Kokubun-ji
Temple 28: Dainichi-ji
40
30
20
10
0

PREVIOUS STOP From Temple 28: Dainichi-ji, walk northwest, crossing the Monobe-gawa and the Kōchi plain.

Temple 29: Tosa Kokubun-ji

It's a 9km walk west across the plain from Temple 28 to **Temple 29: Tosa Kokubun-ji** (土佐国分寺; *tosakokubunji.org; @tosakokubunji.official*), the second of the national temples on your pilgrimage that were set up in each of Japan's provinces in 741 CE. The pleasant walk passes through agricultural fields and rice paddies, with numerous greenhouses producing vegetables such as tomatoes, eggplants, peppers and cucumbers. Just after crossing the Kokubu-gawa, Kokubun-ji and its grounds appear as an oasis of tall trees, standing out from their surroundings. This is a peaceful place, with beautifully maintained grounds, gardens and attractive buildings.

Tosa Kokubun-ji is a National Historic Site, sometimes referred to as the 'moss temple of Tosa' for its beautiful cedar moss garden. The temple runs a cafe; enjoy a matcha green tea as you prepare for the next step on the journey.

Temple 30: Zenraku-ji

Walk west for 7km from Temple 29 to get to **Temple 30: Zenraku-ji** (善楽寺; *zenrakuji30.jp; @kaoriya_zen*). Pilgrims are often surprised to hear that a most embarrassing and unholy row went on for decades over which temple was the real Temple 30. Zenraku-ji is in the precincts of Tosa Shrine and when the Meiji Restoration of 1868 restored the emperor to the top job, he was seen as a divine figure in Shintō, deemed the national religion. The revival of Shintō created antagonism towards Buddhism, and the Kōchi authorities went at it with great enthusiasm. Zenraku-ji was demolished in 1870, with its central images of Amida and Kōbō Daishi sent to Temple 29: Kokubun-ji for safekeeping.

A temple in Kōchi city, **Anraku-ji**, somehow acquired the Amida statue, the principal image and essence of a temple, and in 1893 declared itself Temple 30. Then in 1929, Zenraku-ji was re-established, got the Kōbō Daishi statue back and demanded that Anraku-ji (meaning 'Temple of Peaceful Enlightenment') return the Amida statue. Its demand was refused and an embarrassing controversy as to which was the real Temple 30 was all on until 1994, when a truce

Niōmon, Temple 29: Tosa Kokubun-ji

JESSICA KORTEMAN/LONELY PLANET

AMEHIME/SHUTTERSTOCK

Temple 28:
Dainichi-ji

Temple 29: Tosa Kokubun-ji

9km

7km

Pass greenhouses growing vegetables

The second of the national temples

Pagoda (p108), Temple 31: Chikurin-ji

and deal established Zenraku-ji as Temple 30 and Anraku-ji as its *okunoin* (inner sanctuary).

When you go to Temple 30: Zenraku-ji, perform your *mairi* (rituals before a visit) and have your *nōkyō-chō* (book of stamps) stamped, but don't forget to drop in next door and look around the grounds of **Tosa Shrine** (土佐神社), Kōchi Prefecture's main Shintō shrine.

Temple 31: Chikurin-ji

Staying to the east of central Kōchi city, it's a 6.5km walk directly south from Temple 30 to **Temple 31: Chikurin-ji** (竹林寺; *chikurinji. com; @chikurinji.temple*), which sits at 120m in elevation, atop Godai-san (五台山), a hill

BEST PLACES TO EAT

Temple 29: Tosa Kokubun-ji ¥
The temple runs a cafe where you can sit looking out on the beautiful gardens with a matcha set (¥700); ask at the temple office.

Takesaki Shōten, by Temple 31 ¥
Right outside the main gate of Temple 31: Chikurin-ji, fuel up on noodles, curry or *donburi* (dishes served over rice) for the next stretch of walking. 竹崎商店; *9am-5pm Tue-Sun*

Umi-no-Terrace, Katsurahama ¥
Good eating options at Umi-no-Terrace, the small shopping centre at Katsurahama (p110), including places offering noodles, set meals, coffees and desserts. It's a short walk from Katsurahama Beach.

**Temple 30:
Zenraku-ji**

**Temple 31:
Chikurin-ji**

6.5km

Next to Kōchi Prefecture's most important shrine

of parkland. With Monju, deity of wisdom, as its central image, Chikurin-ji is popular with students (and parents!), who come to pray for success in exams. It's well-known in Kōchi that the prefecture's name 高知, which translates to 'high intelligence', was bestowed upon it by the high priest of Chikurin-ji so that Monju would look favourably upon the local populace.

Temple 31 is extremely proud of its scenic garden, deemed a National Place of Scenic Beauty, and its **Treasure Museum**; a combined ticket to the two will set you back ¥800. The attractive 31m-high five-storey **pagoda** was built in 1980, replacing a three-storey one that was destroyed in a typhoon. It's constructed of *hinoki* (cypress) in the architectural style of the early Kamakura period. Although the characters for Chikurin-ji 竹林寺 translate to 'Bamboo Forest Temple', it is the maples and ginkgo trees that are impressive here, especially during autumn.

Temple 32: Zenjibu-ji

A 6km walk southeast from Temple 31 is **Temple 32: Zenjibu-ji** (禅師峰寺). There's a bit of up and down until you reach the temple at an elevation of 76m, not far from the coast. This is one storm- and wind-battered place, with glorious views of the coastal plain and the Pacific Ocean below. Kōbō Daishi is said to have visited here in 807 CE and carved an 11-faced Kannon as a prayer for safety in the seas around Kōchi. That statue became the principal image of the temple, known as Fun-adama Kannon (Boat Spirit Kannon), revered by sailors and fishers.

During the Edo period (1603–1868), the feudal lords of Tosa prayed here before sailing from Urado-wan, Kōchi's protected harbour, to Edo (Tokyo).

Although there's no evidence that the legendary, travelling haiku poet Matsuo Bashō

BRESTER IRINA/SHUTTERSTOCK

Along the Way We Met...

SOLOMON & RUBY We finished work for the season in Hokkaidō and had three weeks to spare. So we came to Shikoku and have walked from Temple 1 to Temple 30 this year. We're planning to finish the pilgrimage in either one or two more visits in the future. One Japanese pilgrim kindly walked with us for a few days and explained about the pilgrimage and what to do at each temple.

Solomon and Ruby are ski instructors from New Zealand.

SOLOMON & RUBY'S TIP: *Ask a Japanese person where you are staying to call ahead to the next place to make a booking for you in Japanese.*

**Temple 31:
Chikurin-ji**

Don't miss the pagoda

6km

**Temple 32:
Zenjibu-ji**

5km

This stretch features gorgeous coastal views

Temple 33: Sekkei-ji

(1644–94) ever made it to Shikoku, one of his poems is inscribed on a stone in front of the *hondō* (main hall): *kogarashi ni / iwa fuki togaru / sugi ma kana* (The winter gust / sharpening a rock with its blow / through the cedars).

Temple 33: Sekkei-ji

These days it's a nice, easy 8km walk from Temple 32 to **Temple 33: Sekkei-ji** (雪蹊寺) thanks to the existence of Rte 14 and the Urado-ōhashi, completed in 1972. The alternative is to do what *henro* did for centuries before the bridge was built – take the tiny ferry (it's free!) from Tanezaki to Nagahama. The crossing only

Continues on page 112

BEST PLACES TO SLEEP

Ohenrosan-no-yado Kōchi-ya ¥
Set up for *henro*, right in front of Temple 33: Sekkei-ji, with meals and a laundry service for walking pilgrims. *min88.jp/inn/en/11502*

Guesthouse Onaka ¥¥
Good location 4km west of Temple 33: Sekkei-ji on the way to Temple 34: Tanema-ji; book online with optional breakfast. *booking.com*

Henro Guesthouse Lilian ¥
Great location on the western side of the Usao-bashi near Temple 36: Shōryū-ji; stay here and catch the ferry the next morning. *lilian-guesthouse.studio.site*

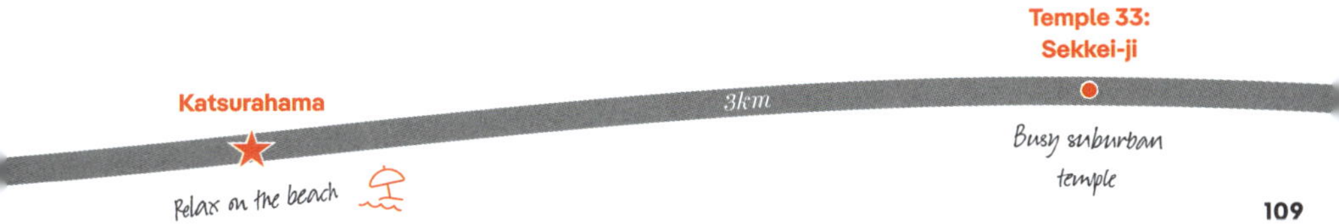

Katsurahama

3km

Temple 33: Sekkei-ji

Relax on the beach

Busy suburban temple

Take a Break at Katsurahama

This popular beach park on the southern side of the Urado-ōhashi, virtually right on the pilgrim path, is a good spot to take a break on the beach, check out the ruins of Urado Castle and visit the museum celebrating Kōchi's favourite son, Sakamoto Ryōma.

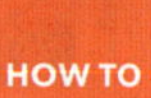

HOW TO

Nearest stop: Temple 32: Zenjibu-ji

Getting here: The park encompasses the peninsula to the east of Rte 14 on the southern side of Urado-ōhashi

When to go: The park is open 24 hours

Cost: Free

Tip: While maps make everything look flat, it's actually quite hilly in the park.

More info: katsurahama-park.com

When you come down off Urado-ōhashi, the bridge over the entrance to Urado-wan, carry on until you get the opportunity to turn left into Katsurahama Park. This is a very popular Kōchi destination for Japanese visitors, who have it on their list of must-sees when they come here. All Japanese learnt the name Sakamoto Ryōma during their school days.

Sakamoto Ryōma Memorial Museum

After only a few hundred metres, turn left for the **Sakamoto Ryōma Memorial Museum** (*ryoma-kinenkan.jp; adult/child ¥500/free*), which sits high on the hill and has exhibits dedicated to the life of a local hero who was instrumental in bringing about the Meiji Restoration in the 1860s. Born in Kōchi in 1835, Sakamoto brokered the Satchō alliance between the Satsuma (modern-day Kagoshima) and

Chōshū (Yamaguchi) domains that eventually brought down the Tokugawa shogunate. He was killed in Kyoto in 1867, aged 32. There is a statue of Sakamoto at the museum entrance.

Katsurahama Beach

While there are some nice walking trails in the park and the beach is attractive, swimming is prohibited due to strong currents and you'll cause much consternation if you head in for a dip. At the beach's western end, on a small promontory is **Wakatsumi-jinja**, a tiny shrine with beautiful coastal views down towards Muroto-misaki,

URADO CASTLE RUINS

While there's not a lot left to see, the famous temple-burning Chōsokabe Motochika (1539–99) once had his home castle, **Urado-jō**, here on the peninsula. Right at the entrance to Urado-wan, it was the perfect spot to base a naval force and manage the comings and goings into the protected bay. When Motochika died, Kōchi-jō gained prominence and Urado-jō was demolished. There's signage and small monuments at the old castle site on the hill by the Sakamoto Ryōma Memorial Museum.

Left: Katsurahama Beach
Below: Sakamoto Ryōma Memorial Museum

especially on a good day. At the eastern end of the beach, just back in the trees, is a towering 5.3m-high **statue of Sakamoto Ryōma** standing on an 8m-high pedestal, looking out towards the ocean. It was unveiled in 1928 with great fanfare.

Umi-no-Terrace Shopping Centre

As befits a spot popular with Japanese tourists, **Umi-no-Terrace** has souvenir shops, a few small restaurants, cafes and a tourist information centre. It's almost at the end of the peninsula, back from the eastern end of the beach.

HENRO WITH WHEELS

- Those with cars should allow two days for the temples, plus as much time as needed to explore the vibrant prefectural capital.
- Kōchi city is a great place to base yourself to explore the city and the nine temples around it.
- Make sure you choose a place to stay in the city that offers car parking.
- Temple 28: Dainichi-ji is only 23km east of central Kōchi city.
- Temple 36: Shōryū-ji is 26km west of central Kōchi.

Continued from page 109

takes a few minutes and shortens the walk by 1.5km, but outside of commuter times, there's only one departure every hour at 10 minutes past the hour. It's a fun option though, and breaks up the walk.

Somewhat surprisingly, there are three temples of the Zen sect of Buddhism on this very Shingon pilgrimage: Temple 11: Fujii-dera, Temple 15: Awa Kokubun-ji and this one, Temple 33: Sekkei-ji. Though all are now Zen temples, earlier they were associated with the Shingon sect.

Founded by Kōbō Daishi, Sekkei-ji has had a long and vacillating history. By the late 1500s, it had fallen on hard times, only to be saved and rebuilt by one of Tosa's greatest heroes, warlord and temple-burner Chōsokabe Motochika, who

famously conquered and ruled Shikoku in the early 1580s. Motochika changed Sekkei-ji from Shingon to his own sect, Zen, and invited the Zen monk Geppō to be its chief priest. Sekkei-ji became his family temple and, when Motochika died, his statue was installed in the main hall and the name of the temple was changed to his posthumous name. More upheaval was to come though, and in the early 1870s, the temple was burnt during *haibutsu-kishaku,* the anti-Buddhist movement at the beginning of the Meiji era.

Nowadays, Sekkei-ji is a nice little suburban temple with a big history.

Temple 34: Tanema-ji

Heading west from Temple 33, in 6.5km you'll reach **Temple 34: Tanema-ji** (種間寺), known far and wide as a sacred place where pregnant women and their families come to pray for a safe delivery. Pregnant women bring a wooden ladle to the priest, who knocks the bottom out of it so that the ladle can hold no water, symbolising hope that the baby will come out as easily as water will pass through the bottomless ladle. The woman treasures the ladle until she has a safe birth, then writes her name and age on the handle before presenting it to the temple. Countless ladles are on display and the temple is resplendent with small statues of Jizō, the guardian deity of children.

Rural and southwest of central Kōchi city, Tanema-ji, meaning 'Between the Seeds Temple', is in an area said to be one of the most productive in Kōchi, thanks to Kōbō Daishi bringing the seeds of five different grains from China and planting them around the temple.

**Temple 33:
Sekkei-ji**

**Temple 34:
Tanema-ji**

6.5km

9.5km

Pray for a safe delivery here

Temple 35: Kiyotaki-ji

From Temple 34, it's a 9.5km walk north-west, with the last section involving a steep climb up to **Temple 35: Kiyotaki-ji** (清滝寺), which sits at an elevation of 150m. The temple's name, meaning 'pure waterfall', comes from the legend of Kōbō Daishi striking his staff in the ground to create a spring of pure water that became the waterfall at the temple. This pure water is important for its role in processing bark from the paper mulberry bush to make *washi* (traditional Japanese paper), for which Tosa is famous.

A 15m-tall statue of Yakuyoke Yakushi Nyorai (the Buddha of Medicine Who Wards off Bad Luck) stands before the main hall, said to have been donated by a local paper manufacturer in 1933. To learn more about paper-making, take a detour 6km north to the **Ino-chō Paper Museum** *(kamihaku.com; adult/child ¥500/100)*.

Before you leave the temple, gaze south and look for a 'V' in the mountains – your route to the next temple.

Temple 36: Shōryū-ji

It's a 14km walk from Temple 35 to **Temple 36: Shōryū-ji** (青龍寺) and some logistics are about to come into play. Until the 645m-long bridge, Usao-bashi, was completed in 1973, pilgrims took a boat across the entrance of Uranouchi-wan, a narrow 13km-long inlet squeezed between the mainland and the rugged Yokonami Peninsula. These days, it's easy to walk across the bridge, go to Temple 36 and perform your *mairi*.

Shōryū-ji is said to have been named by Kōbō Daishi after the Shōryū-ji in China, at which he trained in esoteric Buddhism (804–06 CE); to repay the kindness of his teacher there, he decided to build a Shōryū-ji on Shikoku. Worshippers pray for a safe voyage, much like the one Kōbō Daishi had on his trip home from China.

From Temple 36, you can avoid 15km of tough walking along the Yokonami Peninsula by taking advantage of the fact that this is the one part of the pilgrimage of which it's said Kōbō Daishi gave permission for *henro* to use a form of transport other than their feet. To avoid the peninsula walk, head back 4km over the Usao-bashi to the Umetate Ferry Terminal and take the ferry run by Susaki City Ferry west to Yokonami Ferry Terminal (¥640) at the far end of the bay. This is a great option, but there are only three departures each day at 7.10am, 10.05am and 2.50pm. Consider staying at the nearby Hostel John Man (p123) the night before to catch the 7.10am ferry. Whatever you do, don't miss the boat!

Temple 35: Kiyotaki-ji

**Temple 35:
Kiyotaki-ji**

14km

**Temple 36:
Shōryū-ji**

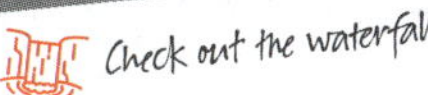

Check out the waterfall

Cross the Usao-bashi
to the peninsula

Shōryū-ji
TEMPLE 36

Did we mention that Kōchi is the pilgrim's testing ground? We hope you enjoyed your time in the city, because once you leave Temple 36: Shōryū-ji, you've got close to 200km of walking to visit the next three temples, including a stop at Shikoku's second great southern cape, Ashizuri-misaki. There are some lovely coastlines, rivers and beaches, but you'll need to do some planning to stay fit and fed as it's pretty remote down here.

Craig McLachlan

Ashizuri-misaki (p124)
6NKEN/SHUTTERSTOCK

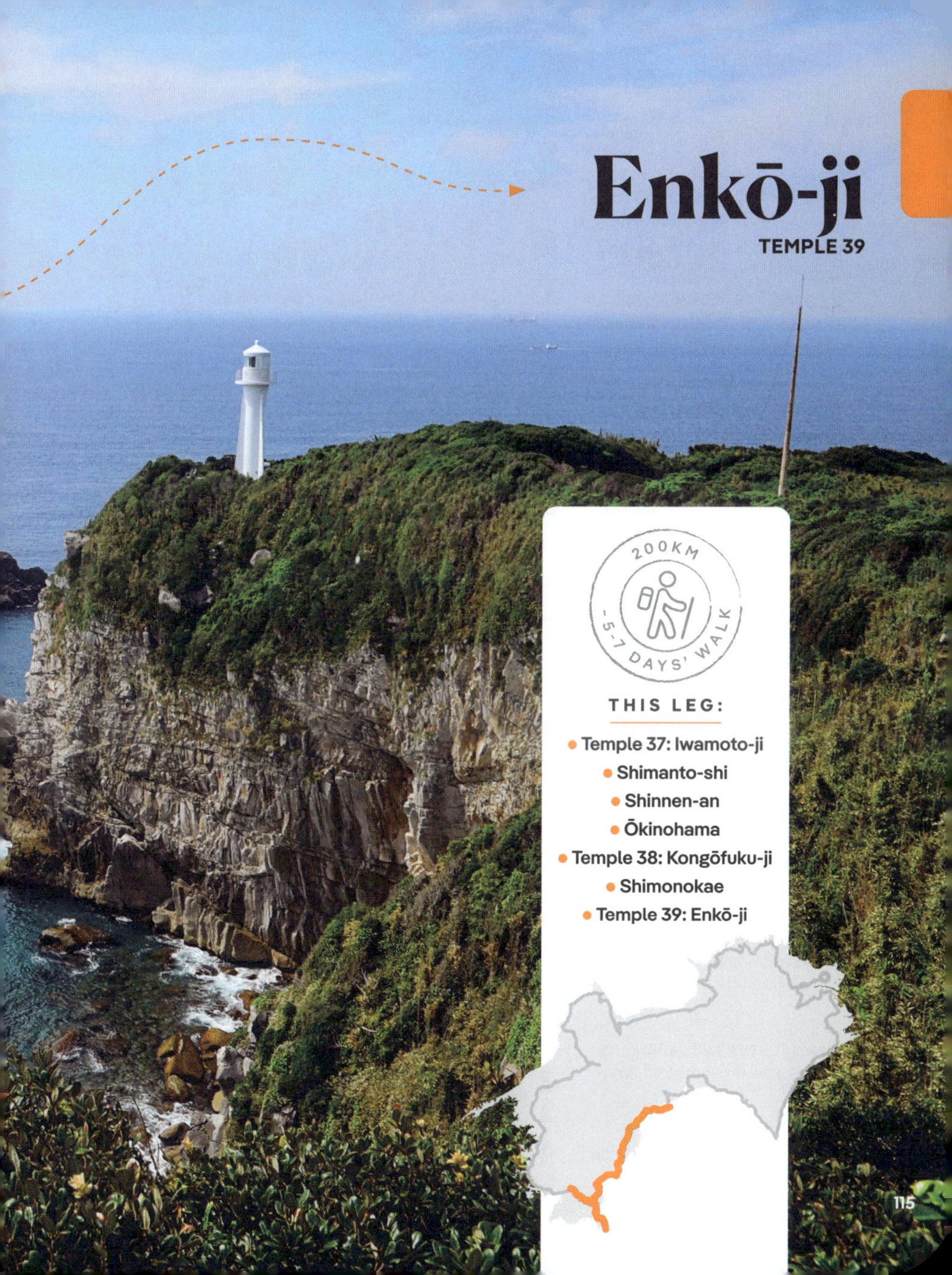

Enkō-ji

TEMPLE 39

200KM
~5-7 DAYS' WALK

THIS LEG:

- Temple 37: Iwamoto-ji
- Shimanto-shi
- Shinnen-an
- Ōkinohama
- Temple 38: Kongōfuku-ji
- Shimonokae
- Temple 39: Enkō-ji

Walking Notes

You'll cover some big distances between temples here, mainly on sealed roads, but with some *henro-michi* (pilgrim track) options. With 57km, 82km, then 53km between temples in a remote part of Shikoku with limited facilities, you'll need to plan ahead.

Breaking Your Journey

Do your homework and plan ahead for places to stay, making bookings a couple of days in advance, while keeping your eye on weather forecasts. Ashizuri-misaki tends to attract trouble when it comes to bad weather. Susaki, Shimanto-chō, Shimanto-shi and Ashizuri-misaki have decent places to stay. There are not many supermarkets or convenience stores once past Shimanto-shi.

Craig's Tips

BEST BEACH It doesn't get any better in Japan than the sand at Ōkinohama (p122).

FAVOURITE VIEW From the walking trails and viewing platforms at Ashizuri-misaki (p124).

ESSENTIAL STOP Temple 38: Kongō-fuku-ji is a beauty at Ashizuri-misaki (p122).

TOP TIP Stay a night at the *shukubō* (temple lodging) at Temple 37: Iwamoto-ji (p118).

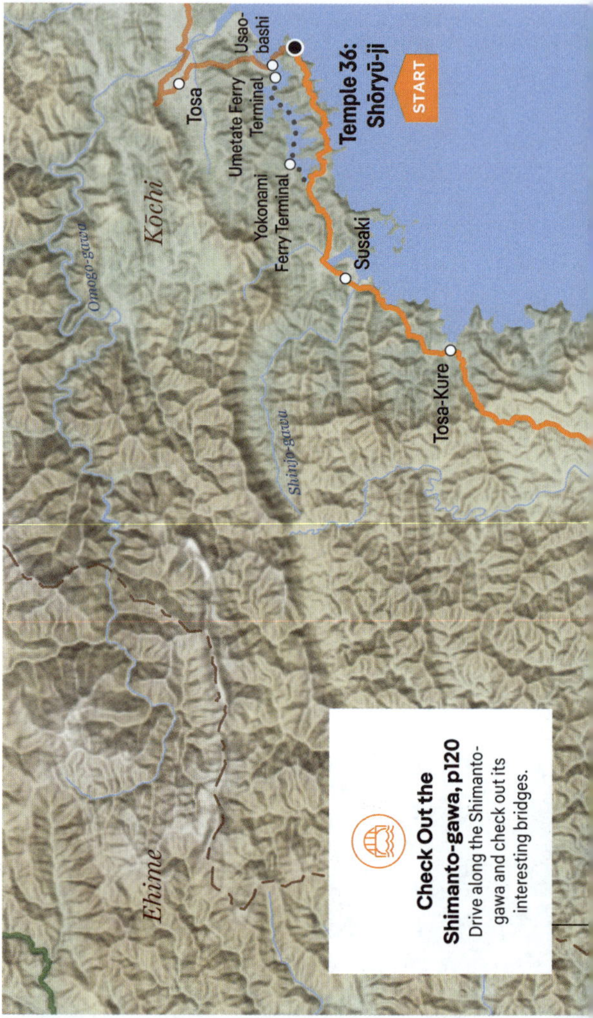

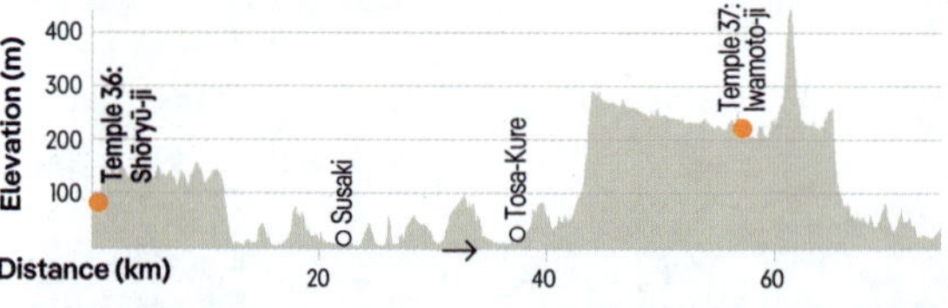

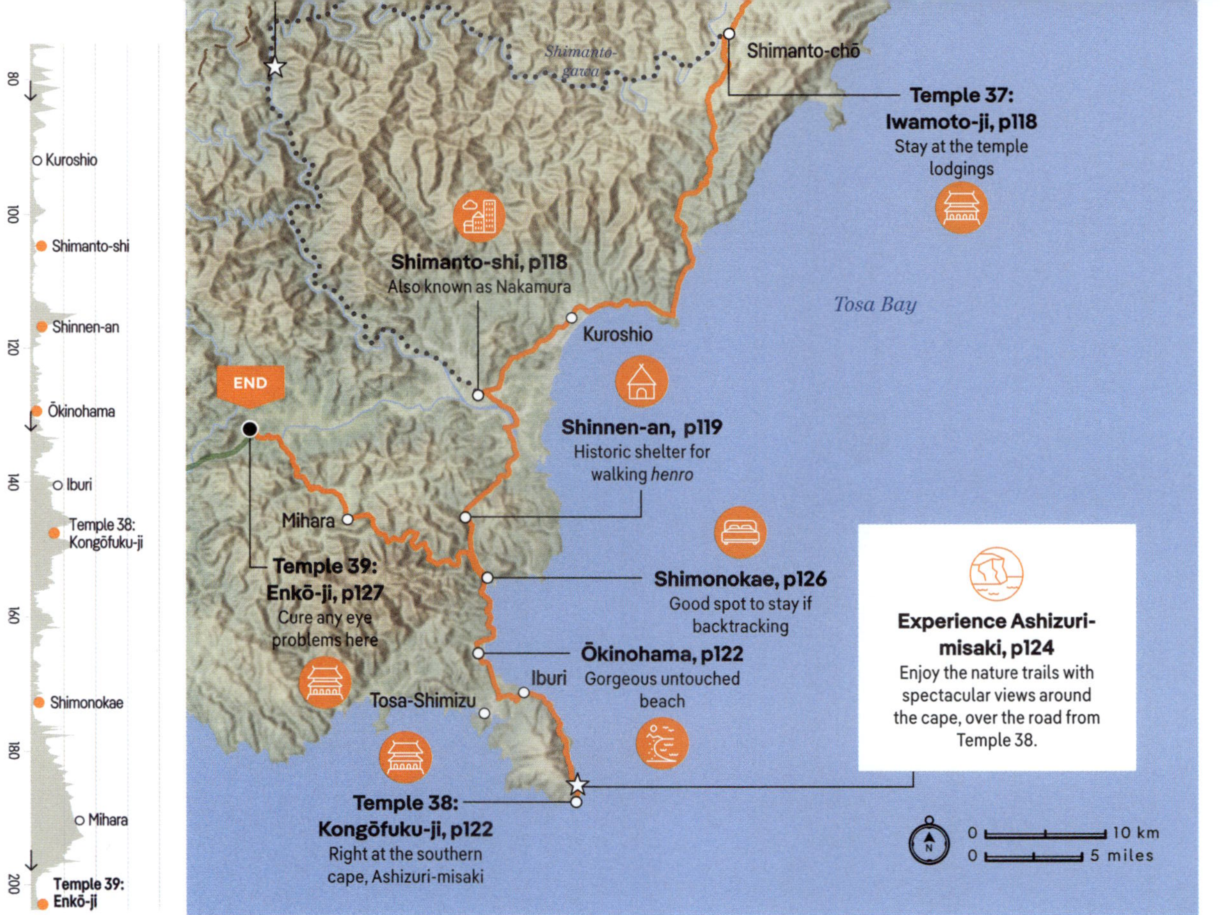

Shimanto-gawa
Shimanto-chō
Temple 37:
Iwamoto-ji, p118
Stay at the temple lodgings
Shimanto-shi, p118
Also known as Nakamura
Tosa Bay
Kuroshio
Shinnen-an, p119
Historic shelter for walking henro
END
Mihara
Temple 39:
Enkō-ji, p127
Cure any eye problems here
Shimonokae, p126
Good spot to stay if backtracking
Ōkinohama, p122
Gorgeous untouched beach
Iburi
Tosa-Shimizu
Temple 38:
Kongōfuku-ji, p122
Right at the southern cape, Ashizuri-misaki
Experience Ashizuri-misaki, p124
Enjoy the nature trails with spectacular views around the cape, over the road from Temple 38.
0   10 km
0   5 miles
Kuroshio
Shimanto-shi
Shinnen-an
Ōkinohama
Iburi
Temple 38:
Kongōfuku-ji
Shimonokae
Mihara
Temple 39:
Enkō-ji
80
100
120
140
160
180
200

AMEHIME/SHUTTERSTOCK

PREVIOUS STOP It's fully 58km and a big haul over mountain passes and on *henro-michi* from Temple 36: Shōryū-ji at the eastern end of the Yokonami Peninsula to Temple 37: Iwamoto-ji, but you can take the boat (p113) to shorten the walk. Along the way, Susaki is the biggest town with lots of places to stay, while another 12km down the trail, Tosa-Kure also has decent overnighting options. Tosa-Kure's Taishō-machi market attracts locals from far and wide for its stalls selling fresh fish, fruit and vegetables.

Temple 37: Iwamoto-ji

Temple 37: Iwamoto-ji (岩本寺; *iwa motoji.or.jp)* is in the town of **Shimanto-chō** (四万十町), previously known as Kubokawa-chō (窪川町) before merging with two nearby small towns to create the larger town of Shimanto-chō in 2006 – much to the everlasting confusion of visitors to the region. The cause of the confusion is that bordering Shimanto-chō to the south is Shimanto-shi (Shimanto city), formed in 2005, when the city of Nakamura merged with a neighbouring village.

Both the new town of Shimanto-chō and the new city of Shimanto-shi were trying to take advantage of their connections to the well-known **Shimanto-gawa**, the river flowing through both that has a huge reputation in Japan as being the last free-flowing river in the country – but confusion reigns, especially for foreign visitors.

Iwamoto-ji is just down the road from JR Kubokawa train station, which retained the old town's name. Iwamoto-ji is known for being the only temple on the pilgrimage that enshrines five principal deities and for the main hall's ceiling, which is decorated with 575 paintings. The temple has a **shukubō** *(iwamotoji.or.jp/ lodging),* one of the few *shukubō* (temple lodgings) left on the pilgrimage and a really good place to stay as you mentally prepare for the longest leg of your journey: the 82km to Temple 38.

Shimanto-shi

From Shimanto-chō it's some 46km of walking to **Shimanto-shi** (Shimanto city; 四万十市), although to keep it straight in your mind, you could use their former names of Kubokawa and Nakamura. JR Shikoku trains from Kōchi city only run as far south as Kubokawa station, before heading west across the island to Uwajima, then linking with JR lines heading north to Matsuyama. South of Kubokawa would have lost out completely in terms of trains in the late 1980s, when Japan National Railways (JNR) was privatised to become Japan Railways (JR), if Tosa Kuroshio Railway (with big input from Kōchi Prefecture) hadn't stepped in to run the less profitable lines from Kubokawa to Nakamura and on to Sukumo, on the west coast of the island. Parts of rural Japan like this have long been losing valuable services such as train lines due to rural population decline.

While *henro* need not walk through Shimanto-shi, as there is another route option nearer the coast, it's worth noting that this is the last sizable city for the next five days or so, with business hotels, restaurants, cafes and a supermarket right on Rte 56 through town. If you're feeling

Hondō (main hall), Temple 37: Iwamoto-ji

the need for some city time before heading out into less-populated areas, Shimanto-shi is the place to overnight. While the route near the coast is a tad shorter, there aren't many services along the trail.

Shinnen-an

After writing the first pilgrimage guide-book in 1687 (p26), the wandering holy man Shinnen, who, it is said, walked the pilgrimage over 20 times, changed his focus. At a track junction passed by *henro* on their way to Temple 38: Kongōfuku-ji at Ashizuri-misaki, and by the many pilgrims who backtrack on their way to Temple 39: Enkō-ji, he built a chapel and shelter
Continues on page 122

BEST PLACES TO EAT

Tomo's Drive-In, Ōkinohama ¥
This little hamburger, doughnut and coffee diner just past the southern end of gorgeous Ōki Beach may feel like a saviour. *11am-5pm Thu-Mon*

Tsubaki, Ashizuri-misaki ¥
Outside the main gate of Temple 38: Kongōfuku-ji, this 2nd-floor place serves tasty *katsuo-tataki* (seared bonito on rice) options. つばき; *9am-6pm*

Funny House, near Temple 39 ¥
This classic Japanese diner may be in desperate need of a paint job, but its generous portions will hit the spot. *7.30am-5pm*

Shimanto-shi

Shinnen-an

15km

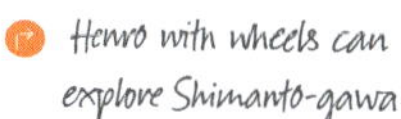

119

Check Out the Shimanto-gawa

The longest river on Shikoku at 196km, the attractive Shimanto-gawa also famously holds the title of Japan's last free-flowing, untamed river. It is known as such throughout Japan.

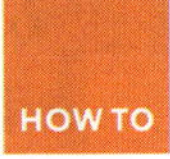

HOW TO

Nearest stop: Temple 37: Iwamoto-ji

Getting here: You'll need your own set of wheels to explore this scenic drive.

Tip: You're driving from Shimanto-chō (town) along the Shimanto-gawa (river) to Shimanto-shi (city); it's helpful to remember this.

More info: Shimanto City Tourist Information *(shimanto-kankou. com)* covers around Shimanto-shi and the lower sections of the Shimanto-gawa; **Oku-Shimanto** *(okushimanto.jp)* covers Shimanto-chō, plus the headwaters and upper/middle sections of the Shimanto-gawa.

Chinkabashi

One of the distinctive features of the **Shimanto-gawa** is its numerous *chinkabashi,* submersible bridges without railings that allow water and debris to flow virtually unimpeded both over the top and underneath when the river swells and floods. There are 22 of these quaint structures over the main river and another 26 over tributaries; crossing them has become a tourist attraction in its own right.

For an extremely scenic drive, *henro* with wheels might consider turning inland on Rte 381 from **Shimanto-chō** (Kubokawa) after visiting Temple 37: Iwamoto-ji, then following the Shimanto-gawa and JR Yodo train line, also known as the Shimanto Green Line, as they curl around to the west. From **Ekawasaki,** you'll lose the train line, which heads over to **Uwajima** on Shikoku's west coast. Continue south now, following the winding river on Rte 441 all the way around to **Shimanto-shi** (Nakamura). It's an 86km drive and along the way you'll see and have the opportunity to drive or walk over a number of *chinkabashi.* Take care as they are one lane and don't have side rails.

River Activities

In the downriver area nearer Shimanto-shi, the river is wide and the expansive scenery makes the perfect setting for a relaxing cruise on a *yakatabune* (flat-bottomed, roofed boat). These cruises are very popular with Japanese visitors. The Shimanto-gawa is also great for a range of outdoor adventure

RIVER CUISINE

Shimanto-shi's cuisine is heavily influenced by its river. One of the top specialities is grilled *unagi* (eel), cooked over charcoal and basted with a rich, slightly sweet soy-based sauce. The river is also famous for its *ayu* (sweetfish), which is often grilled with salt on skewers over an open fire and served with a simple garnish to highlight its delicate flavour. Boiled or deep-fried freshwater prawns from the river are packed full of flavour.

Left: Shimanto-gawa
Below: *Yakatabune* on Shimanto-gawa

activities, including rafting, canoeing, kayaking and stand-up paddleboarding. Cycling alongside the river is popular. Head to the **Shimanto City Tourist Information Center** next to Nakamura Station for info, bookings and rental bikes.

Downriver Bridges

Walking *henro* really only have a couple of options for crossing the Shimanto-gawa as there aren't many bridges. The best option is to do whatever you want in Shimanto-shi, then carry on down the north side of the river and cross on the bridge 4km downriver.

Continued from page 119

and lived there helping *henro*. It's known as **Shinnen-an** (Shinnen's Shelter) and can be visited where Rte 321 meets Rte 346, 500m off the main road, 15km south of Nakamura train station. It's said that Shinnen began the practice of placing stone markers to guide future pilgrims along the trail. Consider Shinnen-an an optional extra for *henro* interested in the history of the pilgrimage; there's no extra credit for visiting here!

Ōkinohama

As you turn the corner some 12km south of Shinnen-an, you'll find yourself blinking in surprise. Is that magnificent white-sand beach for real? It's got to be close to 2km long, backed by subtropical scrub and forest, not condominiums or skyscrapers. **Ōkinohama** (Ōki Beach; 大岐の浜) is absolutely gorgeous and a sight for sore eyes, especially if you like a dip in the ocean. The only souls to frequent this unspoilt stretch are the pick of the region's surfers, some egg-laying turtles and the odd grinning clam-diver. Turn left at signage on the main road for **Takoyaki** (たこ焼) street food, walk through the small car park, then through low-growing forest and head out for a swim in front of the beach gazebo if you're keen. The beach faces directly east, perfect for watching the sun rise.

There are a few places to stay 3km south of Ōkinohama in the small port of Iburi, including **Minshuku Tabiji**.

Temple 38: Kongōfuku-ji

From Temple 37, it's an 82km walk to **Temple 38: Kongōfuku-ji** (金剛福寺; *kongou fukuji.com*) at Ashizuri-misaki, the longest stretch between temples on the pilgrimage. It seems somewhat appropriate that the two longest walks – the 77km from Temple 23:

CRAIG MCLACHLAN/LONELY PLANET

Along the Way We Met...

RAYMOND I'm a Shingon Buddhist priest and now it's time for me to go back to the roots of Shingon and walk the Shikoku pilgrimage. I was worried about walking the Kōchi coast as I heard it was very hard, but the weather was beautiful, the scenery was amazing and I was pleasantly surprised. I've been so impressed with the youth here: young people repairing walking tracks and picking up litter.

Raymond has been a Shingon Buddhist monk at the Seizan-ji Temple in Sydney, Australia for 25 years.

RAYMOND'S TIP: *Go slowly at the start in Tokushima and don't overdo it. You can pick up the pace later when your body gets used to the pilgrimage.*

Shinnen-an

12km

Ōkinohama

17km

 *One of the most beautiful beaches you'll see in Japan*

Temple 38: Kongōfuku-ji

Yakuō-ji to Temple 24: Hotsumisaki-ji and the 82km from Temple 37: Iwamoto-ji to Temple 38: Kongōfuku-ji – are to remote, holy temples at the island's two great southern capes, Muroto-misaki and Ashizuri-misaki.

Breaking left off the main road just south of Ōkinohama, Rte 27, the shortest way for walkers to get to Ashizuri-misaki, heads south along the eastern coast of the peninsula for 15km from Iburi all the way out to the cape. Few cars use this winding, somewhat lonely, road that deposits walkers right out in front of Temple 38.

Kongōfuku-ji is more or less right at the cape, a popular destination for Japanese visitors to

Continues on page 126

BEST PLACES TO SLEEP

Hostel John Man ¥
Ideal location 50m from the Umetate Ferry Terminal for catching the 7.10am ferry (p113) on your way to Temple 37. *hostel-john-mang.jimdosite.com*

Temple 37: Iwamoto-ji Temple Lodging ¥
Good food and facilities here at the relaxed temple *shukubō*, 600m south of JR Kubokawa Station. *iwamotoji.or.jp*

Henro House Taishō-tei ¥
Not many budget options at Ashizuri-misaki; book early and read all the information on the website before you arrive. Pre-packaged meals are provided as *osettai* (gifts and acts of hospitality offered to pilgrims). *henrohouse.jp*

Temple 38: Kongōfuku-ji

Stay on the coast for the walk to the cape

Don't forget to explore Ashizuri-misaki

Experience Ashizuri-misaki

At the southernmost point of Shikoku, Ashizuri-misaki is renowned for Temple 38: Kongōfuku-ji and as the place from where the devout sailed forth in search of Kannon's Pure Land in the South.

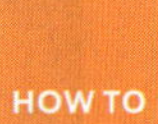

HOW TO

Nearest stop: Temple 38: Kongōfuku-ji

Getting here: It's an 82km walk from Temple 37 to Temple 38 and a 53km walk on to Temple 39.

Where to stay: Henro House Taishō-tei (p123) is 600m west of Temple 38.

Tip: The small Irifune store sells *bentō* (packaged meals) and you may be able to book meals through your accommodation, but there are no supermarkets or convenience stores so come prepared.

More info: **Ashizuri-misaki** *(shimizu-kankou.com)*; **Ashizuri-Uwakai National Park** *(env.go.jp/park/ashizuri)*

Foot Stamping

Ashizuri means 'foot stamping' and the name comes from the story of a proud old monk who, on learning that his young protégé had decided to sail from the cape in search of Fudaraku (the Pure Land of Kannon), stamped his foot in frustration, leaving his footprint forever in the rock at the cape.

While many prayed for rebirth in heavenly realms such as Yakushi's Pure World in the east or Amida's Pure Land in the west, others tried to reach Kannon's Fudaraku, the Pure Land in the south, in this lifetime. They went in search of a physical place, rather than a mental state, most simply disappearing out into the ocean, never to be heard from again. Records in Okinawa indicate that some washed up here.

Ashizuri-Uwakai National Park

Established in 1972, **Ashizuri-Uwakai National Park** is one of only two of Japan's 35 national parks that is part of Shikoku. The other is Setonaikai National Park, in the Inland Sea (Seto-nai-kai), between Shikoku and Honshū.

While the park covers a large area, at the cape there are extensive, well-maintained walking **trails** through thick vegetation starting from the **John Manjirō Statue**, just east of Temple 38: Kongōfuku-ji. Amble out to the **Ashizuri-misaki Viewing Platform** to see the lighthouse,

BRESTER IRINA/SHUTTERSTOCK

JOHN MANJIRŌ

Just to the east of the temple's main gate, you'll find the imposing statue of locally born hero, John Manjirō. Born in 1827 as Nakahama Manjirō, the young fisherman and four friends were swept onto the desolate shores of Torishima, some 800km to the east, in 1841. He and his mates were rescued five months later by an American whaler and taken to Hawaii. After moving to Massachusetts and learning English, 'John' eventually returned to Japan and later played a leading role in diplomatic negotiations with the USA and other countries at the end of the Edo period.

Left: John Manjirō statue, Ashizuri-Uwakai National Park
Below: Ashizuri cape lighthouse

80m-high cliffs and waves crashing on the rocks below. Stroll further afield to **Tengu-no-hana** or out to the **lighthouse** itself.

Tourist Village

Good news for walking *henro* is that as tourists come here to overnight, many at **Ashizuri Onsen Village**, there are quite a few accommodation options at the cape, though you'll still want to book ahead and come prepared. Make use of the free **Manjirō Ashi-yu** *(Foot Bath; 8am-7pm)* in a small building that looks down on the spectacular **Hakusan Natural Arch** rock formation.

AMANA IMAGES INC./ALAMY

Temple 39: Enkō-ji

HENRO WITH WHEELS

- From Kōchi city to Ashizuri-misaki by car is around 150km. Allow three to four hours using the expressway.
- With time up your sleeve, check out the *chinkabashi* on the Shimanto-gawa (p120).
- There are good places to stay at Ashizuri-misaki, such as Ashizuri Kokusai Hotel and Hotel Ashizurien; don't forget to walk the trails at the cape.
- Staying at the cape is a good option, unless you want to press on and finish this leg of the journey in one day.
- Don't backtrack as walking *henro* do; drive Rte 321 west around the coast to Temple 39: Enkō-ji.

Continued from page 123

Shikoku, and gets its fair share of tourists as well as pilgrims. There's a bit of a different vibe here: the temple feels lush, subtropical, surrounded by green, with a big pond and a lovely statue of a sea turtle just inside the main gate. The buildings sit strategically around the pond, as much for fire-fighting purposes as for aesthetic beauty, and while the temple is attractive in its own right, it's all about the location at Ashizuri-misaki (p124).

Shimonokae

Walking from Temple 38: Kongōfuku-ji to Temple 39: Enkō-ji is no easy task and requires some decision making, as there are four possible

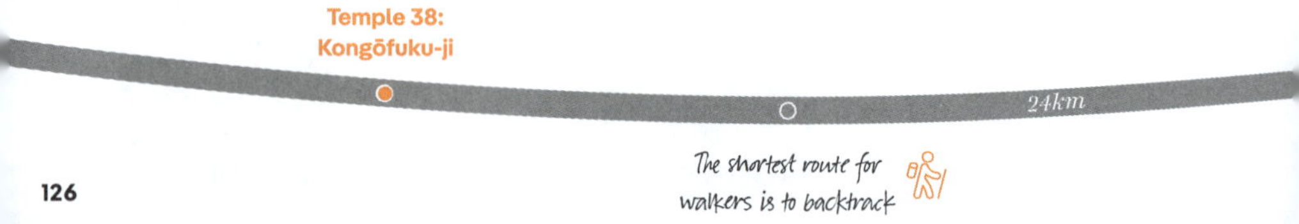

Temple 38:
Kongōfuku-ji

24km

The shortest route for walkers is to backtrack

routes you can take. Check your options on the Henro Helper app.

The shortest, but with limited facilities, is via **Shimonokae** and Mihara (53km). In this case, splitting the walk into two days is a good option and the best way to do it is to backtrack 24km from Ashizuri-misaki, past **Ōkinohama** to **Shimonokae** at the mouth of the Shimonokae-gawa and spend the night here. **Anshuku** (*phone 0880-84-0567; ¥*), right beside the bridge, is a good, cheap spot to stay with a convenience store next door; stock up on supplies for the following day. On day two, you'll walk up a remote river valley through to tiny **Mihara**, then on to Temple 39, for a total of 29km.

If you don't like backtracking or are just happy walking extra hours, the 70km route to Enkō-ji via **Tosa-Shimizu**, the scenic Tatsukushi coast, the small town of **Otsuki** and **Sukumo** is the way to go. All up, it's an extra three to four hours of walking, but Tosa-Shimizu, 15km northwest of Ashizuri-misaki, has eateries, supermarkets and overnighting options, the coastal scenery is picturesque and Rte 321 is nowhere near as remote. Overnighting in Sukumo is a good option; stay there, leave your bags, then do a piston walk (15km return to Temple 39: Enkō-ji).

The other two routes are slightly shorter than the picturesque route, but involve walking to Tosa-Shimizu, then cutting through very remote mountainous areas.

Temple 39: Enkō-ji

From Ashizuri-misaki it's a minimum of 53km of walking to get to the last temple in Tosa, **Temple 39: Enkō-ji** (延光寺). That's 200km of walking to get from Temples 36 to 39, a far cry from the easy first 10 temples on the north side of the Yoshino-gawa in Tokushima. No wonder *henro* have always sighed in relief at getting through Tosa.

Enkō-ji is known for its bell, said to have been carried to the temple by a turtle from the Palace of the Sea; don't miss the lovely statue of the turtle with the bell on its back. The grounds are extensive, peaceful and beautifully maintained, with tall trees and shade, up an agricultural side valley off Rte 56. The temple is popular with worshippers afflicted with eye problems. It's said that Kōbō Daishi dug the *mearai-ido* (eye-washing well) here with his staff, and many come to pray for relief from their eyesight issues.

From Enkō-ji, it's only a 14km walk west through the town of Sukumo to the prefectural border, where *henro* can breathe a sigh of relief at successfully getting through Tosa and into the third prefecture on their pilgrimage.

Turtle with bell statue, Temple 39: Enkō-ji

Staying at Shomonkae breaks the walk into two manageable days

A long walk through the Mihara mountains

Pray for eye issues here

Discovering Spirituality on the Shikoku Pilgrimage

Learn about the inner workings of the Shikoku pilgrimage from one of its priests, including why people walk the route, how how pilgrims are viewed by the Shikoku people, and what to expect along the way.

WORDS BY **KIM KAHAN**
Kim is a Japan-based writer and translator.

Bench erected as an act of *osettai*

WASHU EBIZUKA, THE head priest of Temple 31: Chikurin-ji, has walked the route himself and greets numerous pilgrims every day.

'Tired and in pain from walking for so long, I lay down beside the road, relieving myself of my luggage. I turned and saw a ladybug, right next to me. I looked up at the sky, and thought to myself: "this must be the world that the ladybug sees,"' Washu Ebizuka remembers. Taking up the mantle at the tender age of 21, the now-67-year-old has led Chikurin-ji for over 45 years. During that time, he's welcomed countless pilgrims through the temple grounds, and has also accompanied numerous believers, often for short parts at a time.

Walking the Route

Chikurin-ji is the 31st temple stop on the pilgrimage journey when the circular route is taken in a clockwise direction.

Being a priest is a family business, but Ebizuka wasn't such a willing practitioner at first. He rebelled, growing his hair long and leaving the temple to do 'a whole manner of different things,' he says. But fate ran its course. After his father passed away, Ebizuka made a deal with his mother: he could spend one year doing whatever he wished, then go to Kyoto and begin his studies. It was while studying in Kyoto that he discovered the beauty of his inherited profession, and by the time his training was up, he was converted, walking the whole of the Shikoku pilgrimage when he returned.

JESSICA KORTEMAN/LONELY PLANET

The experience, he says, opened up another channel in his heart. 'We always hear birds, don't we? And we always see flowers. But have we ever truly listened to the birdsong?' He reflects, 'I realised I had never done that because I'd always been in a hurry.' Spending the time walking the course made him appreciate how small his own daily worries are, and how they pale within the wider context of the human world.

Open to All

The path close to Temple 31: Chikurin-ji is relatively easy. It's flat and close to civilisation, so Ebizuka believes that the temple acts as a place to untie any tension that a pilgrim has been feeling until that point. It's a fitting position, as he wants Chikurin-ji to be a temple for everyone, a promise that he made to himself when he became the head priest all those years ago.

> 'We always hear birds, don't we? And we always see flowers. But have we ever truly listened to the birdsong?'

By Ebizuka's reckoning, roughly 80,000 people undertake the pilgrimage each year, and that number is constantly increasing. Of these, only about 5000 actually walk the entire course. The rest cycle or take cars, buses or public transport – the main idea is to show dedication and respect, rather than the method of completion. Others will take the pilgrimage in stages. In Japan, it's hard for people to take leave for the 12 days required for the bus tour, let alone the six weeks required to walk the entire circuit. Ebizuka estimates that a large proportion of the walkers are visitors from overseas.

Osettai: The Art of Hospitality

One can tell if someone is a pilgrim by the clothes they wear. For the Shikoku pilgrimage, this means a white stole and a staff, sometimes with a pointy straw hat, too. People in Shikoku hold pilgrims in high regard, and they'll look after them as they go, in a custom called *osettai*.

Pilgrims are believed to embody the spirit of Kōbō Daishi himself. So when locals offer something, they are offering it directly to Kōbō Daishi.

Thanks to the pilgrim's uniform, it's easy for residents to spot a traveller and this works as an easy conversation starter – something that the chatty people of Shikoku are more than happy to use. An elderly woman might spark up a conversation, asking the pilgrim where they're off to next. A local shopkeeper might give mandarins as fuel. A passerby may offer the pilgrim a lift or somewhere to stay. In other instances, Ebizuka says, jumping into a stranger's car or crashing at a random house may not be the safest bet, but all this changes in Shikoku.

For him, encounters with people along the way are the best part of the pilgrimage. He recalls a time he was walking down a hill in the pilgrim's path when he met an elderly woman at the bottom, who pressed a 100 yen coin into his palm. The coin was warm. 'She had been there... since morning, waiting for the first pilgrim she could give it to. That 100-yen coin carried the warmth of her body and her heart. It wasn't just a coin. I felt that it was something far more precious than 100 yen.'

The hospitality works both ways – Ebizuka welcomes his fair share of pilgrims, too. He may offer them a lift, a bottle of Pocari Sweat, or ask if they have somewhere to stay for the night. If they don't, he's happy to offer them a bed at his place, a common offering from the Shikoku people to their pilgrims.

In the words of Ebizuka, undertaking the Shikoku pilgrimage is to experience the welcoming heart of the Japanese people. 'If you want to see modern Japan, you should go to Tokyo. If you want to experience Japan's history and beauty, go to Kyoto. And why do people seek out Shikoku? Because here, you can encounter the true spirituality of the Japanese people.'

第四十一番霊場
龍光寺本堂

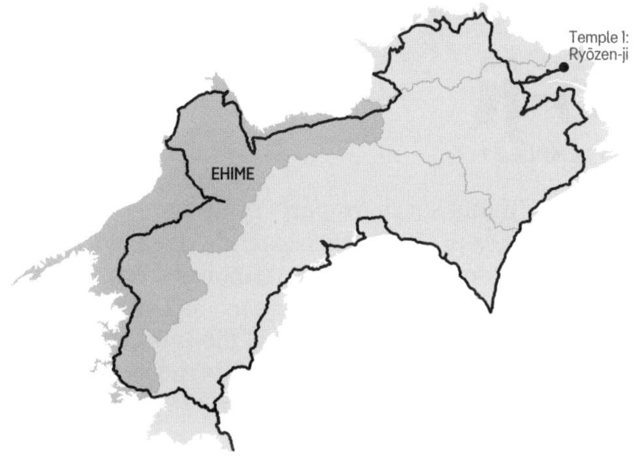

EHIME PREFECTURE

Known as the province of Iyo in times past, Ehime Prefecture is *Bodai-no-dōjō* (the Place of Attainment of Wisdom) and home to 27 of the 88 temples. Much like Kōchi, its southern parts are thought of as wild and remote, while Matsuyama, the prefectural capital and Shikoku's largest city, is a refined and cultured place, home to the legendary hot springs of Dōgo Onsen and eight of the temples. This is where many pilgrims get a boost of energy, knowing that another tough stage of the pilgrimage is behind them. The trail curls around the prefecture's northern coast, preparing pilgrims for their final prefecture, Kagawa.

Temple 41: Ryūkō-ji (p136)
AMEHIME/SHUTTERSTOCK

Enkō-ji

TEMPLE 39

Chances are that you'll find southern parts of Ehime Prefecture to be as remote as the capes of Kōchi; there are big distances between temples down here and some tough mountainous terrain. You'll pass some interesting cities along the way, such as Uwajima, Ōzu and Uchiko, but then a foray into the central mountains will bring you back on your toes before advancing towards the beckoning prefectural capital of Matsuyama (p146).

Craig McLachlan

Temple 40: Kanjizai-ji (p136)
AMEHIME/SHUTTERSTOCK

Jōruri-ji
TEMPLE 46

205KMS
~6-8 DAYS' WALK

THIS LEG:

• Temple 40: Kanjizai-ji
• Temple 41: Ryūkō-ji
• Temple 42: Butsumoku-ji
• Temple 43: Meiseki-ji
• Sleeping Kūkai
• Temple 44: Daihō-ji
• Temple 45: Iwaya-ji
• Temple 46: Jōruri-ji

Walking Notes

You'll find more big distances and lots of *henro-michi* (pilgrim track) options, especially in the southern parts, then again in the mountainous interior on the way to Temple 44: Daihō-ji and Temple 45: Iwaya-ji. It seems like you're constantly choosing between sealed roads in the valleys or old *henro-michi* over the mountains.

Breaking Your Journey

There are a lot of places to stay along this route, including in the interesting towns of Uwajima (p137), Ōzu (p140) and Uchiko (p142). Plan and book ahead for the mountains though, as there's not much between Uchiko and Temple 44: Daihō-ji at Kuma Kōgen.

Craig's Tips

BEST MEAL Stop for traditional sweets at CotoCoto in Uchiko (p142).

FAVOURITE STORY Sleeping Kūkai, where legend says the Daishi slept under a bridge (p139).

ESSENTIAL STOP Temple 45: Iwaya-ji is one of the most atmospheric holy places on the pilgrimage (p143).

TOP TIP Leave your bag near Temple 44, then pick it up after going to Temple 45 and back.

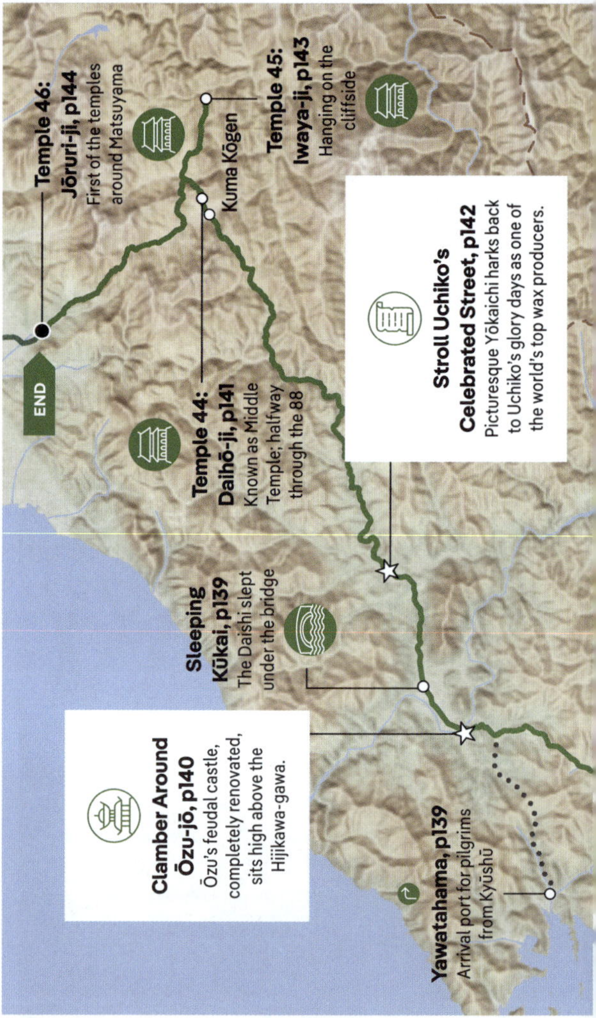

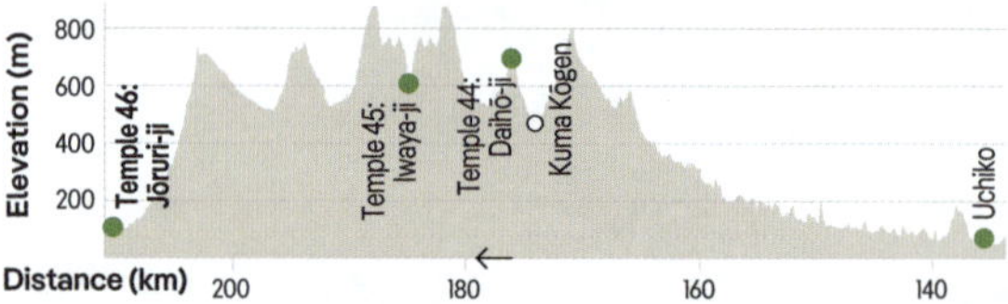

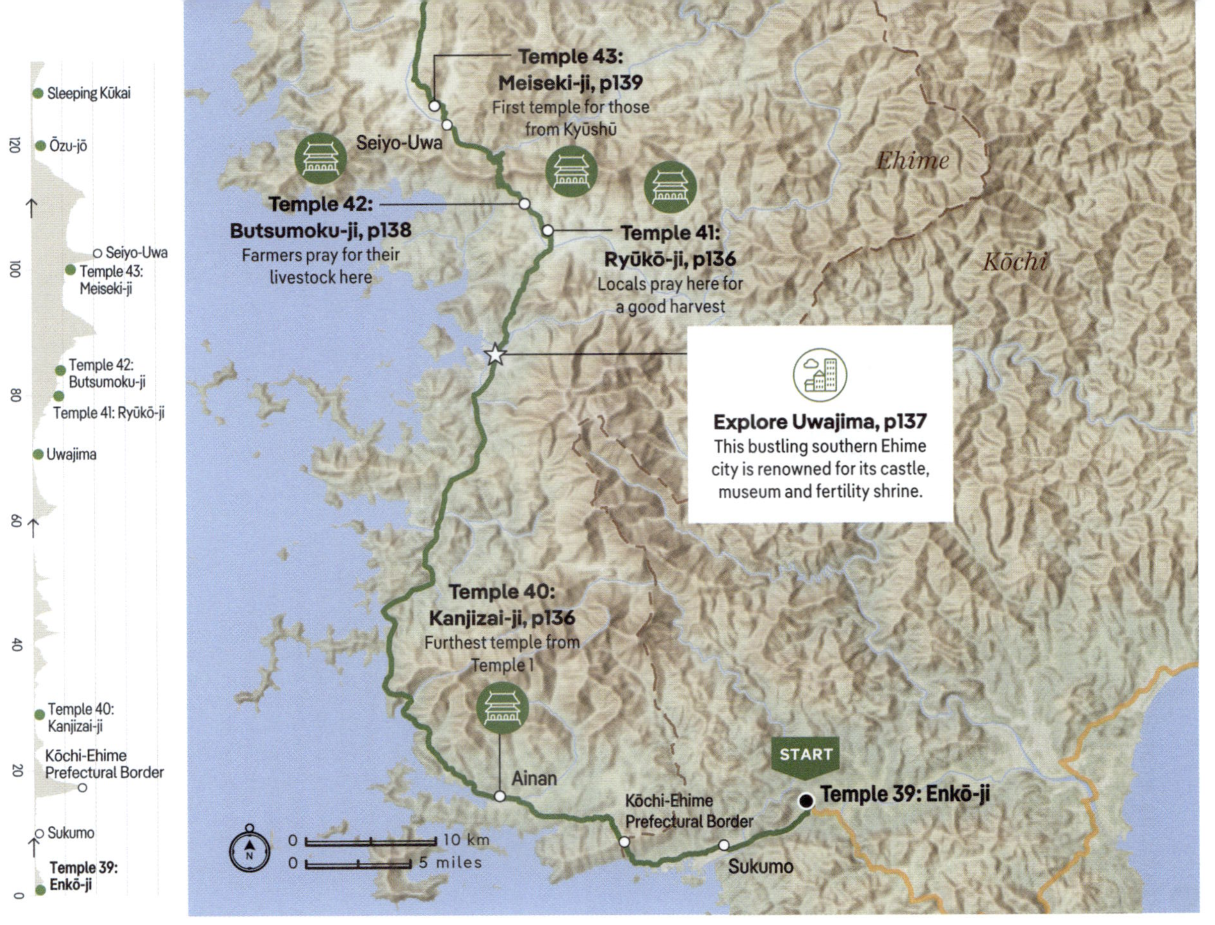
Ehime
Kōchi
Explore Uwajima, p137
This bustling southern Ehime city is renowned for its castle, museum and fertility shrine.
Temple 43: Meiseki-ji, p139
First temple for those from Kyūshū
Temple 41: Ryūkō-ji, p136
Locals pray here for a good harvest
Temple 42: Butsumoku-ji, p138
Farmers pray for their livestock here
Seiyo-Uwa
Temple 40: Kanjizai-ji, p136
Furthest temple from Temple 1
Ainan
Kōchi-Ehime Prefectural Border
Sukumo
START
Temple 39: Enkō-ji
10 km
5 miles
0
0
N

Sleeping Kūkai
Ōzu-jō
Seiyo-Uwa
Temple 43: Meiseki-ji
Temple 42: Butsumoku-ji
Temple 41: Ryūkō-ji
Uwajima
Temple 40: Kanjizai-ji
Kōchi-Ehime Prefectural Border
Sukumo
Temple 39: Enkō-ji
120
100
80
60
40
20
0

PREVIOUS STOP From Temple 39: Enkō-ji, the last temple in Tosa, it's a 27km walk west to Ehime Prefecture's first temple, Temple 40: Kanjizai-ji. *Henro* (pilgrims) walk west via *henro-michi* to the town of Sukumo, then cross the prefectural border into Ehime on a mountain path over the 370m Matsuo-tōge (Pine Tree Pass), continuing on to Ainan on the old Sukumo-kaidō route.

Temple 40: Kanjizai-ji

Temple 40: Kanjizai-ji (観自在寺; *kanjizaiji.com*) is geographically the furthest temple from Temple 1: Ryōzen-ji. Here you can complete a mini-walk of the entire pilgrimage as there are tiles around the Daishi-dō (Daishi Hall) representing all the temples. Temple 40's buildings were destroyed by fire in 1675, rebuilt by the Date feudal lords of Uwajima in 1678, only to burn down again in 1959. The main hall was rebuilt in 1964 and the Daishi-dō in 1993.

PEARL & FISH FARMING

As you head around the coast towards Uwajima, the sea offshore is known as Uwakai, part of Ashizuri-Uwakai National Park, and home to some serious fish farming and pearl cultivation. This is one of Japan's top areas for red sea bream farming in large submerged cages. The sea here, influenced by the Kuroshio Current, is rich in nutrients, has optimal water temperatures and produces a quality firm-fleshed fish thanks to its strong currents and tides. The area is also a leading producer of Akoya pearls, known for their quality, and Koshi-mono pearls, which require a longer cultivation period.

Consider staying at Yamashiroya Ryokan (p145), which will, for a fee, pick up your gear from your accommodation near Temple 39, relieving you of the need to carry it.

Temple 41: Ryūkō-ji

It's a 50km walk from Temple 40: Kanjizai-ji, via **Uwajima** (right) to **Temple 41: Ryūkō-ji** (龍光寺), at 200m in elevation on the Mima agricultural plain, some 10km north of the city. While you've passed out of Tosa, this is the rugged southern part of Ehime and there are still big distances between pilgrimage temples. The 40km stretch from Temple 40 to the largest city in southern Ehime, Uwajima (population 70,000), starts off flirting with the coast, but then turns north and inland, up and down river valleys to the bustling city.

Ryūkō-ji was founded by Kōbō Daishi in 807 CE and is dedicated to rice growing. It is known locally as Mima-no-Oinari-san, a name showing its roots in both Shintō and Buddhism. It's worth noting that the temple gate is a *torii*, normally only seen at a Shintō shrine, and visitors are greeted by *komainu* (guardian dogs) in place of the *Niō* guardian statues usually found at temple gates. In the precincts of the temple, stone statues of a fox (Shintō) and Jizō (Buddhism) are side by side in harmony. Farmers come here to pray for a good rice harvest.

Continues on page 138

Temple 39:
Enkō-ji

Temple 40:
Kanjizai-ji

27km

Cross the border into Ehime Prefecture

Uwajima

40km

10km

Check out the castle, one of 12 originals left in Japan

Temple 41:
Ryūkō-ji

Explore Uwajima

Southern Ehime Prefecture's largest city, Uwajima, is right on the pilgrim trail and features both interesting and intriguing historical highlights. It's worth breaking your journey here.

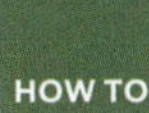

HOW TO

Nearest stop: Temple 41: Ryūkō-ji

Getting here: The pilgrim trail passes through Uwajima. Uwajima is 40km north of Temple 40: Kanjizai-ji and 10km south of Temple 41: Ryūkō-ji.

More info: Uwajima Sightseeing Guide (uwajima.org)

Uwajima-jō (adult/child ¥200/ free) is one of Japan's celebrated 12 original castles, dating from 1601. Almost all of the country's castles were demolished after 1868, when samurai rule came to an end with the Meiji Restoration, or were destroyed during WWII. Most of the castles that visitors see in Japan today are modern replicas. Uwajima-jō is a small three-storey affair, but stands atop a hill in **Shiroyama Park** in the middle of the city and has excellent views. A few blocks from the castle's southern *Nob-oritachi-mon* (gate) is the **Date Museum** (adult/child ¥500/250; 9am-5pm Wed-Mon), dedicated to the Date family, who ruled Uwajima from the castle during the Tokugawa period.

There are a number of fertility-related objects of worship at **Taga-jinja** (多賀神社) shrine – where people pray for longevity, good health and fertility – including a 2m-long wooden phallus. Such explicit fertility objects were common at shrines across Japan before the import of foreign puritanical values led to their removal during the Meiji period (1868–1912). Here you'll also find the notorious three-storey **sex museum** (admission ¥800; 8am-5pm).

FUMOTO_S/SHUTTERSTOCK

Uwajima-jō

Temple 42: Butsumoku-ji

BEST PLACES TO EAT

Isshin, Uwajima ¥¥
A top spot to try the local speciality, *tai-meshi* (sea bream on rice), below the castle Uwajima-jō. 一心; *issin-uwajima.sakura.ne.jp; 11.30am-2pm & 5-10pm Mon-Sat*

Sakami Kigetsu-dō, Uchiko ¥
Try Uchiko's beloved local *wagashi* (confectionery), and *manjū* (sweet bun filled with chestnut paste), on the town's main street. 坂見輝月堂; *9am-6pm*

Garden Time, Kuma Kōgen ¥
Close to Temple 44: Daihō-ji, this place doubles up with simple rooms and a good roadside restaurant known for its hearty meals. *garden time-ehime.com; 11am-9pm*

Continued from page 136

If you've been to Fushimi Inari in Kyoto, the main shrine of thousands throughout Japan that are dedicated to Inari, the Shintō god of rice, prosperity in agriculture and in business, you'll have seen the fox statues before. Foxes are thought to be Inari's messengers, so it's not at all surprising to find a fox statue at Mima-no-Oinari-san. Ryūkō-ji showcases the blending of Shintō and Buddhist beliefs in Japan.

Temple 42: Butsumoku-ji

If Temple 41 was a temple at which to pray for a good rice harvest, **Temple 42: Butsumoku-ji** (佛木寺), only 3km away, is the temple at which to pray for the health of farm

Temple 41:
Ryūkō-ji

Temple 42:
Butsumoku-ji

Temple 43:
Meiseki-ji

3km

11km

Locals pray for a good harvest here

Statues of Shichifukujin
(Seven Lucky Gods)

animals, particularly cattle and horses, and success in animal husbandry. A sport that is particularly popular in Uwajima, just down the road, is *tōgyū,* a kind of bovine sumo, where bulls lock horns and try to force each other to retreat. The bulls are given ring names, just like in sumo, and are treated like big pets by their owners, many of whom come to Butsumoku-ji to pray for success before tournaments. Worshippers also pray for lost pets.

Don't miss the marvellous set of statues here of the **Shichifukujin** (Seven Lucky Gods), a group of deities popular in Japanese folklore who are believed to bring good luck and fortune. They are often depicted on a *takara-bune* (treasure ship), which is said to visit at New Year and bring fortune for the coming year. Visits to temples and shrines dedicated to the Shichifukujin are a popular activity, particularly during New Year.

Butsumoku-ji translates to 'Tree Buddha Temple', after the theory that everything in the universe has the capability of attaining Buddhahood, even a tree.

Temple 43: Meiseki-ji

Sitting on a hill at close to 300m in elevation, **Temple 43: Meiseki-ji** (明石寺) is an 11km walk from Temple 42. This is the closest temple to Yawatahama, where, over the centuries, *henro* from Kyūshū arrived at the port by boat. Just as Ryōzen-ji is Temple 1, as it's the first temple pilgrims came to after visiting Kōya-san and arriving on Shikoku by boat, Meiseki-ji was number one for pilgrims from Kyūshū. Their goal was to go right around the island, complete the circle, then head back to Kyūshū by boat.

The temple is spread out, not lacking for space, with large, ancient trees, stone walls and steps, and a *henro-michi* over the hill that allows *henro* to carry on without backtracking down the way they came up and going around.

DETOUR: **Yawatahama**

Though it's west of the most direct walking route for *henro* on their way to Temple 44: Daihō-ji, Yawatahama, on the coast, is still an important transport hub in this part of Ehime Prefecture. The train lines that head north to Matsuyama and south to Uwajima pass through the port town's **JR Yawatahama station**, and ferries still depart from here for Beppu and Usuki on Kyūshū. These days, there are no ferries from Uwajima to Kyūshū, but the ferries that depart Yawatahama are run by **Uwajima Unyu Ferries** (*uwajimaunyu.co.jp*) and **Orange Ferry** (*orange-ferry.co.jp*). The ferries also carry cars, motorbikes and bicycles.

Sleeping Kūkai

It is likely that *henro* will have heard the story that they shouldn't tap their *kongō-zue* (staff) on a bridge when crossing it as Kōbō Daishi could well be sleeping underneath. **Tōyogahashi** (Ten Nights Bridge), 5km northeast of Ōzu-jō (p140), at the small temple **Eitoku-ji**, is said to be that spot. Eitoku-ji is Temple 8 of the *Bekkaku* (p16), the extra set of 20 distinguished temples for pilgrims to visit.

Of course, there's a big concrete bridge now, but this is where the Daishi is said to have slept when no-one would give him lodging. It was only for one night, but it was so cold that it felt like

Continues on page 141

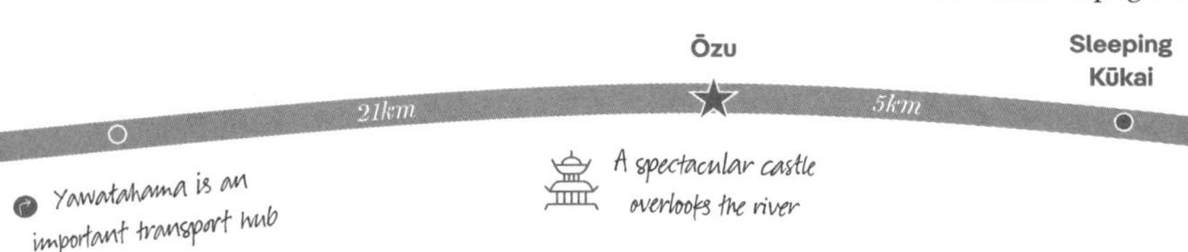

Clamber Around Ōzu-jō

Virtually right on the *henro* trail, beautiful Ōzu-jō sits high above the river Hiji-kawa and has its origins set in the 1300s.

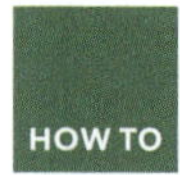

HOW TO

Nearest stop: Ōzu-jō is 5km from Sleeping Kūkai.

Getting here: Ōzu-jō is located in Ōzu, 2km from JR Iyo-Ōzu Station.

When to go: 9am–5pm daily

Cost: Adult/child ¥550/220

More info: ozucastle.jp

Like many castles in Japan, the prominence of **Ōzu-jō** faded with the Meiji Restoration in 1868 when regional rulers were stripped of their powers and lands. The Kato family, rulers of the Ōzu Domain for 13 generations from 1617, vacated the castle and it soon fell into disrepair, the main tower being demolished. The current castle was reconstructed in phases from the 1950s and, unlike in many other castles that were rebuilt in the 20th century using ferro concrete, the main keep of Ōzu-jō was crafted mainly with wood and traditional construction techniques. It was completed in 2004.

Inside the castle buildings there are exhibits on the history of Ōzu, local maps, castle models, and displays of armour and items belonging to the feudal lords. Head to the top of the four-storey main keep for superb views over the river and city. In a Japan-wide first, **Ōzu Castle-Stay** *(castlestay.ozucastle. com; ¥¥¥)* allows visitors to spend a night in the castle, and have the entirety of castle hill to themselves, though it may well be beyond the budget of a wandering *henro*.

Ōzu-jō

RAICHO/SHUTTERSTOCK

Along the Way We Met...

STEPHEN I've been living in Aomori in northern Japan for the last two years. I got two weeks off work, so rode my motorbike – a 400cc Kawasaki Ninja – for two days on the expressways to get to Shikoku. I've got 10 days to ride around the 88 temples, then two days to get back to Aomori. When locals see the registration plates on my bike, it's a great icebreaker! I did some preparation, but I believe in learning from doing, rather than research.

Stephen, from the USA, is hoping to learn more about Japanese culture and Buddhism during his time on the road.

STEPHEN'S TIP: *Stay patient when problems pop up on the pilgrimage. Everything seems to work out well in the end.*

Continued from page 138

10, leading to its name. There's a statue of the Daishi in a reclining pose under a bridge, known as *nōjuku Daishi* (the Daishi sleeping out), but the site doesn't feel particularly holy, at a busy modern road junction. Entirely appropriately, considering the story, the redeeming aspect for walking *henro* is that there is a *tsuyado* (basic lodging for pilgrims), where you can overnight for a small donation.

Temple 44: Daihō-ji

After a few temples reasonably close together, it's a bit of a shock to face a 73km hike from Temple 43 to **Temple 44: Daihō-ji** (大寶寺). While it's a fairly straightforward walk as far as the town of **Uchiko** (p142), after that *henro* are heading straight into remote mountainous territory in order to get to Temple 44, at 580m in elevation. You can either walk on roads in river valleys or go over mountain passes on *henro-michi,* but either way stock up for this 40km stretch from Uchiko as there are no convenience stores and only the occasional tiny shop for food until you get to Kuma Kōgen, just before the temple. The Henro Helper app lists a number of accommodation options along the way; order meals when you make a booking.

Often referred to as Naka-fudashō (Middle Temple), *henro* are halfway through the 88 temples when they reach Daihō-ji, but with about two-thirds of the total distance covered.

This serene, sacred place, enclosed in dense trees on the side of a mountain at Kuma-kōgen, has had more than its share of mishaps since Kōbō Daishi was here in 822 CE, changing the sect of the existing temple to his Shingon sect. It has been destroyed by fire at least three times in the last 1000 years, most recently in 1874.

Continues on page 139

Stroll Uchiko's Celebrated Street

This small town's historic district of Yōkaichi tells the story of its prosperous past as a producer of wax during the late Edo and early Meiji periods.

HOW TO

Nearest stop: Uchiko is 9km from Sleeping Kūkai.

Getting here: One of two *henro-michi* options in Uchiko passes through Yōkaichi; it's a 15-minute walk from JR Uchiko Station.

Tip: Stop for refreshments at CotoCoto in Yōkaichi, a traditional Japanese sweets cafe.

More info: We Love Uchiko (*we-love-uchiko.jp*)

This small town became famous for its high-quality wax, winning awards for best-quality wax at world fairs in Chicago in 1894 and in Paris in 1900. As you'll be walking through Uchiko, take time to stroll down its picturesque 600m historic street in **Yōkaichi**, which has a number of interesting buildings, many now

serving as museums, souvenir stalls, craft shops and charming teahouses. The old buildings typically have cream-coloured plaster walls and 'wings' under the eaves to prevent fire spreading from house to house.

Before you get to the historic street, drop into the helpful **Uchiko Town Visitor Centre** (*uchikogenic.com*), housed in a 1936 art deco building. **Uchiko-za** is a magnificent restored traditional kabuki theatre that regularly holds productions. Heading north in Yōkaichi, visit **Ōmori Wa-rōsoku** (*omoriwarosoku.jp*) where they still make traditional Japanese candles by hand; **Hon-Haga-tei**, a fine example of a rich wax merchant's home; and the **Japanese Wax Museum & Kamihaga Residence** (*uchikogenic.com/en/visit/kamihaga*).

Uchiko streetscape

AMEHIME/SHUTTERSTOCK

Pilgrims reading sutras, Temple 45: Iwaya-ji

HENRO WITH WHEELS

- *Henro* with wheels should allow two to three days for this leg.
- It's a 70km drive from Temple 39: Enkō-ji in Kōchi to Uwajima (p137), which is an interesting city in which to base yourself.
- If you want to get further up the island, it's another 60km from Uwajima to historic Uchiko (left).
- From Uchiko, it's 60km through the mountains on valley roads to Temples 44 and 45, then 40km into the prefectural capital of Matsuyama.
- In particular, give Temples 44 and 45 plenty of time as it's only an hour's drive into the city from there.

Continued from page 141
Daihō-ji enshrines a statue of Kannon, made of copper and gold, that was found in 1934 beneath 130 stones with the Lotus Sutra written on them. The statue is said to possess the power to heal illnesses and drive evil spirits away.

Temple 45: Iwaya-ji

It's 9.5km to **Temple 45: Iwaya-ji** (岩屋寺; *shikoku88-iwayaji.com),* which has one of the most dramatic locations and ranks as one of the most spiritually atmospheric of the sacred places on the pilgrimage.

While it's easy enough to walk around the road and enter the temple from the front gate, the best approach is using the well-marked *henro-michi* off Rte 12 that goes up and over the

Temple 44:
Daihō-ji

Temple 45:
Iwaya-ji

9.5km

Take the henro-michi over the mountain and drop into Temple 45

Along the Way We Met...

DAVE & BLUE Dave: My wife couldn't come, so I invited Blue to join me on the pilgrimage. We met on the Appalachian Trail in the US. I read about the Shikoku pilgrimage on a poster in a coffee shop on the Camino in Spain in 2012. And here we are in 2025! The people and the food are wonderful.

Blue: The scenery is great, but it's the kindness of the people and the food that make this a really great long hike. I like the history and the idea of trying to improve yourself and seek enlightenment.

Dave (76) and Blue (64) are retired Americans and have been buddies since meeting while hiking.

DAVE'S TIP: *Try and learn some Japanese before you come; it will make things a lot easier. And don't carry too much. You can get almost everything you need along the way.*

BLUE'S TIP: *Try to understand what you're getting yourself into before you come to Shikoku. This is a long, long hike. It's not a walk in the park.*

mountain behind the temple and drops into it from above. This is a *nanshō*, a difficult place for pilgrims to reach, so watch your step. You'll be coming back the same way to move on to Temple 46: Jōruri-ji, so if you stay at an inn on the way from Temple 44, such as Haccho-zaka Japanese Inn (right), ask to leave your gear there while you go to Temple 45 and back.

The temple virtually hangs on the mountainside, high above the valley floor, with its buildings erected into the cliffsides. It's a bit like a fantasy world of sculpted rocky cliffs, with a steep wooden ladder climbing to a precarious sacred ledge, a natural altar. You can feel the presence of Kōbō Daishi and 1200 years of his followers. Ancient cedars, lots of stone steps, countless statues of Jizō, pock-marked cliffs and a truly spectacular location; this is a place to take your time. At 600m in altitude, it can get bitterly cold and even snowy here in winter, adding to the feeling of sacredness.

Temple 46: Jōruri-ji

From Temple 45, *henro* are looking at 26km of walking to get to **Temple 46: Jōruri-ji** (浄瑠璃寺), coming down out of the mountains,

Temple 46:
Jōruri-ji

approaching Matsuyama (p146) and the eight pilgrimage temples in and around Shikoku's largest city. There's a bit to do in the mountains first, including passing by the local ski area, **Kuma Ski Land**, but then a *henro-michi* drops into a narrow valley that gradually widens to deposit you at Temple 46. The grounds here are lush, with even a feeling of being overgrown, pride of place being taken by a massive 20m-high, 1000-year-old juniper tree, beneath which are Buddha handprints and footprints believed to prolong life and produce a bountiful harvest.

A stone at the temple is engraved with a haiku by one of Japan's greatest poets, Masaoka Shiki (1867–1902), who was born nearby in Matsuyama: *How long the spring day is / remembering Emon Saburō / at Jōruri-ji.*

Henro will soon pass by **Monju-in** (p162), where Emon Saburō, the man who became the first pilgrim, was given absolution by Kōbō Daishi and died below Temple 12: Shōsan-ji (p57).

BEST PLACES TO SLEEP

Yamashiroya Ryokan, Ainan ¥
Excellent location near Temple 40: Kanjizai-ji. They will transfer your gear from your accommodation around Temple 39 for a fee, allowing you to cross Matsuo Pass with no gear. *yamashiroyaryokan.jp*

Omeguri-an, Seiyo-Uwa ¥
Right on the trail 2.5km southeast of Temple 43: Meiseki-ji, Omeguri-an offers vegan meals. *omeguri.com*

Haccho-zaka Japanese Inn ¥
Ideal location between Temples 44 and 45. Leave your gear here to visit Temple 45, then pick it up on your way to Temple 46. *8-cho-zaka.jp*

Temple 46: Jōruri-ji

JOHN S LANDER/GETTY IMAGES

CITY GUIDE:

Matsuyama

Matsuyama (松山), the capital of Ehime Prefecture, holds a great romanticism for its past – from the city's Edo-era castle to historic Dōgo Onsen, and the streetcars that run between them. Among it all, you'll find shopping arcades and souvenir stores celebrating the prefecture's plentiful citrus fruits.

WORDS BY **JESSICA KORTEMAN**

Jessica is an Australian writer specialising in Japanese travel and culture.

Arriving

By foot Walking pilgrims will arrive in Matsuyama from Temple 50: Hanta-ji, around 4km from central Matsuyama.

By bus The bus from Ehime Prefectural Rd 40 into Matsuyama's city centre takes around 20 minutes.

By train It's possible to bridge the gap between Temple 43: Meiseki-ji and Matsuyama on a JR rail line, then dart southeast using buses and walking to cover Temples 44 to 50.

By car It's a 15-minute drive from Temple 50: Hanta-ji to central Matsuyama. Think about parking ahead of time – paid parking may be the only option even if you're staying in a hotel.

By air From Matsuyama Airport (MYJ), it's a 15- to 20-minute ride on the limousine bus to the city centre.

HOW MUCH FOR A

Citrus juice on tap ¥200

Sea bream rice ¥1500

Bath at Dōgo Onsen Honkan from ¥700

Getting Around

Tram Matsuyama is a city that's well served by its tram network, conveniently shuffling passengers between central Matsuyama and Dōgo Onsen for a flat rate of ¥230 per ride. Use an IC card (accepted on any Iyotetsu tram, train or bus) to receive a small discount.

Train Iyotetsu rail services departing in and out of Matsuyama City Station give quick and easy access to Mitsu Station (for Mitsuhama) and Takahama Station (for Takahama Port and the ferry to Gogo-shima). JR Matsuyama Station is your coastal connection to Imabari in the northeast (paper tickets only).

Ferry Regular ferries departing from Takahama Port can transport you to Gogo-shima in 10 to 15 minutes. Simply jump aboard; staff will collect ticket payment en route.

Bicycle Gogo-shima is most conveniently explored by bicycle, best rented from the Island Station at Yura Port.

For trip planning, download the **Iyotetsu Route Map:**

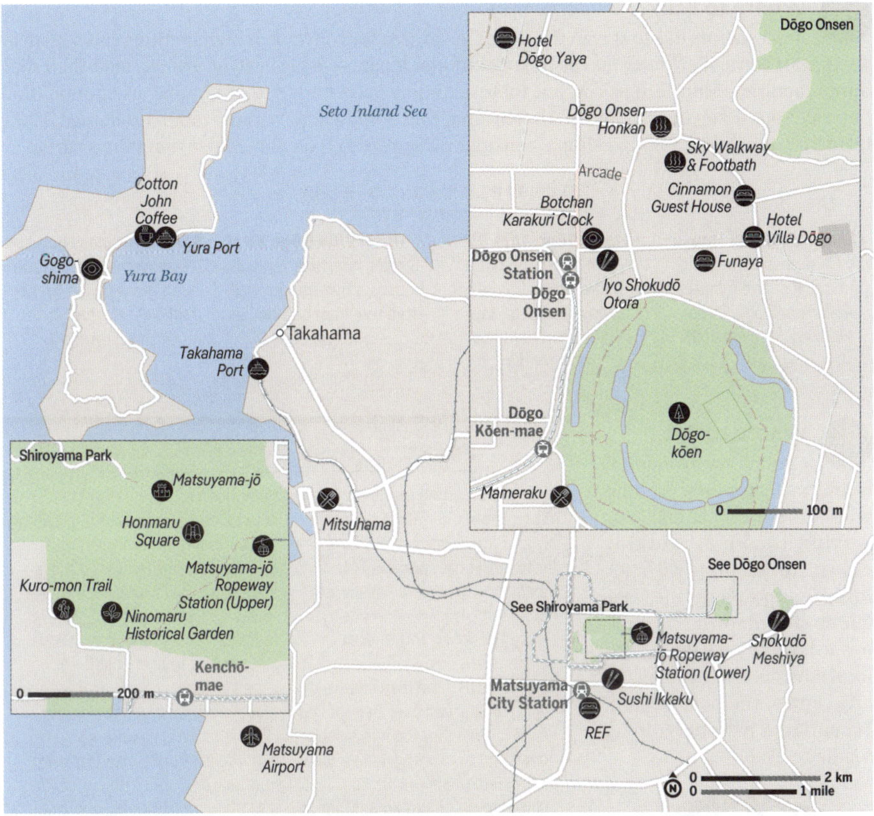

Dōgo Onsen

A DAY IN MATSUYAMA

Board a morning ferry from **Taka-hama Port** to **Yura Port** on nearby island **Gogo-shima** (p151). Rent an e-bike to explore the undulating coastline and admire the Inland Sea (Seto-nai-kai) from various vantage points. Grab lunch on the island or head to the culinary port precinct of **Mitsuhama** (p148) on the Matsuyama mainland.

Take a short train ride back to central Matsuyama. Ride the ropeway up to **Matsuyama-jō** (p150) to self-tour the castle and marvel at the city views. If you have time, take the walking trail down to **Ninomaru Historical Garden**, before hopping on a tram to **Dōgo-kōen** to explore the castle ruins of Yuzuki-jō.

Enjoy dinner and the special night-time atmosphere around the main bathhouse, **Dōgo Onsen Honkan** (p149). Stroll the *shōtengai* (shopping arcade) among kimono-clad visitors and then take a steaming bath in the city's restorative waters. Afterwards, take in the bathhouse from above at **Sky Walkway & Footbath** (p151).

Where to Stay

Most visitors like to stay in the Dōgo Onsen area for convenient night bathing (plus it's near Temple 51: Ishite-ji). Numerous *ryokan* (traditional Japanese-style inns) and hotels have their own onsen facilities. Many are pricey, but there are some good budget to midrange accommodation options, too. If staying in central Matsuyama, find somewhere within walking distance of the tram line. If heading to Gogo-shima, consider proximity to Iyotetsu's Matsuyama City Station.

BEST PLACES TO STAY

Cinnamon Guest House ¥ Cheapest dorm beds around, just two minutes' walk from Dōgo Onsen Honkan. *booking.com*

Hotel Dōgo Yaya ¥¥ Value midrange hotel with free *mikan* (mandarin orange) juice on tap and Imabari towel bar. *yayahotel.jp*

Hotel Villa Dōgo ¥¥ Simple *minshuku* (guesthouse), a five-minute walk from the main bathhouse. *booking.com*

REF ¥¥ Business hotel by Matsuyama City Station with great Ehime breakfast. *vessel-hotel.jp/ref/matsuyama*

Where to Eat

Central Matsuyama has numerous shopping arcades with quick and cheap eats serving the city's working crowd. In keeping with the historic atmosphere, the Dōgo Onsen side of town errs more towards traditional dining and local cuisine. Just north of the city centre, the port town of Mitsuhama is undergoing a foodie revival.

EHIME'S MOST-LOVED CUISINE

In Japan's leading producer of wild-caught and farmed sea bream, you won't need to look far to find local speciality *tai-meshi* (sea bream rice; pictured below left). The fish and rice are typically cooked together in an earthenware pot, while the Uwajima version of the dish involves laying *tai* sashimi over the cooked rice and then dipping it in a sauce consisting of raw egg, *shōyu* (soy sauce) and *dashi* broth.

Head to a convenience store or souvenir shop and Ehime's reputation as the 'citrus state' doesn't go unnoticed. With warmer coastal climates ideal for growing *mikan* (mandarin oranges; pictured below right) and the more acidic *Iyo-kan* (a reference to the region's old name of Iyo), visitors to Matsuyama can access citrus juice from a faucet at self-service juice stations.

Just north of town, don't miss Mitsu Port's *Mitsuhama-yaki*, an *okonomiyaki*-style dish featuring noodles, beef, beef tallow, *chiku-wa* (a type of fish cake) and egg.

FROM LEFT: KARIPHOTO/SHUTTERSTOCK, NISHIHAMA/SHUTTERSTOCK

BEST PLACES TO EAT & DRINK

Iyo Shokudō Otora ¥¥ Traditional Japanese restaurant at Dōgo Onsen serving local specialities. *noon-3pm & 5-10pm*

Sushi Ikkaku ¥ Top-notch city-centre sushi on the 2nd floor. *11.30am-2pm Mon-Fri, 5-9.30pm Mon-Sat*

Shokudō Meshiya ¥¥ By Temple 51: Ishite-ji, choose between hamburger steak or fish set menu. *11am-4pm Tue-Wed & Fri-Sun*

Mameraku ¥¥ Soybean restaurant by Dōgo-kōen, homemade tofu and soy milk products. *8.30am-6pm Tue-Sat*

Bathe at Dōgo Onsen

Just the ticket for a weary pilgrim: take a relaxing soak at Dōgo Onsen Honkan, the city's main bathhouse and most photographed building in Matsuyama.

HOW TO

Getting here: Dōgo Onsen Honkan is a five-minute walk from tram terminus Dōgo Onsen Station.

When to go: Most comfortable in cooler weather, but it's open for a hot bath year-round.

Cost: From ¥700

Tip: Check live wait times on the website and bring your own towel, or rent or buy one onsite. Soap and shampoo are provided.

More info: dogo.jp/en

According to legend, **Dōgo Onsen** (道後温泉) has been a source of restorative power for locals for some 3000 years. **Dōgo Onsen Honkan** (道後温泉本館), the hot spring's main bathhouse, was constructed in 1894 and has been canonised in the collective Japanese consciousness thanks to famed 1906 novel *Botchan* by Natsume Sōseki, in which the bathhouse appears.

Despite a recent restoration, the Honkan maintains its iconic wooden-castle-like facade and traditional interior, featuring two popular and extremely hot public baths: **Kami-no-Yu** (Bath of the Gods) and **Tama-no-Yu** (Bath of the Spirits).

The basic plan gives one-hour access to Kami-no-Yu on the ground floor. There's an additional fee to use Tama-no-Yu, the rest area and private rooms on the upper floors. Some plans include viewing the Yūshinden (the bath reserved for exclusive use by the Imperial family). Some accommodation provides *yukata* (light-weight cotton kimono) to wear to and from the baths.

Dōgo Onsen

Take a Ride to Matsuyama-jō

The city's Edo-era watchtower perched atop Mt Katsuyama, Matsuyama-jō is one of Japan's last surviving original castles.

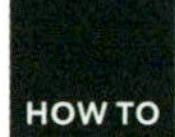

HOW TO

Getting here: Matsuyama-jō is a 10-minute walk from Matsuyama-jō Ropeway Station (Upper) or 30 minutes on foot.

When to go: Best in clear weather – steps get slippery and the open-air chairlift closes in inclement weather.

Cost: Matsuyama-jō ¥520, Ropeway one-way/return ¥270/520, Ninomaru Historical Garden ¥200

More info: matsuyamajo.jp

Built over a quarter of a century and finally completed in 1627, **Matsuyama-jō** (松山城) stands tall among Japan's 12 original castle keeps. Interestingly, no one ever lived there; it was purely a strategic structure used as a last line of defence.

As one of the larger of Japan's castles, the interior is well signposted and includes a few small experience corners, like the opportunity to try on armour. If you're unable to negotiate the castle's steep interior stairs, the area in front of the castle tower, called **Honmaru Square** (本丸広場), is free and provides views almost equally as superb as from the main citadel.

Most hitch a ride up to the square from the **lower ropeway station** on the shopping street to the east of the castle precinct, where you can choose between a thrilling open-air chairlift or an enclosed gondola. Alternatively, there are four pleasant walking paths (20 to 30 minutes), with the **Kuro-mon Trail** (黒門口登城道) from the south connecting with **Ninomaru Historical Garden** (二之丸史跡庭園) on the site of the second bailey.

Matsuyama-jō

SHIKOKU 4K/SHUTTERSTOCK

PHOTO JAPAN/ALAMY

Botchan Karakuri Clock

Take a Foot Bath

Soothe your pilgrim feet at one of Dōgo Onsen's numerous complimentary *ashi-yu* (足湯; footbaths). Next to Dōgo Onsen Station, try the popular footbath at famed landmark **Botchan Karakuri Clock** (坊っちゃんカラクリ時計). Next to Dōgo Onsen, **Sky Walkway & Footbath** (空の散歩道) has a direct view over the main bathhouse and is especially atmospheric at night. Just 250m away, **Funaya** (ふなや) welcomes nonguests to use the *ashi-yu* in the *ryokan's* exquisite central garden, complete with running stream. Funaya provides towels, but have one on hand for the other locations.

LINEGOLD/SHUTTERSTOCK

Ferry to Gogo-shima

Cycle a Matsuyama Island

For a quieter take on Ehime's prefectural capital, hop on a 10- to 15-minute **Gogoshima Ferry** (*gogoshima-ferry.com*) from Matsuyama's **Takahama Port** (高浜港) to nearby island **Gogo-shima** (興居島). Rent a bike at **Yura Port** (由良港) and take in the island's incredible panoramas on two wheels. Only a couple of hours is needed to circumnavigate the island, but allocate more time for stops and soaking in the view. Beginner riders and those with limited time can curate a short route within the vicinity of the port. Ask at portside coffee shop and informal tourist information **Cotton John Coffee** for advice.

DŌGO'S WATER BARISTAS

The origins of Dōgo Onsen (p149) are believed to go back several thousand years to the age of the gods. The story goes that a heron placed its injured leg in a pool of the hot spring's water and was cured of its ailment. Locals who witnessed the heron's miraculous recovery started bathing in the waters themselves and the rest, as they say, is history.

The water for Dōgo Onsen Honkan today is blended from up to 17 different sources to reach the desired 42°C temperature without any artificial heating or cooling. In a job that is done manually, a city-employed engineer *(kikanshi)* is tasked with maintaining the temperature throughout the day's operations.

Sometimes likened to a 'water barista', the *kikanshi* make adjustments based on the day's weather and the air temperature of the baths, which are coolest first thing, having been emptied overnight. At 3.30am, they start sending the water from the supply facility to the baths, expertly accounting for the cooling that will take place as it proceeds through the pipes, ready for the 6am opening time.

The 88 Temples

THE SHIKOKU HACHI-JŪ-HAKKASHŌ MEGURI (四国八十八ヶ所巡り), as it is known in Japanese, is a serious religious pilgrimage. None of the temples are grand or ostentatious, most being small, serene places that serve their local communities. People turn up to pray concerning everyday issues; for the ability to conceive or have a safe childbirth; for relief from medical issues such as blindness, diabetes or a sore leg; or for success in school exams or in business. This isn't a 'tourist pilgrimage', though all are welcome, as long as they show respect. Enjoy the temples. The good people of Shikoku are proud of both them and their pilgrimage.

Below left: The *nōkyō* (temple stamp) of Temple 88: Ōkubo-ji (p231) in a pilgrim's *nōkyō-chō* (temple stamp book).

Below right: *Shikoku Hachi-jū-hakkashō* in Japanese characters – The 88 Sacred Temples of Shikoku.

Right: Temple 88: Ōkubo-ji, high in the mountains of Kagawa Prefecture.

MASAYUKI NAKAYA/LONELY PLANET

MASAYUKI NAKAYA FOR LONELY PLANET

MASAYUKI NAKAYA FOR LONELY PLANET

MASAYUKI NAKAYA FOR LONELY PLANET

MASAYUKI NAKAYA FOR LONELY PLANET

MASAYUKI NAKAYA FOR LONELY PLANET

Above: After entering the temple through the main gate, pilgrims cleanse their hands and mouth at the *chōzuya* (wash basin).

Right: Many of the temples are guarded by two fierce warriors (*niō*) at the main gate (*niōmon*); the *niō* protect the temple and ward off evil.

MASAYUKI NAKAYA FOR LONELY PLANET

Left: The *hondō* (main hall) at Temple 1: Ryōzen-ji (p48) is known for the atmospheric lanterns hanging from its ceiling.

Below: The *niōmon* (main gate) at Temple 1: Ryōzen-ji; pilgrims bow before entering the temple.

IKE-YAMA/SHUTTERSTOCK

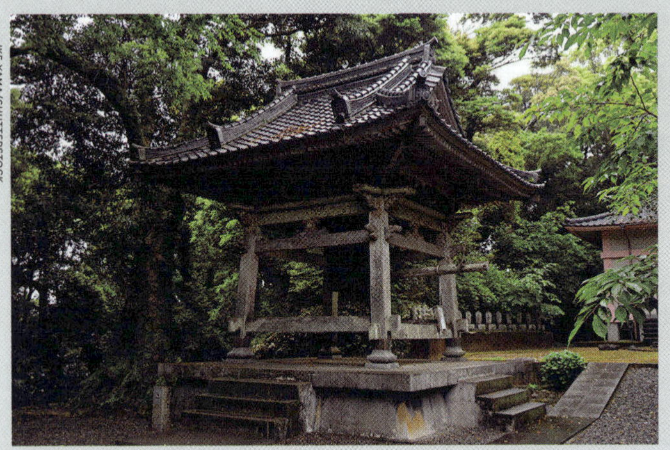

Left: *Henro* signal their arrival by ringing the bell in the bell tower – like this one at Temple 24: Hotsumisaki-ji (p85) – once. Note: set ringing hours may apply.

Below: The *hondō* at Temple 37: Iwamoto-ji (p118) in Kōchi Prefecture.

Right: Get ready to climb plenty of stone steps, such as these at Temple 65: Sankaku-ji (p186).

MASAYUKI NAKAYA FOR LONELY PLANET

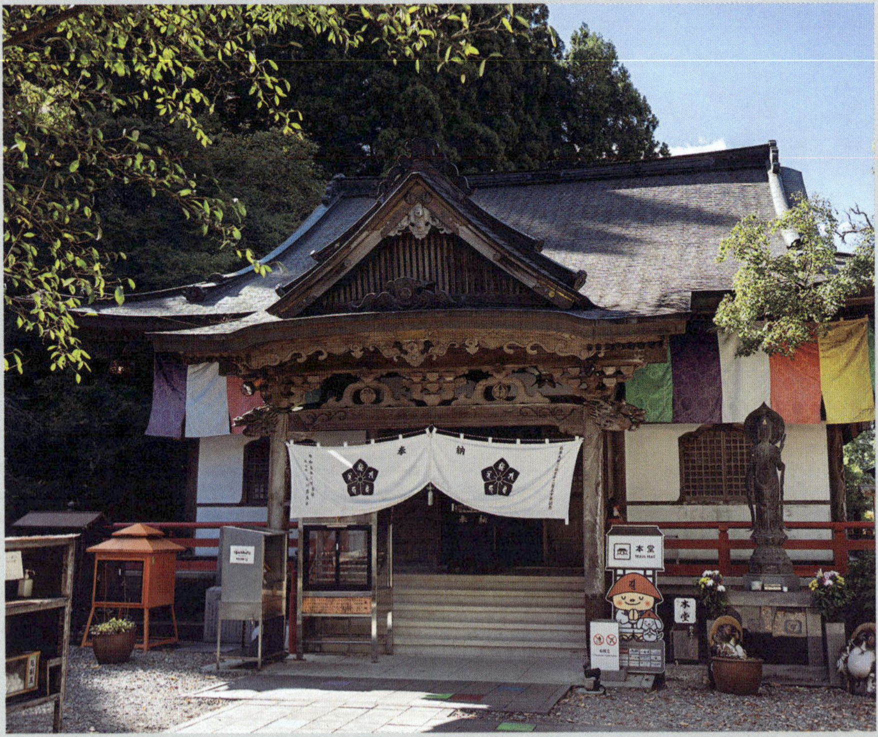

MASAYUKI NAKAYA FOR LONELY PLANET

Jōruri-ji

TEMPLE 46

Eight pilgrimage temples await around Ehime's capital city of Matsuyama, the most populous city on the island. They seem like a prize for all the hard work done in Kōchi and southern Ehime Prefecture. Take some time to soak in legendary Dōgo Onsen and prepare your body and mind in the knowledge that the big distances in the south are over, but it's definitely not time to lose focus.

Craig McLachlan

Temple 49: Jōdo-ji (p164)
AMEHIME/SHUTTERSTOCK

Enmei-ji

TEMPLE 54

Walking Notes

Pilgrims have no choice but to walk on sealed roads through busy Matsuyama city. There's a lot going on, but there's little pressure as there are so many places to stay and eat. Once through Matsuyama, it's a long enjoyable walk up the coast to Imabari city.

Breaking Your Journey

Henro (pilgrims) with wheels should consider basing themselves in Matsuyama city (p146) or the Dōgo Onsen area (p149) for a few days as they visit the temples. Walking *henro* won't have issues finding places to stay around Matsuyama and Imabari; check the Henro Helper app for places to overnight when walking up the coast.

Craig's Tips

FUN BREAK Go for a ride on the Shimanami Kaidō (p170).

FAVOURITE VIEW Look out over Matsuyama city from Temple 50: Hanta-ji (p165).

ESSENTIAL STOP The tunnel through to the *okunoin* (inner sanctuary) out the back at Temple 51: Ishite-ji (p165).

TOP TIP Soak your bones in Dōgo Onsen Honkan as you pass through (p149).

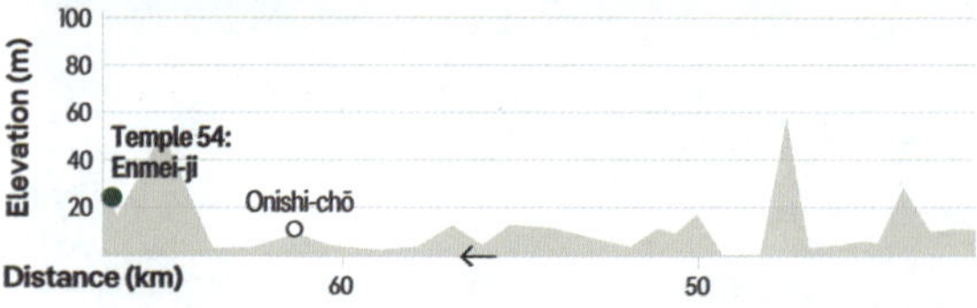

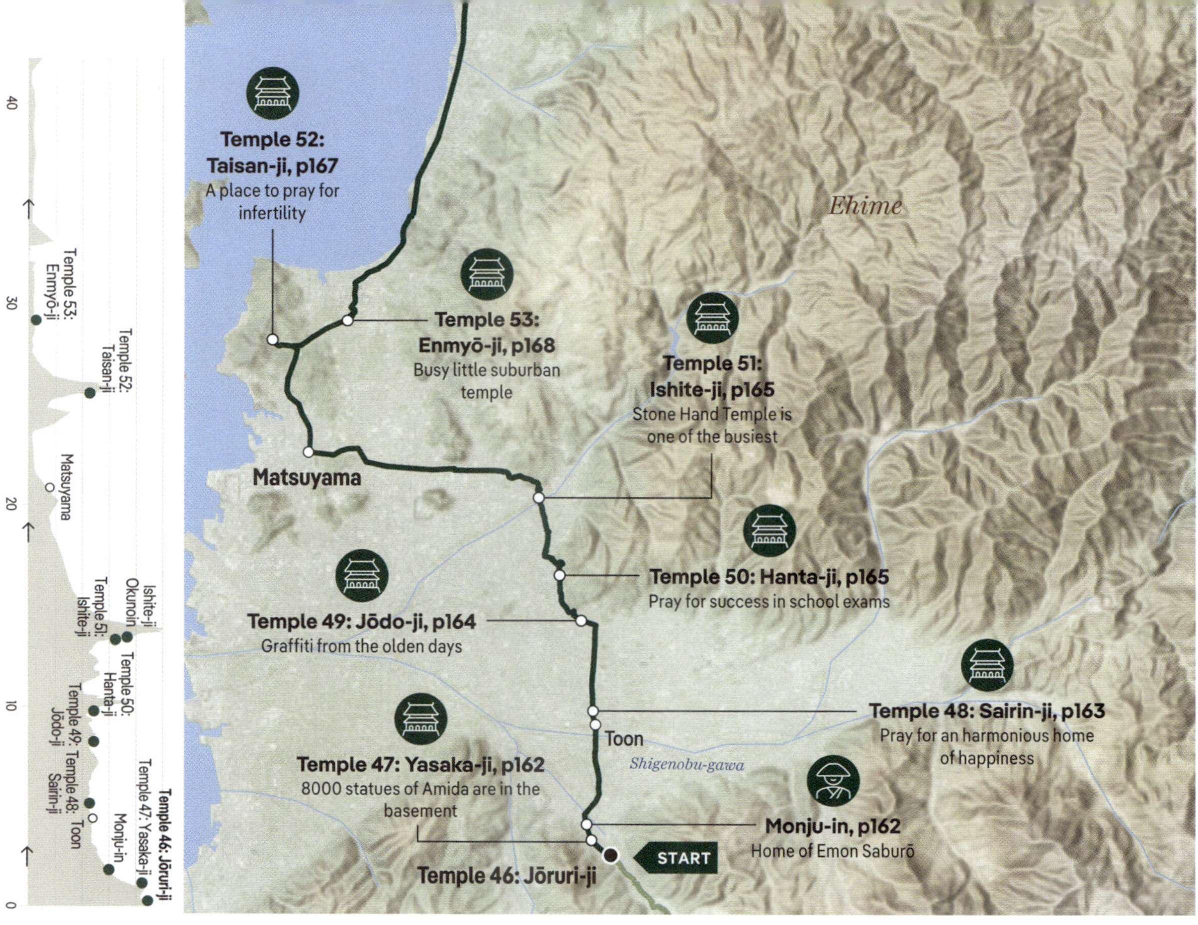
Ehime
Temple 52: Taisan-ji, p167
A place to pray for infertility
Temple 53: Enmyō-ji, p168
Busy little suburban temple
Temple 51: Ishite-ji, p165
Stone Hand Temple is one of the busiest
Matsuyama
Temple 50: Hanta-ji, p165
Pray for success in school exams
Temple 49: Jōdo-ji, p164
Graffiti from the olden days
Temple 48: Sairin-ji, p163
Pray for an harmonious home of happiness
Temple 47: Yasaka-ji, p162
8000 statues of Amida are in the basement
Toon
Shigenobu-gawa
Monju-in, p162
Home of Emon Saburō
START
Temple 46: Jōruri-ji
40
30
20
10
0
Temple 53: Enmyō-ji
Temple 52: Taisan-ji
Matsuyama
Ishite-ji Okunoin
Temple 51: Ishite-ji
Temple 50: Hanta-ji
Temple 49: Jōdo-ji
Monju-in
Temple 48: Toon
Temple 47: Yasaka-ji
Sairin-ji
Temple 46: Jōruri-ji

PREVIOUS STOP It's just a short stroll, slightly less than 1km, up the road towards Matsuyama from Temple 46: Jōruri-ji to the next temple.

Temple 47: Yasaka-ji

The short distance from Temple 46 to **Temple 47: Yasaka-ji** (八坂寺) is hard to fathom after the hard toil of 60km, 70km and even 80km distances between temples in Kōchi and southern Ehime Prefecture. It's likely to start *henro* wondering how the 88 sacred sites were chosen. According to scholars, there is no evidence that Kōbō Daishi deliberately started a pilgrimage and chose its sacred places. The pilgrimage grew in the wake of his enlightenment, with pilgrims visiting places associated with the Daishi, trying to do the same. While there is plenty to ponder about how a temple

got to be one of the 88, in the 21st century the identity of the 88 temples is well set.

With a history of 1300 years, Yasaka-ji means 'Temple of Eight Slopes', though there is a theory that the name also came from the word *iyasaka* (increasingly prosperous). The basement of the main hall here is home to 8000 statues of Amida Nyorai (Buddha of Limitless Light and Life), dedicated by believers from all over Japan.

Monju-in: Home of Emon Saburō

Although not included in the 88 sacred temples of the pilgrimage, this small temple is one of the *Bekkaku* (p16), the 20 'extra' temples that pilgrims are not required to visit to complete their pilgrimage. **Monju-in** is, however, hugely significant as the place where Emon Saburō lived. It's only 700m past Temple 47: Yasaka-ji.

Legend has it that Saburō, a rich man known for his hatred of begging holy men, broke the Daishi's begging bowl when he came asking for alms. Saburō's eight children died in the following eight days, so, in grief, Saburō went in search of the Daishi to beg his forgiveness. Legend says that Saburō circuited Shikoku over 20 times, then decided to walk around the other way (*gyaku-uchi*) to increase his chances of meeting the Daishi. Near death, he met Kōbō Daishi below Temple 12: Shōsan-ji (p57), sought absolution and asked to be reborn to serve the world. Legend has it that the Daishi took a pebble, wrote 'Emon Saburō reborn' on it,

Temple 47: Yasaka-ji

Temple 46:
Jōruri-ji

1km

700m

Head worth, down the
widening valley

Temple 47:
Yasaka-ji

Temple 48: Sairin-ji

placing the pebble in Saburō's hand as he died. Some time later, a child was born clasping a small stone with 'Emon Saburō reborn' written on it, leading to Temple 51 (p165) being named Ishite-ji (Stone Hand Temple).

Temple 48: Sairin-ji

An attractive, compact suburban temple 4.5km north of Temple 47, **Temple 48: Sairin-ji** (西林寺) sits right on busy Rte 40, well and truly out on the plain to the north of the Shigenobu-gawa. It's said that in 807 CE, when Kōbō Daishi was here and the area was suffering through drought that, by a miracle, he found limitless fresh water by thrusting his staff into the ground and that the water has never run dry.

BEST PLACES TO EAT

Ramen Ikko, by Temple 49: Jōdo-ji ¥
Right out the front of the temple, this is a good spot for a break with filling ramen, *gyōza* (dumplings) and *donbu-ri* (dishes served over rice) options. ラーメン一興; *11am-11pm*

Temple 51: Ishite-ji ¥
Try *yakimochi*, the temple's famous grilled *mochi* (rice cake) that's filled with sweet bean paste; vendors sell it like a street food outside the front gate. *9am-5pm*

Ebisuya, up the coast ¥
It doesn't look like much from the outside, but expect top *okonomiyaki* (savoury pancakes) and *yaki-soba* (stir-fried noodles) from a friendly mother-and-daughter team. えびす屋; *11am-3pm Wed-Sun*

Monju-in: Home
of Emon Saburō

Temple 48:
Sairin-ji

The legend of Emon Saburo continues

4km

Cross the Shigenobu-gawa

HENRO WITH WHEELS

- Allow one to two days to complete this stretch.
- The eight temples in and around Matsuyama are easily visited while basing yourself in the prefectural capital. The furthest away, Temple 46: Jōruri-ji, is only 13km from the middle of the city.
- The six temples to the east and southeast of Matsuyama (Temples 46 to 51) can be visited in one day.
- Either allow a day for Temples 52 and 53 while staying in Matsuyama, or visit them on your way north to Imabari city.
- It's a 42km drive from Matsuyama to Temple 54, 50km if you drive via Temples 52 and 53.

That spring is in **Jōnofuchi Park**, where there is a clear pond with carp and water birds, along with a large statue of the Daishi, some 300m southwest of the temple. This is a lovely park for families, with a children's playground, and a good spot for *henro* to take a rest. The pure water here was selected as one of Japan's 100 top springs, further enhancing the legend of the Daishi.

Somebody at Sairin-ji likes gardening, as the grounds are immaculate. It is believed that if worshippers pray to the bamboo of filial piety Kokotake (said to be a happy 'parent and child bamboo' growing close together), that they will live in a harmonious home of happiness, just like the bamboo. There is also a Jizō statue that is said to grant one wish to those who come to pray.

Temple 49: Jōdo-ji

From Temple 48, *henro* are in for a short 3km walk to **Temple 49: Jōdo-ji** (浄土寺), a suburban temple hemmed in by housing on three

Statue, Temple 51: Ishite-ji

CRAIG MCLACHLAN/LONELY PLANET

sides and a forested hill behind. Interestingly, there is handwritten graffiti here on a small shrine in the main hall that dates from the Muromachi (1336–1573) and Edo (1603–1868) periods, considered to be valuable historical records.

Just as modern *henro* are carrying name slips to leave at each temple and give to people who present them with *osettai* (small gifts of generosity), in the distant past, when pilgrims visited a temple they would nail a wooden or bronze name slip on the main temple gate or building – an early form of graffiti. The temple would remove them when room was needed for more. Others would write on the building itself and, after paper *osame-fuda* slips became the fashion, many literally plastered their name slips on temple buildings in places difficult to reach in the hope that they'd be there forever. You'll see them on old temple buildings all over the island.

Temple 50: Hanta-ji

Nice easy distances here bring pilgrims close to Matsuyama city; it's only 2km from Temple 49 to **Temple 50: Hanta-ji** (繁多寺), sitting above the plain, backing onto forested foothills and offering panoramic views out over the city. The car park sits between two large water reservoirs, with the temple tucked in behind. Legend has it that the temple was first built in the mid-700s and was already here when Kōbō Daishi came to visit.

It's a competitive world out there for temples in this part of the city, and coming up next, only 3km away, is one of the most popular, busiest and best-known of the pilgrimage temples, Temple 51: Ishite-ji. Hanta-ji competes well for worship-pers by having its own wide range of specialities for which they come to pray.

People come here to pray to the statue of Kangiten, a protective deity, who is said to help with success in school exams, as well as warding away misfortune, having a prosperous business and assuring a harmonious relationship at home between a husband and wife. Needless to say, this temple is popular with the people of Matsuyama and certainly appears prosperous.

Temple 51: Ishite-ji

It's only a 3km walk almost directly north from Temple 50 to one of the busiest temples on the pilgrimage, **Temple 51: Ishite-ji** (石手寺). This temple is both busy and prosperous for a couple of reasons, one being that it is only a 15-minute walk east from Dōgo Onsen (p149), one of the top hot springs destinations in Japan, a drawcard for countless visitors.

The other reason is that Ishite-ji means 'Stone Hand Temple', and this is the place where the baby was born clutching a pebble with 'Emon Saburō reborn' written on it (p66). Originally constructed around 680 CE, it's said that the temple's name was changed in 892 to Ishite-ji, based on the legend about the rebirth of Saburō.

These days, Ishite-ji specialises in fertility. Couples having problems conceiving turn up to pray for a new arrival. They choose a stone from a pile and, after praying for conception and an easy birth, take it home with high expectations. After a successful birth, they return the stone with the baby's name on it and give thanks. The returned stones are proudly displayed at the temple for all to see.

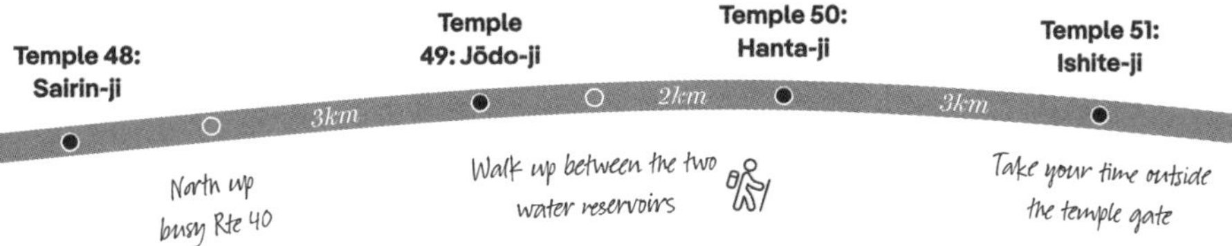

At the other end of the scale, people also come to Ishite-ji for the prevention of senility. If you're having foot issues, cure them by praying for your feet and poking a coin into the huge straw sandals at the *niōmon* (main gate).

At the front of Temple 51, the stone bridge at the street entrance, which is roped off to visitors, is said to have been crossed by the Daishi himself, while there's a veritable mall of souvenir shops and *mochi*-sellers leading up to the main gate. The *mochi* speciality here is *yakimochi,* made by wrapping *anko* (sweet red bean paste) in a dough made from rice flour and grilling until it is crispy. Everyone loves it, and enjoying *yakimochi* after visiting Ishite-ji is a custom for both locals and pilgrims alike. On the temple grounds are a recently renovated three-storey pagoda, and Treasure House. A giant 16m-tall **statue** of the Daishi sits high on the hill behind the temple.

Ishite-ji Okunoin

Behind the *hondō* (main hall) at Temple 51: Ishite-ji, you'll come across the **Mantora Cave** entrance to a mysterious 200m-long tunnel that passes through the mountain on the way to the **okunoin** (inner sanctuary). Make sure to go straight when you enter the dimly lit tunnel, which is lined with statues, carvings and drawings. It may feel a bit creepy, but keep going to the far end. Once you're out of the tunnel, cross the road and go left to find the inner sanctuary, which features a large, golden dome-shaped hall and some near-skeletal statues of the Buddha Shaka, reduced to bones just before he gained enlightenment. The 16m-tall statue of the Daishi on the hill is now towering above you. You can walk back around to the front of the temple on the road.

AMEHIME/SHUTTERSTOCK

Along the Way We Met...

CHARLES I'm out here taking this one step at a time, trying to appreciate the here and now. Mostly walking, but I hired a bicycle this morning. [We met Charles riding up to Temple 50.] This is Day 31 for me. I've camped out on 24 nights, but I try to stay indoors when it's raining. Acts of random kindness by local people have been unbelievable. One family invited me in for dinner in their home as *osettai.*

Charles is a merchant sailor from the USA taking some time out in Japan.

CHARLES' TIP: *Wear comfy shoes and if you're coming in spring, be prepared for rain. The weather can be very changeable.*

Temple 51:
Ishite-ji

Ishite-ji
Okunoin

Temple 52: Taisan-ji

Temple 52: Taisan-ji

The 11km walk west from Temple 51 to **Temple 52: Taisan-ji** (太山寺) is very different from any of the other trails *henro* have faced between temples so far. It runs directly through Dōgo Onsen and Matsuyama city on busy urban roads until the final climb up to Temple 52, which is tucked up into forested hills, above suburbia. Legend says that the main hall here was built in one night.

While Temple 51: Ishite-ji and a number of other temples on the pilgrimage specialise in fertility, Taisan-ji is a place to pray for infertility; worshippers come here to pray for no more children. They pray and leave sewing needles,

BEST PLACES TO SLEEP

Minshuku Mikan, Matsuyama ¥
Close to Temple 51: Ishite-ji, Mikan is a good budget option with simple, immaculate facilities; visit the temple early morning or late. *minshukumikan. crayonsite.net*

Hotel Eco Dogo, Dōgo Onsen area ¥
A great option for *henro* on a budget in Dōgo Onsen; just a short stroll for a soak in Dōgo Onsen Honkan, the historical hot spring building. *ecodogo.com*

Masuya Ryokan, Onishi-chō ¥
Just 4km west of Temple 54: Enmei-ji, this places surprises, even having its own French restaurant; popular with pilgrims. *masuya-auberge.com*

**Temple 52:
Taisan-ji**

11km

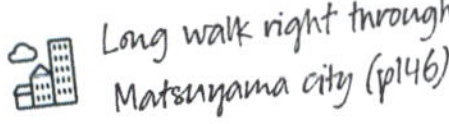

Along the Way We Met...

PAUL I don't have the time to commit to walking the whole pilgrimage, but I've always wanted to do it since I read Oliver Statler's *Japanese Pilgrimage* when I was young and travelling around the world. So, I'm doing it by rental car with one of my buddies. We're allowing two weeks. As we've got a car, it's easy finding places to eat and stay along the way. Most Japanese *henro* we see seem to be in cars, taxis or buses.

Paul, from Hawai'i, is a fan of the poet Matsuo Bashō. His favourite haiku is 'Fleas, lice, a horse peeing near my pillow'.

PAUL'S TIP: *Read Statler's book before you go for a better understanding of the background of the pilgrimage.*

said to guarantee future infertility. This has led to a slightly bizarre custom in which women having problems conceiving come to Taisan-ji and pick up sewing needles left by other women who don't want any more children, supposedly improving their own fertility in the process. Apparently, wearing underwear sewn with these needles is helpful when it comes to conceiving.

Temple 53: Enmyō-ji

Last in the cluster of eight temples around Matsuyama city, **Temple 53: Enmyō-ji** (圓明寺) is only a 2.5km walk northeast from Temple 52. Unlike Taisan-ji though, Enmyō-ji is a busy little suburban temple surrounded by businesses and housing down on the flat land.

As well as being known for Dr Frederick Starr (right) discovering a brass name plate dated 1650, Enmyō-ji also boasts a 40cm-high stone lantern adorned with what is believed to be an image of the Virgin Mary. During the Edo period

(1603–1868), Christianity was outlawed by the Tokugawa shogunate, but it seems that Enmyō-ji allowed local *kakure-kirishitan* (hidden Christians) to worship here. While most of the 'hidden Christian' communities were in western Kyūshū, it's believed that there were also groups in the area around Matsuyama.

Initially, the Meiji Restoration of 1868 stringently made Shintō the national religion, but in the ensuing years, things relaxed and there was a certain degree of religious freedom. In the 1889 Constitution (Article 28), freedom of belief was fully established.

Temple 54: Enmei-ji

It's time for a long walk, 35km from Temple 53, northeast along the Inland Sea (Setonai-kai) coast to **Temple 54: Enmei-ji** (延命寺; *enmeiji.info)*, first in a cluster of six temples in and around the city of Imabari. In good weather, this is a pleasant walk, with views out over the

Temple 52: Taisan-ji	Temple 53: Enmyō-ji	Temple 54: Enmei-ji
2.5km	*35km*	

The place to pray for infertility

Go back down to a busy suburban temple

It's a long haul along the coast

Inland Sea and its countless islands, and over to Hiroshima Prefecture on Honshū.

Originally built in the early 700s atop 244m-high Chikamiyama as a mountain temple, Enmei-ji suffered at the hands of the Tosa warlord and temple-burner Chōsokabe Motochika when he conquered Shikoku in the early 1580s. Razed to the ground, it was moved to its present location at the foot of the mountain in 1727. Over the years, a number of temples were relocated from remote places to locations that made them more accessible to the populace.

The temple gate here was originally one of the gates of Imabari-jō (p176), made entirely of *keyaki* (zelkova); it was moved to Enmei-ji when the castle was demolished in 1873, in the early Meiji period.

It's said that the bell at Enmei-ji was once taken to reside at Matsuyama-jō but that, when rung, its tone sounded like the word 'home', leading to its swift return to the temple.

FIRST FOREIGN HENRO

In 1921, Dr Frederick Starr (1858–1933), anthropology professor at the University of Chicago, became, in all probability, the first foreigner to complete the pilgrimage. Starr, who visited Japan 15 times, was a celebrity in Japan at the time and his pilgrimage was featured in the national press as he travelled on foot, by rickshaw and train. Starr had a fascination with *osamefuda* (pilgrim name placards), and at Temple 53 he is credited with discovering a brass plate dated to 1650, testifying to the pilgrimage of a man from Kyoto – the oldest such pilgrimage plaque yet discovered.

Temple 54: Enmei-ji

CRAIG MCLACHLAN/LONELY PLANET

Cycling the Shimanami Kaidō

Grab a rental bike and cycle as far as you'd like on this wondrous 70km cycling trail connecting islands in the Inland Sea (Seto-nai-kai) from Imabari on Shikoku to Onomichi on Honshū.

HOW TO

Nearest stop: Temple 54: Enmei-ji

Getting here: Sunrise Itoyama is 15km north of Temple 54: Enmei-ji. There is no train link between Shikoku and Honshū here; the only train link is via the Seto Ōhashi bridge from Kagawa Prefecture to Okayama.

Tip: An easy ride, not far from the pilgrim trail, is to hire a bike at Sunrise Itoyama and cycle the bridge bicycle path across the Kurushima Strait for a 15km round trip to Ōshima, where you can have lunch.

More info: visitshimanami.com

This is island-hopping by bicycle on bridges, and the trail crosses six islands along the 70km journey, with picturesque views of the Inland Sea. The **Shimanami Kaidō** is part of the Nishiseto Expressway, the westernmost of three bridge systems linking Shikoku to Honshū that were opened between 1988 and 2000. What makes the Shimanami Kaidō special is that it has a dedicated cycling path alongside the toll road. It's hard to get lost as the route is well-marked on the road with a blue line and there are plenty of information boards and maps along the way, as well as a multitude of places to pause or detour to.

Sunrise Itoyama

In a perfect spot, more or less right where the Shamanami Kaidō arrives on Shikoku, **Sunrise Itoyama** (*sunrise-itoyama.jp*) is a great spot to rent a bike, overnight, eat, bathe, do your

laundry or store gear in lockers while you're out riding. This place is really set up for cyclists with everything you could need. Views out over the Kurushima Kaikyō Bridge are enticing.

Imabari Station Cycling Terminal

You can also start your ride at the **i.i.imabari! Cycle Station** some 6km south, by JR Imabari station, right next to **Imabari Tourist Information Centre** (*city.imabari.ehime.jp/kanko/cycling*). Imabari has become a hub for cyclists; there are plenty

WEST_PHOTO/SHUTTERSTOCK

CYCLING WITHOUT BAGGAGE

If the idea of cycling the full Shimanami Kaidō without carrying your gear appeals, check out **Sagawa Hands-free Travel** (*sagawa-exp. co.jp*). They have set up an excellent system for 'Shimanami Kaidō Cycling Without Baggage'. There are affiliated facility pick-up and drop-off points for baggage delivery at both Imabari and Onomichi and at four of the islands along the way, so you can turn the ride into a multiday trip and have all your gear when you want it.

Cyclist, Shimanami Kaidō

of hotels set up to host visiting cyclists near the station.

Shimanami Rental Cycle

This operation rents bikes of all shapes and sizes, both regular and e-bikes, and has 10 locations where you can rent and return bikes. You can change the location for the return of your bike if you strike bad weather or your situation changes, as long as it is during business hours. Book ahead online in English at shima nami-cycle.or.jp to avoid disappointment, especially during Japanese holiday seasons.

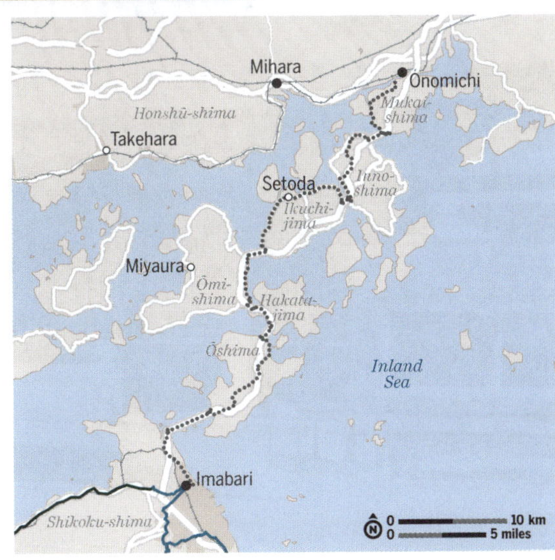

Enmei-ji

TEMPLE 54

Northern Ehime covers a large, sprawling area. There are six pilgrimage temples in a cluster around Imabari city, but it pays not to get complacent as the climb up to Temple 60: Yokomine-ji in the mountains awaits. Next, there's a smaller cluster of four temples down near the coast in Saijō city, then a long haul along Ehime's industrial northern coast to Temple 65: Sankaku-ji, the last temple in the prefecture.

Craig McLachlan

Temple 59: Iyo Kokubun-ji (p179)

JOHN S LANDER/GETTY IMAGES

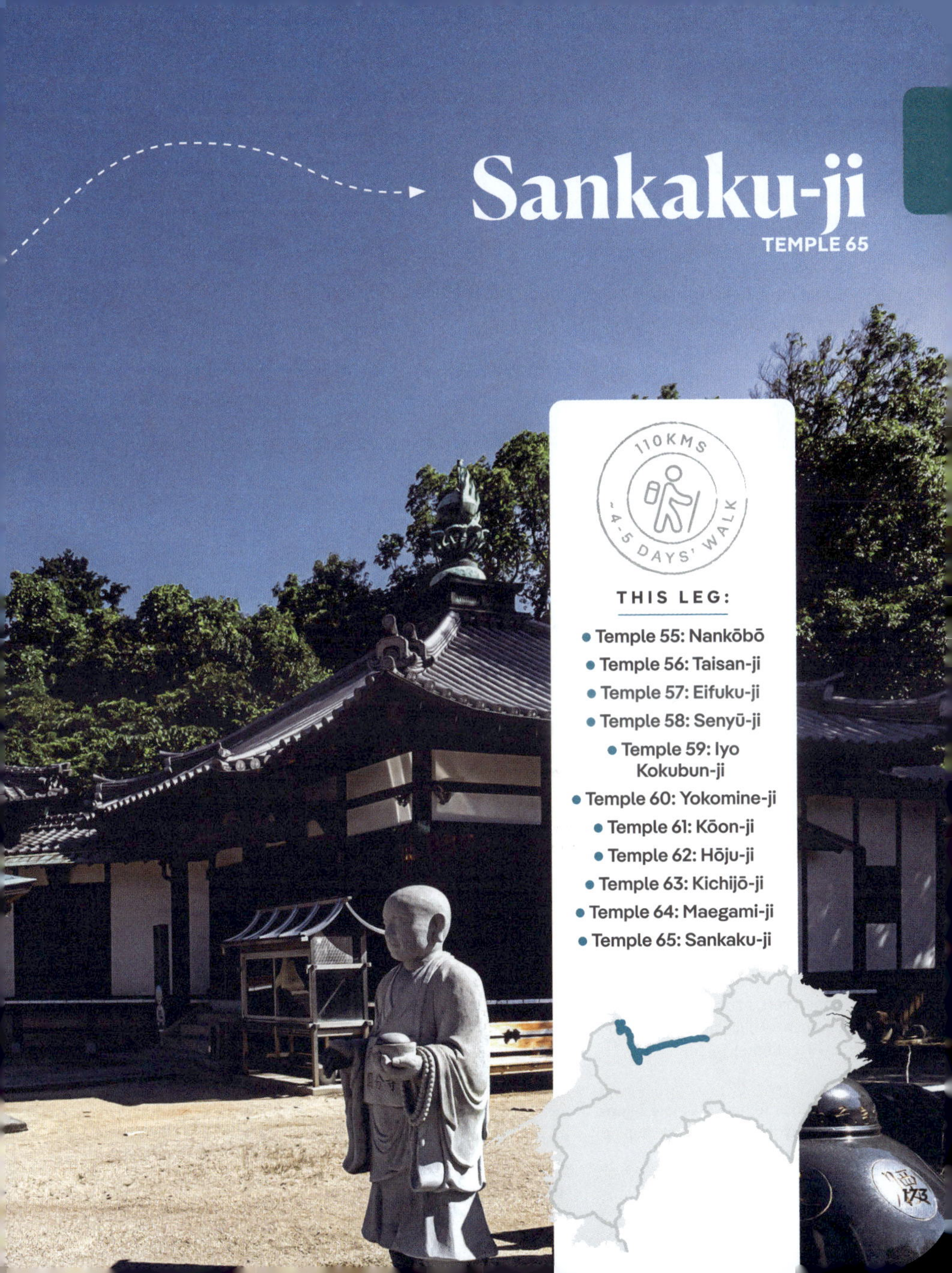

Sankaku-ji

THIS LEG:

- Temple 55: Nankōbō
- Temple 56: Taisan-ji
- Temple 57: Eifuku-ji
- Temple 58: Senyū-ji
- Temple 59: Iyo Kokubun-ji
- Temple 60: Yokomine-ji
- Temple 61: Kōon-ji
- Temple 62: Hōju-ji
- Temple 63: Kichijō-ji
- Temple 64: Maegami-ji
- Temple 65: Sankaku-ji

Walking Notes

There are two clusters of temples here: six in Imabari and four in Sajō. There are, however, also two climbs on *henro-michi* (pilgrim tracks); the first to Temple 58: Senyū-ji is only 200 vertical metres, though Temple 60: Yokomine-ji sits at 772m, the third-highest temple on the pilgrimage.

Breaking Your Journey

There's an almost constant urban landscape around the northern coast of Ehime, from Imabari around to Shikoku-chūō, where you'll find Temple 65: Sankaku-ji. Consequently, there are lots of places to stay and eat, though you'll want to plan your day up to Temple 60: Yokomine-ji carefully.

Craig's Tips

BEST PLACE TO STAY The *shukubō* at Temple 58: Senyū-ji (p179).

MEAL PLANNING Buy enough food for a few days before climbing up to Temple 65: Sankaku-ji (p186).

ESSENTIAL STOP The unusual, modern main building at Temple 61: Kōon-ji (p184).

TOP TIP Visit Temple 61 before Temple 60; leave your gear and pick it up on return (p181).

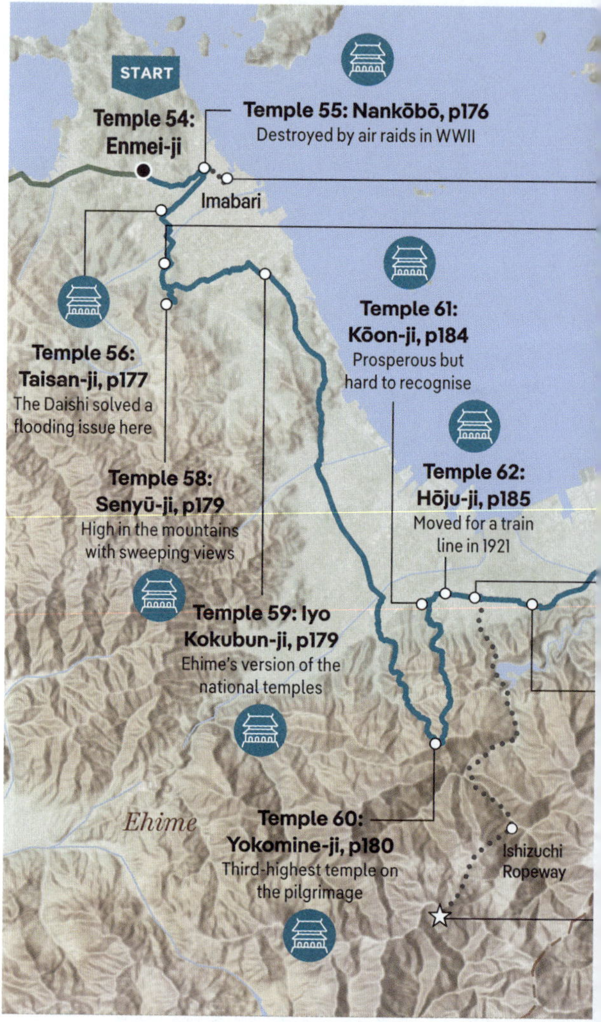

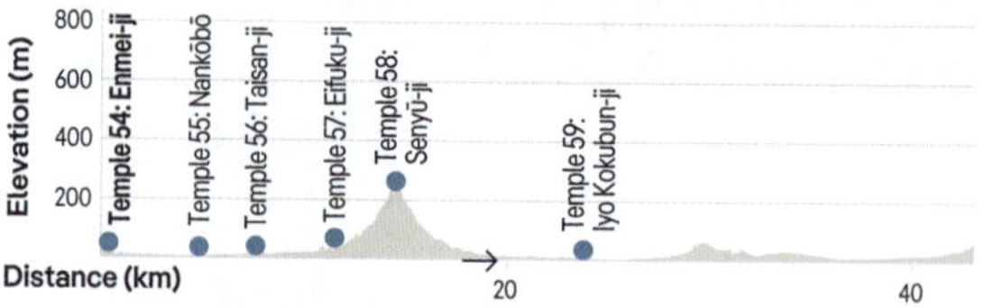

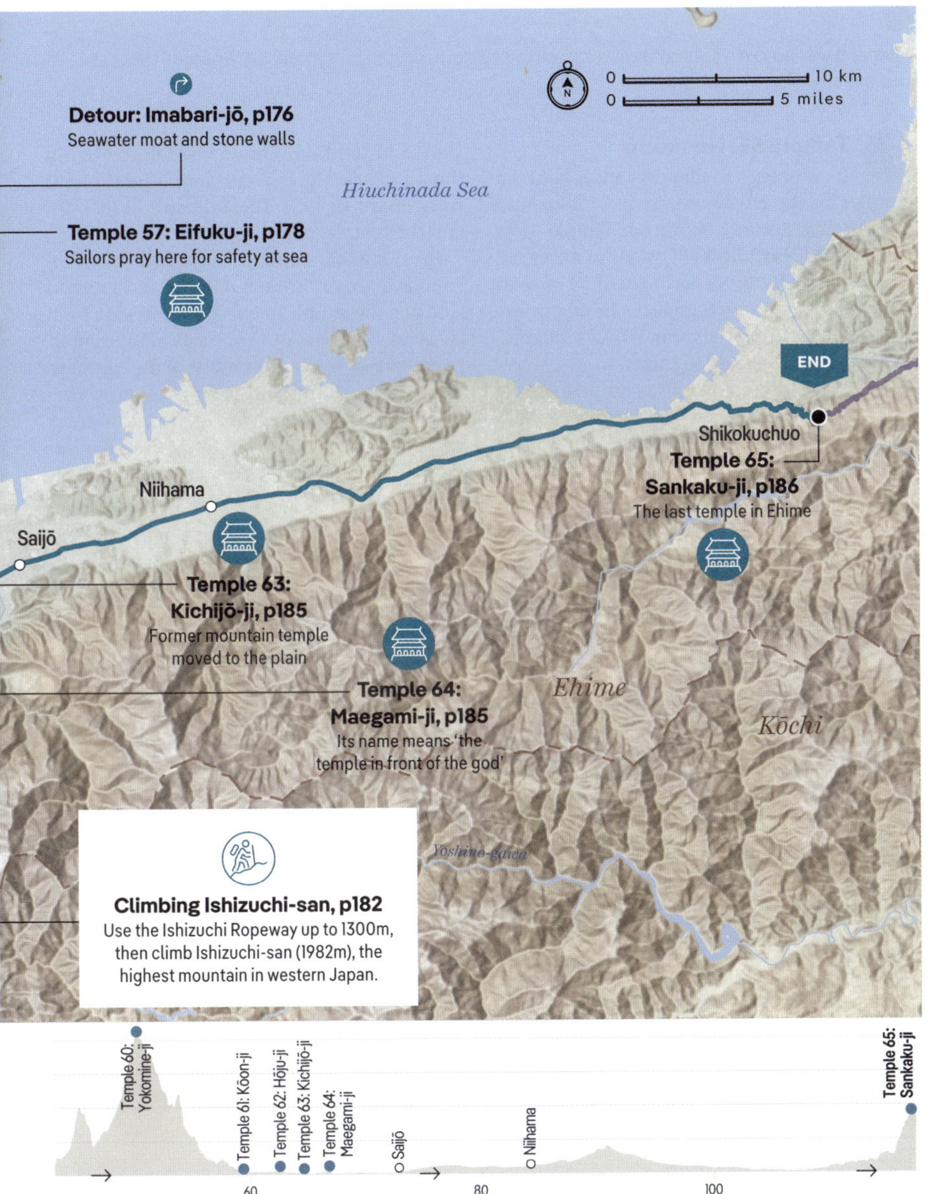
Detour: Imabari-jō, p176
Seawater moat and stone walls
Hiuchinada Sea
Temple 57: Eifuku-ji, p178
Sailors pray here for safety at sea
0   10 km
0   5 miles
N
END
Shikokuchuo
Temple 65:
Sankaku-ji, p186
The last temple in Ehime
Niihama
Saijō
Temple 63:
Kichijō-ji, p185
Former mountain temple
moved to the plain
Temple 64:
Maegami-ji, p185
Its name means 'the
temple in front of the god'
Ehime
Kōchi
Yoshino-gawa
Climbing Ishizuchi-san, p182
Use the Ishizuchi Ropeway up to 1300m,
then climb Ishizuchi-san (1982m), the
highest mountain in western Japan.
Temple 60:
Yokomine-ji
Temple 61: Kōon-ji
Temple 62: Hōju-ji
Temple 63: Kichijō-ji
Temple 64:
Maegami-ji
Saijō
Niihama
Temple 65:
Sankaku-ji
60
80
100

PREVIOUS STOP An easy 4km walk almost directly east from Temple 54: Enmei-ji takes you into the city area of Imabari.

Temple 55: Nankōbō

It's now back to short distances between temples in the cluster of six in and around Imabari city. It's only 4km from Temple 54 to **Temple 55: Nankōbō** (南光坊), in an urban setting only about 500m northeast of JR Imabari station. This is the only temple on the pilgrimage with -*bō* in its name, meaning 'priest's lodging', as in *shukubō* (temple lodgings).

This whole area is made up of post-WWII buildings as some 80% of **Imabari's central city** was destroyed in 1945 by incendiary bombs, designed to obliterate the city's ship-building and textile industries. At Nankōbō, all the buildings except the Daishi-dō (Daishi Hall) and the Kompira-dō were destroyed in the air raids. The current *hondō* (main hall) was rebuilt in 1981, the Yakushi-dō in 1991, and the temple gate in 1998.

One thing that's interesting here is that Nankōbō is a 'drive through' temple, with a road splitting the temple in two. Cars carrying local parishioners arrive from one side of the temple, park more or less in the middle of the complex, worshippers jump out, perform their *mairi* (rituals), then hop back in their cars and carry on through and out to the road on the other side. It's a remarkably efficient system for locals if the goal is to get in and out of there in the shortest time possible.

DETOUR: **Imabari-jō**

A 2km walk southeast of Temple 55: Nankōbō, **Imabari-jō**, from a distance, is an impressive sight. While you've likely seen amazing original wooden castles along the journey in Kōchi city, Uwajima and Matsuyama, what you're looking at here is a postwar, reinforced concrete reconstruction. The keep and other buildings were destroyed in the WWII air raids of 1945.

What is original here, surviving WWII and making it absolutely worthwhile to come and look at Imabari-jō, is the vast seawater moat that surrounds the castle and the incredible stone walls that support the 'island' in the moat that the castle sits on. They are mostly unchanged since the castle was completed in 1608 and are

Temple 55: Nankōbō

FROM LEFT: AMEHIME/SHUTTERSTOCK, BEAUTY-BOX/SHUTTERSTOCK

Imabari-jō

an impressive sight. Two bridges cross the moat, which is connected to the Inland Sea (Seto-nai-kai), only some 100m away.

Saltwater moats are unusual among Japanese castles and Imabari-jō has the distinction of being one of Japan's Mizujiro (Three Great Water Castles), all located on the coast. Reconstruction of the castle by Imabari City began in 1980.

Temple 56: Taisan-ji

Relocated from its former mountaintop home, **Temple 56: Taisan-ji** (泰山寺) is only a 3km walk inland, pretty much straight down the road from Temple 55. Recognise the name? Yes, Temple 52 was also a Taisan-ji, but with its name

BEST PLACES TO EAT

Toribayashi, Imabari ¥¥
Excellent, tiny *yakitori* place only a few hundred metres east of Imabari station; friendly atmosphere and service. 鳥林; *5-10pm Mon-Sat*

10taro (Jutaro), near Temple 62 ¥¥
Out front of iyo-Komatsu Station, this little place is a haven for *henro* with all sorts of creative cuisine. *11am-3pm & 6-11pm Wed-Mon*

Lawson Convenience Store, Rte 11 ¥
Henro may well want to stock up on a couple of days' worth of food here when walking the shortest route to Temples 65, 66 and 67, as it's the last chance to buy food.

**Temple 56:
Taisan-ji**

3km

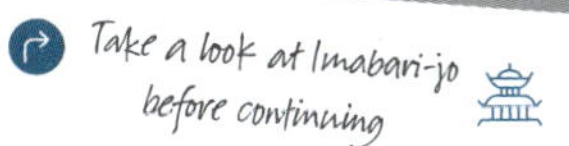
Take a look at Imabari-jo before continuing

HENRO WITH WHEELS

- Allow two days for this stretch.
- The cluster of six temples in and around Imabari city is best visited while basing yourself in the city; there are good accommodation and eating options around JR Imabari Station.
- Consider taking a day off and going for a cycle on the Shimanami Kaidō (p170).
- Saijō city, with its cluster of four temples, is 30km south of Imabari.
- It's an 18km drive from Saijō up to Temple 60: Yokomine-ji, with a ¥2000 road toll.
- It's a 55km drive east along the base of the mountains from Temple 61: Kōon-ji to Temple 65: Sankaku-ji.

written with differing kanji characters. This Taisan-ji may have mountain 山 as the second character in its name, but it no longer sits on a mountain and is down on the flats, though built up slightly higher than the Sōja-gawa plain, with magnificent stone walls.

When Kōbō Daishi was here in around 815 CE, it's said that the area was being flooded every year by the Sōja-gawa, washing away houses, rice paddies, livelihoods and people. Scared locals had nicknamed the river *hitotori-gawa* (the river that takes away people) and pleaded with the Daishi for help. Legend has it that the Daishi blessed the soil, then helped the locals build embankments, and the problem was solved.

Temple 57: Eifuku-ji

There's now another 3km walk, this time from Temple 56 to **Temple 57: Eifuku-ji** *(栄福寺; eifukuji.jp)*, a short climb up off the plain into forested foothills. The first thing to catch

Priest's residence, Temple 57: Eifuku-ji

CRAIG MCLACHLAN/LONELY PLANET

your eye will be the head priest's architecturally designed house, the big building looking well and truly out of place, a blight on the temple's lovely traditional buildings.

Surprisingly for a temple that's 6km inland, Eifuku-ji became a place for sailors to pray for safety after Kōbō Daishi conducted a ritual for the gods of the sea, praying for protection from wind and waves on the Inland Sea. Keep your eye out for a *hako-guruma* (box-shaped cart) left here in 1933, along with his crutches, by a 15-year-old boy who was cured of his crippling leg issues by a miracle, attributed to the Daishi.

With a history of syncretism of Buddhism and Shintoism, the temple used to be at the top of the small mountain, sharing a compound with the shrine **Iwashimizu Hachiman-gū**, but when the Meiji Restoration came along and Shintō became the designated national religion, the temple was demoted to halfway down the mountain. Most of the buildings were erected in the early Meiji period.

Temple 58: Senyū-ji

While the last few temples may have induced some complacency by being easy to get to on foot due to having been relocated off mountaintops to more accessible locations, **Temple 58: Senyū-ji** (仙遊寺; *shikoku88-58senyuji.com*) brings *henro* back to reality with a thud. Though it's only a 3km walk from Temple 57, there's a 200m gain in elevation, mostly in a short, sharp, breathtaking climb on a *henro-michi,* more or less straight up in the final section to the temple, after passing through the lower gate. It's worth the effort though, because views out over the plain and Inland Sea are superb.

Temple 58: Senyū-ji

Legend says that Kōbō Daishi dug a well here, known as the **Well of Blessings**, to help people suffering from various illnesses, and it is still revered today. Suffering somewhat from inaccessibility compared to its neighbours down on the flats, Senyū-ji is a practical mountain temple, surrounded by forest, that has developed a number of revenue streams to survive. One is a *shukubō,* and this temple lodging is a great place to overnight. There's a ¥400 road toll if you drive up.

Temple 59: Iyo Kokubun-ji

The pilgrims' prize for climbing up to Temple 58 is a knee-knocking initial descent on the 6km walk out to **Temple 59: Iyo Kokubun-ji** (伊予国分寺), the third of the national temples along the route. Out on the coastal plain, only a kilometre or so

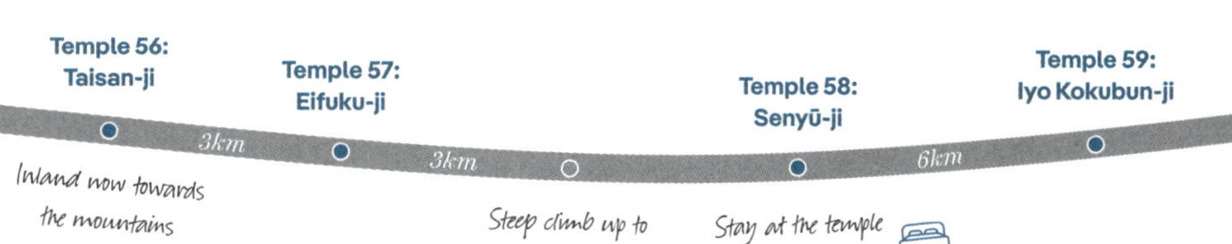

from the coast, it was burnt on three separate occasions during wars between the 10th and 14th centuries, before the forces of Chōsokabe Motochika turned up in the late 1500s to do it again. Enthusiasm to rebuild must have been minimal as the temple was described in the first pilgrimage guidebook of 1687 as 'a small hut with a thatched roof'. It took a couple of centuries to be completely rebuilt. These days, the compound is pleasant, without being overly inspiring, and *henro* may also enjoy a visit to the shrine **Kasuga-jinja** among the trees next door.

While 68 Kokubun-ji were built around the country as the national temples from 741 CE, when Japan moved into its feudal period in the late 10th century, the Kokubun-ji lost all national funding and many simply disappeared. Some were eventually restored by local governments, but in many locations, all that remains is a place name. On Shikoku, however, the four Kokubun-ji have survived, and even thrived, from having a constant source of pilgrims due to being four of the 88 pilgrimage temples.

Temple 60: Yokomine-ji

From Temple 59, it's a 28km walk to **Temple 60: Yokomine-ji** (横峰寺), but that doesn't really tell the story. This is the third-highest temple on the pilgrimage, the trail up to it is one of the *henro-korogashi* (*henro* fall down trails), and it's the spiritual barrier temple for Iyo. If *henro* aren't pure of intention, they should go back to Temple 1: Ryōzen-ji and start again! The good news for walking *henro,* is that, while this is the holy temple for Ishizuchi-san (p182), the highest mountain in western Japan at 1982m, the temple isn't at the top! At 772m, it's still a tough climb, though.

AMEHIME/SHUTTERSTOCK

Along the Way We Met...

EIKICHI I'm 39 and I finally decided to quit my stressful job in Tokyo and go out and see Japan with Puchi, my five-year-old corgi. We go everywhere together as I try to decide what to do with the rest of my life. I now understand that every moment in life is precious. I'm surprised to see so many foreigners walking the pilgrimage and learning about my country. It makes me feel proud.

Eikichi is easy to spot with Puchi in his backpack as he visits the 88 temples by car.

EIKICHI'S TIP: *Please make an effort to learn about Japanese etiquette before coming to Shikoku so that the local people will be happy to host you.*

Temple 59:
Iyo Kokubun-ji

Head back down and out to the coastal plain

28km

South now, towards the big mountains

Temple 60: Yokomine-ji

Climbing up to the temple requires some thought. The temple itself is glorious, in a beautiful clearing in a forest of cedars on the side of the mountain. It's known for its flowering *shakunage* (rhododendron bushes) that bloom in May and *ajisai* (hydrangeas) in early summer.

A 20-minute walk up from Temple 60 will bring you to **Okunoin Hoshigamori**, the inner sanctuary, where there's a *torii* (Shintō shrine gate) and a gorgeous view of Ishizuchi-san.

If you've got wheels, there's a long, winding drive up to a parking area 500m from the temple with a ¥2000 road toll for the privilege. The road is closed in midwinter, from late December to late February.

Continues on page 184

LOGISTICS FOR TEMPLE 60

Climbing up to Temple 60: Yokomine-ji, which sits high in the mountains at 772m in elevation, requires some planning. Over the years, pilgrims have found it a lot easier to visit Temple 61: Kōon-ji, at the foot of the mountains first, stay in the vicinity of the temple, leave their gear, and then climb up to Temple 60 piston-style, 9km up, 9km down, without a backpack. Some also visit Temples 61, 62 and even 63 (the three are only 2.7km apart) before making a day trip up to Temple 60 and back. It depends on where you arrange accommodation.

Temple 60: Yokomine-ji

Consider going to Temple 61 before 60

Don't carry your gear up to Temple 60

Climbing Ishizuchi-san

At 1982m, Ishizuchi-san is known as 'the roof of Shikoku' and is the highest peak in western Japan. With a name meaning 'stone hammer mountain', Ishizuchi has long been a centre for mountain worship, attracting pilgrims and climbers alike. Ishizuchi Ropeway whisks climbers from 455m up to 1300m.

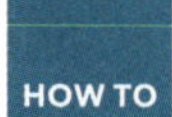

HOW TO

Nearest stop: Temple 60: Yokomine-ji

Getting here: It's a 20km drive from Saijō city to Ishizuchi Ropeway's Shimo-dani lower station. For walking *henro*, there are four buses each day to the lower station with **Setouchi Bus** *(setouchibus.co.jp),* departing from JR Iyo-Saijō Station at 7.10am, 10am, 1.10pm and 3.50pm. Return buses are at 9.12am, 12.02pm, 3.17pm and 5.20pm.

Cost: Ishizuchi Ropeway *(ishizuchi.com; return adult/child ¥2200/1100; hours vary by season)*

More info: ishizuchisankei.com

This is one of Japan's great hikes, made all the more do-able in a day thanks to the **Ishizuchi Ropeway**, which will deposit you at its upper station at 1300m. From here, you'll want to allow five to seven hours for the 7.2km return journey to the peak.

A Walk in the Park

From the top of the ropeway, follow the signs to the shrine **Ishizuchi-jinja Jōju-sha**. From there, after an initial descent, head uphill through the forest to reach **Zen-ga-mori**, from where a zig-zagging track continues up to **Yoakashi-tōge** (pass) at 1652m.

Up the Chains

Ichi-no-kusari is your first and easiest of three sets of chains, 33m in length. This is an opportunity for hikers to test their mettle, something that mountain ascetics have done for centuries. Don't feel you have to haul yourself up the chains though, as there's a bypassing track. After a small hut, the challenge kicks in, as, although there's a trail all the way to the top, the most popular way to make the final ascent is up the *kusari* (heavy chains) that are draped down the rock faces.

Clambering up the chains is the approved pilgrimage method and good fun. **Ni-no-kusari** is 65m long, followed by **San-no-kusari** at 68m. Avoid the chains in inclement weather by taking the track; the mountain has been tamed somewhat by the installation of steel steps.

YOSHINORI OKADA/SHUTTERSTOCK

STAY AT THE PEAK

Perched at the peak, **Ishizuchi-san Chōjō Sansō** *(Ishizuchi Summit Hut; sanso. ishizuchisan.jp)* is open from the start of May to the start of November. You can eat here, buy snacks or stay the night (room only/with meals ¥9000/13,000); the hut sleeps 50. It's nothing luxurious, just hot meals, bedding on a tatami mat in a warm, shared room and a solid roof and walls. This is a real Japanese mountain experience.

Left: Ishizuchi-san
Below: Ishizuchi Ropeway

When you hit the first peak, **Misen** (1974m), you'll find the shrine **Ishizuchi-jinja** and the **summit hut**.

Tengu-dake

There's one final test. **Tengu-dake** (1982m), the highest point, is reached by carefully climbing along a sharp ridge with a big drop-off to the left. On a good day, it's clearly visible and will take 10 minutes, but is best avoided in bad weather and strong winds. On a blue-sky day, the views are incredible and it's easy to understand why Ishizuchi is called 'the rooftop of Shikoku'.

AMANA IMAGES INC./ALAMY

SAIJŌ SPRING WATER

As well as being known for its spectacular harvest festival in mid-October, featuring decorated floats and *taiko* drumming, the city of Saijō is famous for its artesian spring water. It's said that there are 3000 springs across the city, called *uchinuki* (meaning to 'punch through'), as natural pressure in large underground reservoirs forces the water to the surface through wells. The highest of quality, its not a coincidence that Coca-Cola and Asahi Breweries have factories in Saijō. The water is said to come from deep in the Ishizuchi mountains; try some at various locations about Saijō.

Continued from page 181

Temple 61: Kōon-ji

Though you may well have come here before going to Temple 60: Yokomine-ji (p180), it's worth noting that it's a 9.5km hike down from Yokomine-ji at 772m to **Temple 61: Kōon-ji** (香園寺; *koyasudaishi.or.jp)* at 24m above sea level. When you finally see it, there's a fair chance you won't recognise Kōon-ji as being a temple. The concrete edifice, one-of-a-kind among the pilgrimage temples, looks more like a city museum than a temple – a bit like a big shoebox made of cement.

This is, however, a very prosperous temple, thanks to specialising in safe childbirth. It's said that when Kōbō Daishi was here, he burnt incense and prayed for a pregnant woman who was in great pain at the temple gate; when the woman subsequently gave birth to a healthy baby boy, the temple flourished as a place of worship for safe childbirth.

Temple 63: Kichijō-ji

AMEHIME/SHUTTERSTOCK

The 16m-high box-shaped main building was built in 1976. It features a large lecture hall on the 1st floor, with the *hondō* and Daishi-dō together on the 2nd floor. To get in there, climb the stairs at the right-hand end of the building. A lovely statue of Koyasu Kōbō Daishi, the protector of children, with the Daishi holding a baby in his left hand, stands front right.

Temple 62: Hōju-ji

There's a cluster of four temples in Saijō city at the foot of the mountains and there's only 6km between them. From Temple 61 it's a 1.5km walk to **Temple 62: Hōju-ji** (宝寿寺). Sitting right on busy Rte 11, Hōju-ji hasn't got a lot of land to play with, after being forced to move slightly south in 1921 to accommodate construction of the Yosan Line rail tracks, now about 100m away.

This little temple has had a lot of ups and downs. After flourishing as a temple in support of Oyamazumi Shrine, somewhat ironically, it was destroyed in 1585 when Toyotomi Hideyoshi conquered Shikoku, taking the island from the temple-burner Chōsokabe Motochika. The temple was rebuilt, closed during the movement to abolish Buddhism at the beginning of the Meiji period, only to be rebuilt again, then relocated due to the railway.

Intriguingly, Hōju-ji has taken on the mantle of being a reduced-labour high-tech temple, selling amulets, charms, candles, souvenirs and even temple stamp books out of vending machines. **Nojima House** (*@nojima_house*), 500m north of the temple, is a good place to stay; its owner is a strong supporter of the **Henro Help Desk** (*henrohelpdesk.com*).

Temple 63: Kichijō-ji

Only 1.5km from Temple 62, **Temple 63: Kichijō-ji** (吉祥寺) was originally a mountain temple, moved to its present location after Toyotomi Hideyoshi burnt it down in 1585. It was rebuilt at its current site in 1659.

Kichijō-ji is the only temple on the pilgrimage with Bishamonten as its principal image, said to have been carved by the Daishi. Bishamonten, one of the four heavenly kings, is believed to be the Buddha of worldly benefits. The temple was named for Kichijō Tennyo (boddess of beauty), the consort of Bishamonten, revered as a deity who brings great wealth.

Good fun here is the big stone with the hole in the centre to the right of the hand-washing basin. Legend says that if you can walk from the *hondō* with your eyes closed and poke the end of your pilgrim staff through the hole, that your wish will be fulfilled. Good luck!

Temple 64: Maegami-ji

From Temple 63, it's a nice, 3.5km amble to the last in the cluster of four temples in Saijō city, **Temple 64: Maegami-ji** (前神寺). While the last couple of temples were little urban ones short on space, there's no such issue here: Maegami-ji sits in the foothills of Ishizuchi-san, backed by forested mountains. This is an unmistakably holy place, the head temple of the Ishizuchi School of Shingon Buddhism and a training centre for Shugendō, a syncretic religion of Buddhism and Shintō based on mountain worship and ascetic practice. Ishizuchi-san itself is revered as a god or *kami*, and Maegami-ji means 'the temple in front of the god'. Ishizuchi-san's annual **Oyama-biraki**

Temple 60: Yokomine-ji — 9.5km — Temple 61: Kōon-ji — 1.5km — Temple 62: Hōju-ji — 1.5km — Temple 63: Kichijō-ji — 3.5km — Temple 64: Maegami-ji

Cluster of four temples around Saijō city

Along the Way We Met...

JOE I've always been interested in Japan and in hiking, so it seemed natural to come here and walk the pilgrimage. I wanted to visit Japan, but not the crowded, touristy places. I'm keen to see the authentic culture out in the countryside. When you're walking, you talk to everyone you meet on the trail and all sorts of opportunities pop up. A group of locals that was having a party under the cherry blossoms invited me to join them. I'll never forget it.

From Missouri, Joe is 19 and taking a gap year before starting college.

JOE'S TIP: *Try to make accommodation reservations three days ahead if you can. I'm using the Henro Helper app a lot.*

(mountain opening) on 1 July is held at the temple, with Shugendō practitioners coming from all over Japan.

Consider climbing Ishizuchi-san (p182), not quite as arduous a task as it was before the opening of Ishizuchi Ropeway in 1968.

It's said that the temple was founded in the late 600s CE by En no Gyōja (also known as En the Ascetic), the founder of Shugendō. After Emperor Kanmu (r 781–806) was cured of an illness, successive emperors prayed at the temple here and it gained great fame. When Shintō and Buddhism were separated with the Meiji Restoration in 1868, the temple was forced to close, but was reopened in 1889.

The temple extends up a narrow valley, with the *hondō* in a truly spectacular setting with a mountain and forest backdrop.

Temple 65: Sankaku-ji

It's a 46km walk east along the foot of the mountains to get to **Temple 65: Sankaku-ji** (三角寺). The Median Tectonic Line (MTL), which passes east–west across northern Shikoku, is Japan's longest fault line system and is particularly obvious in the stretch of land across northern Ehime between Saijō city and Shikoku-chūō city. The narrow coastal plain meets a wall of towering mountains only a few kilometres inland, with an elevation difference of around 1000m. While there hasn't been a major earthquake in Ehime since the 16th century, Japan – on the Pacific Ring of Fire – is one of the most seismologically active countries on the planet. There's a lot of heavy industry along the coast here, and you'll pass the cities of Saijō, Niihama and Shikoku-chūō (Central Shikoku City), a city made up of four local entities that merged

Temple 64:
Maegami-ji

Temple 65:
Sankaku-ji

46km

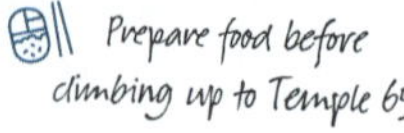

in 2004. It's hard to believe that Kōbō Daishi would be impressed with the huge billowing industrial smokestacks down near the coast.

This is the pilgrim's last temple in Ehime, sitting high at 360m in elevation on a forested hillside; needless to say, it's a decent climb to get up there. If you're planning to follow the standard pilgrim route after Temple 65 on the way to Temple 66, take note that there's nowhere to buy food until after Temple 67: Daikō-ji; stock up accordingly before you leave the city area.

Sankaku-ji means 'Triangle Temple', said to be named for the shape of the altar at which the Daishi performed a fire ceremony for 21 days to pray for the safety of the nation and the welfare of its people. The remains of this altar are an island in the Sankaku-no-Ike (Triangular Pond).

The Yakushi-dō at Sankaku-ji is the place to go if you're having issues with warts and foot corns. Pray here and it's said that warts will simply fall off and corns will disappear. Good news, as you've got one whole prefecture to go.

Temple 64: Maegami-ji (p185)

BEST PLACES TO SLEEP

Shimanami Guesthouse Cyclo-no-ie, Imabari ¥
Set up for cyclists and pilgrims, this place is by JR Imabari station, only 700m from Temple 55: Nankōbō; there's lots going on around here. *www.cyclonoie.com*

Temple 58: Senyū-ji Temple Lodging ¥
Spectacular views from the *shukubō*, up high in the mountains overlooking the coastal plain; there's a natural onsen up here too. *shikoku88-58senyuji.com*

Yunotani Onsen, Saijō ¥¥
Give your feet some love. Superb hot springs hotel 500m east of Temple 64: Maegami-ji; visit Temples 61 to 64 while staying here at the base of the mountains. *yunotani-saijo.com*

AMEHIME/SHUTTERSTOCK

厄年表
16 19 22 25
28 33 34 37
40 42 44 49
52 55 58 61
いたしております
女坂
男坂
本堂
大師堂
四国霊場

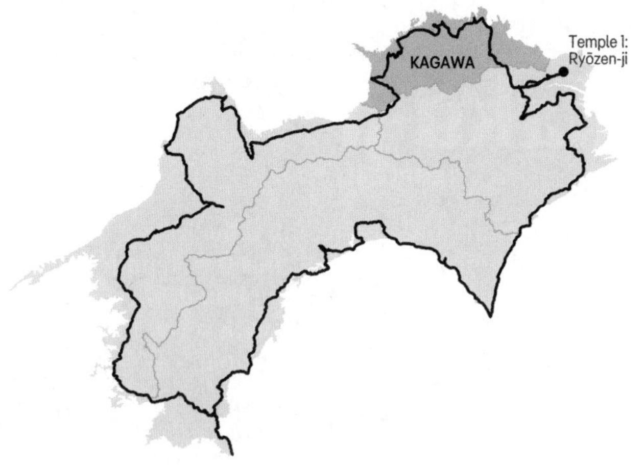

KAGAWA PREFECTURE

The smallest of Japan's 47 prefectures, Kagawa, previously known as Sanuki, is *Nehan-no-dōjō* (the Place of Completion). Pilgrims positively stride down onto the northern plain to visit the last 22 of the temples. Protected by Shikoku's central mountains, Kagawa's weather is warm and welcoming, as are its residents. Most feel a huge sense of accomplishment, and some relief, on heading back into the mountains and reaching Temple 88: Ōkubo-ji, but there is also the understanding that it's not over; there's still the walk back to Temple 1: Ryōzen-ji in Tokushima to close the circle.

Temple 66: Unpen-ji (p196)

AMEHIME/SHUTTERSTOCK

Sankaku-ji
TEMPLE 65

One of our favourite temples is coming up, though it's a big climb to get there. At 900m, Temple 66: Unpen-ji is the 'Temple in the Clouds', the highest of the 88. After tumbling down onto the Kagawa plain, everything gets a lot easier, with seven temples in 16km of walking. Kagawa is the smallest of Japan's 47 prefectures, though there's no room for complacency, as there are still plenty more mountain temples to come.

Craig McLachlan

Temple 75: Zentsū-ji (p203)
BRESTER IRINA/SHUTTERSTOCK

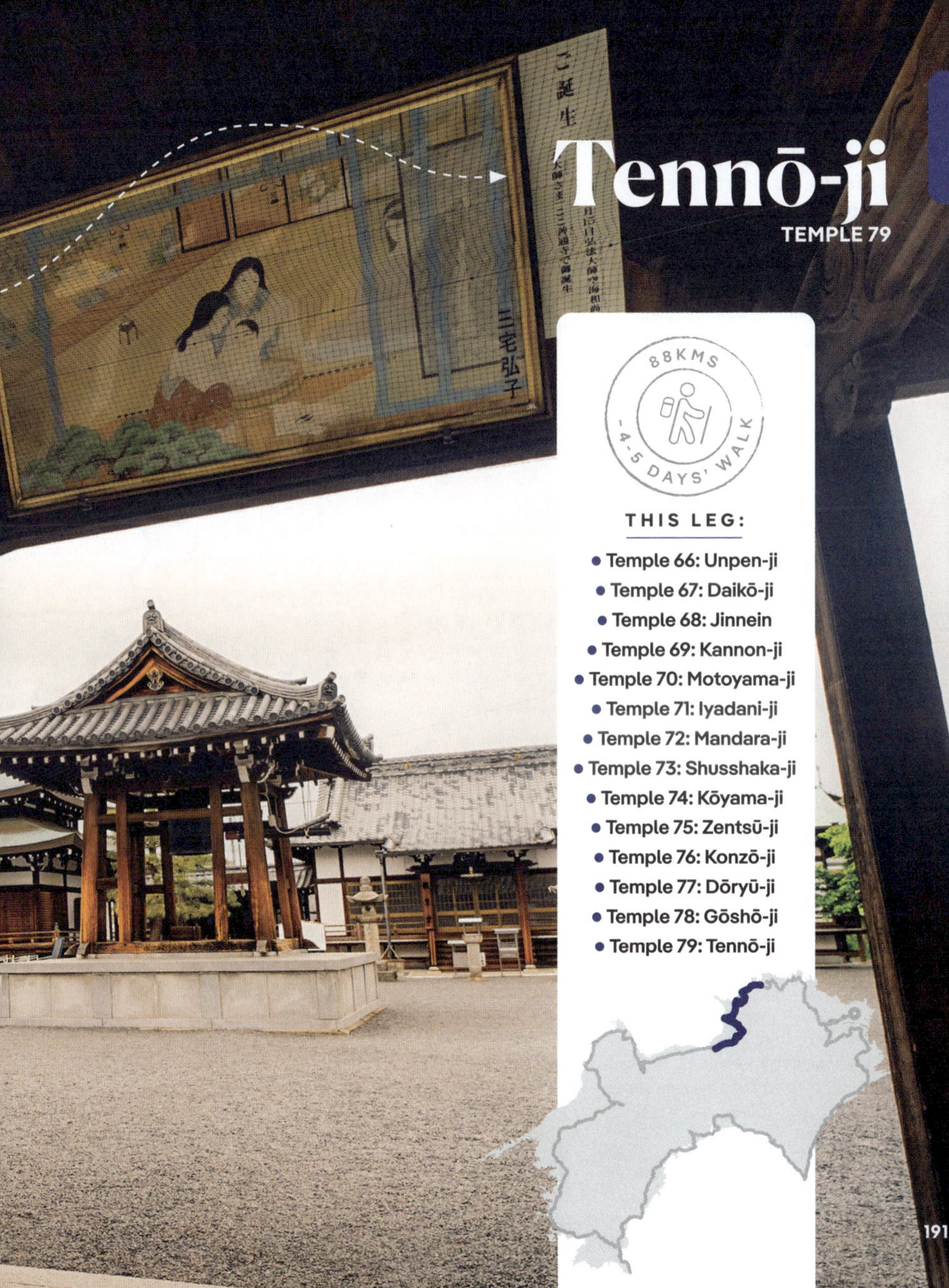

Tennō-ji
TEMPLE 79

THIS LEG:

- Temple 66: Unpen-ji
- Temple 67: Daikō-ji
- Temple 68: Jinnein
- Temple 69: Kannon-ji
- Temple 70: Motoyama-ji
- Temple 71: Iyadani-ji
- Temple 72: Mandara-ji
- Temple 73: Shusshaka-ji
- Temple 74: Kōyama-ji
- Temple 75: Zentsū-ji
- Temple 76: Konzō-ji
- Temple 77: Dōryū-ji
- Temple 78: Gōshō-ji
- Temple 79: Tennō-ji

Walking Notes

After the big climb to Temple 66: Unpen-ji and a similarly large drop into Kagawa, there are a lot of temples without much distance between them. This is a busy, populated part of the island, so as long as you're thinking ahead, you should have no issues finding places to stay and eat.

Breaking Your Journey

While you could race on through Kagawa, this is a place to enjoy welcoming weather and the friendly locals. Take your time. *Sanuki-udon* (noodle) shops are everywhere and there are lots of places to stay. A night around the Daishi's childhood home of Temple 75: Zentsū-ji is a good option.

Craig's Tips

GOOD FUN The path of darkness under the *hondō* (main hall) at Temple 75: Zentsū-ji (p203).

FAVOURITE VIEW The five-storey pagoda at Temple 70: Motoyama-ji can be spotted well before you arrive at the temple (p199).

ESSENTIAL STOP Temple 66: Unpen-ji. The 500 *rakan* statues are a must-see (p196).

TOP TIP *Henro* (pilgrims) with wheels should ride the Unpen-ji Ropeway (p196).

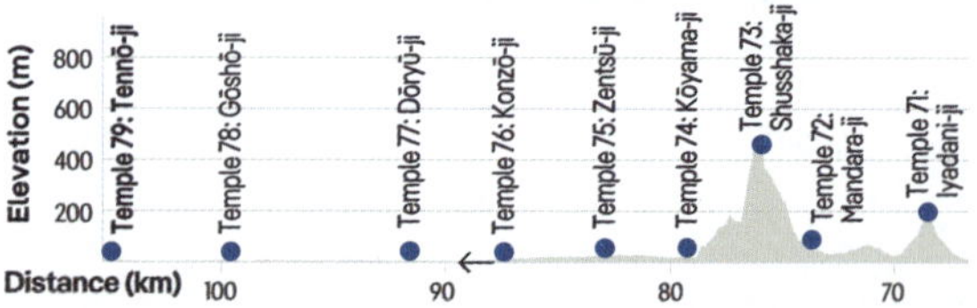

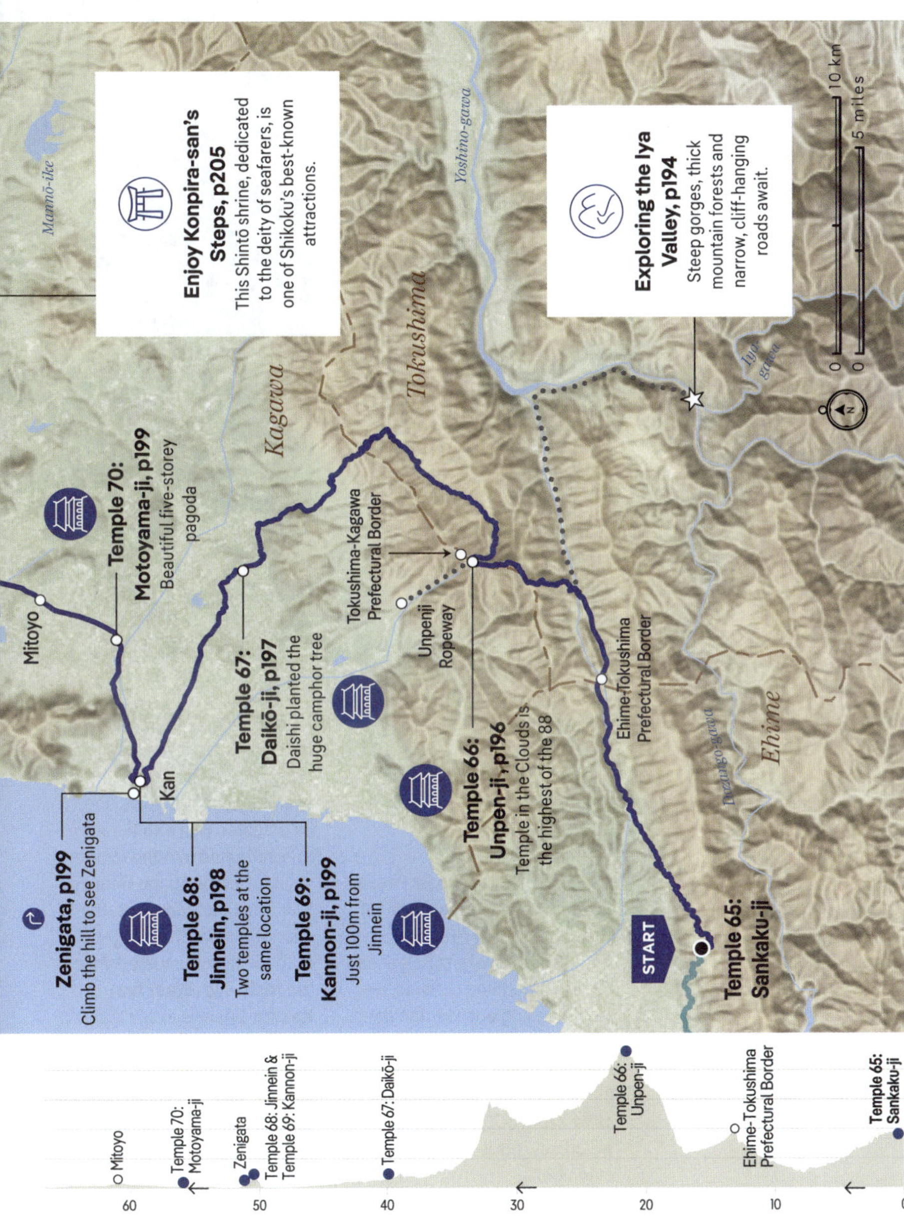
Mannō-ike
Yoshino-gawa
Kagawa
Tokushima
Ehime
Dōzango-gawa
Iiyo-gawa

Enjoy Konpira-san's Steps, p205
This Shintō shrine, dedicated to the deity of seafarers, is one of Shikoku's best-known attractions.

Exploring the Iya Valley, p194
Steep gorges, thick mountain forests and narrow, cliff-hanging roads await.

10 km
5 miles

Mitoyo
Temple 70: Motoyama-ji, p199
Beautiful five-storey pagoda

Kan
Temple 67: Daikō-ji, p197
Daishi planted the huge camphor tree

Tokushima-Kagawa Prefectural Border
Unpenji Ropeway

Zenigata, p199
Climb the hill to see Zenigata

Temple 68: Jinnein, p198
Two temples at the same location

Temple 69: Kannon-ji, p199
Just 100m from Jinnein

Temple 66: Unpen-ji, p196
Temple in the Clouds is the highest of the 88

Ehime-Tokushima Prefectural Border

START
Temple 65: Sankaku-ji

Mitoyo
Temple 70: Motoyama-ji
Zenigata
Temple 68: Jinnein & Temple 69: Kannon-ji
Temple 67: Daikō-ji
Temple 66: Unpen-ji
Ehime-Tokushima Prefectural Border
Temple 65: Sankaku-ji

60
50
40
30
20
10
0

Exploring the Iya Valley

After Temple 65: Sankaku-ji, if you have wheels consider a side trip to explore the remote Iya Valley before heading up to Temple 66: Unpen-ji. Iya-dani is famed for its staggeringly steep gorges, thick mountain forests and narrow, cliff-hanging roads. There's a lot to see, so take your time.

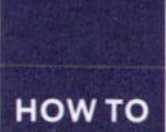

HOW TO

Nearest stop: Temple 65: Sankaku-ji

Getting here: Enter the Iya Valley via the Iya-guchi-bashi bridge, off busy Rte 319 in the upper Yoshino-gawa valley. It's a 56km drive one-way to the chairlift below Tsurugi-san, Shikoku's second-highest mountain (1955m), at the head of the valley.

Tip: Drive very slowly! The first 17km on Rte 32 in particular are on a winding, narrow road that's lucky to still be on the mountain side.

More info: iyatime.com

Peeing Boy Statue

Eleven kilometres of driving will bring you to this landmark **statue** symbolising an old local tradition: young boys would stand on the edge of this 200m-high precipice and urinate into the valley to test their bravado. There's only room for a few cars to stop on this tight outer corner.

Hotel Iya Onsen

A couple of corners past Peeing Boy brings you to the excellent **Hotel Iya Onsen** *(iyaonsen.co.jp, ¥¥)*, a stylish *ryokan* (Japanese-style inn) perched cliffside, almost hanging out over the deep gorge, with its own funicular cable car carrying guests down to its riverside **hot springs** *(adult/child ¥700/300);* day guests are welcome. This is a great place to overnight.

Legendary Vine Bridges

It's said that *kazura-bashi* (vine bridges) were first suspended over the river 800 years ago by defeated Heike samurai as they retreated into the remote valley after losing the Genpei War. They crossed rivers, then chopped down the bridges to outpace their pursuers. While the **Nishi-Iya (West Iya) Kazura-bashi** is easily visited, with a bus parking area that dwarfs the tiny bridge, the place to go is the quiet **Oku-Iya Double Vine Bridge**, 30km further east up the valley. This is a magical spot for a stroll through

CLIMBING TSURUGI-SAN

At the head of the Iya-dani is **Tsurugi-san**, one of Japan's Hyakumeizan (100 Famous Mountains) and the second-highest peak on Shikoku, at 1955m. It's very easy to climb thanks to a single-seater **chairlift** *(return adult/child ¥1900/900)* from the car park at **Minokoshi** (1420m) to 1750m **Nishijima Top Station**. From there to the peak takes less than an hour. Stay at **Tsurugi-san Chōjō Hutte** *(tsurugisan-hutte.com; ¥),* just below the peak. The food tastes great at 1950m!

Kazura-bashi, Iya Valley

the forest, with two secluded 'husband and wife' bridges hanging side by side over the river that are great fun to cross.

Scarecrow Village

Nagoro village is famous for having more *kakashi* (scarecrows) than people. As you drive through, see upwards of 100 **life-size dolls** set up as if doing various everyday activities about town. The *kakashi* were initially made by a local woman who, lonely as the population of her village dwindled, was keen to memorialise former friends.

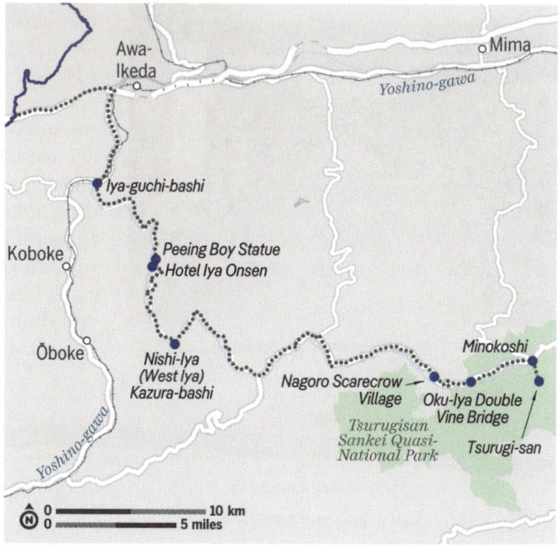

PREVIOUS STOP It's a long 21km walk coming up from Temple 65: Sankaku-ji to Temple 66: Unpen-ji, with nowhere to buy food along the way, so make sure you stock up in Shikoku-chūō. There's still some 14km of walking, initially on winding rural roads, to reach the prefectural boundary and pass back into Tokushima. That's followed by a hefty climb, much of it on *henro-michi* (pilgrim tracks), gaining close to 700m over 7km to get up to the pilgrimage's highest temple at 900m.

Temple 66: Unpen-ji

It's a big 21km walk from Temple 65, the last temple in Ehime Prefecture, to **Temple 66: Unpen-ji** (雲辺寺), which sits high in the mountains at 900m, the highest temple on the pilgrimage. Though almost sitting on the Tokushima–Kagawa prefectural border, Unpen-ji is on the Tokushima side, putting it in the same prefecture as the first 23 temples. Despite this, it is considered the first temple in Sanuki (Kagawa Prefecture).

While its name translates to 'Temple in the Clouds', it's also called the Kōya of Shikoku, after Kōbō Daishi's temple complex of Kōya-san in Wakayama Prefecture. For walkers, it's a big climb and – if you've followed the standard *henro* trail – there's nowhere to buy food along the way (prepare accordingly).

The temple itself is stunning, highlighted by 500 life-size stone *rakan* statues of Buddha's disciples stationed atmospherically among the pole-straight cedars. They convey just about every human emotion in their etched faces and evocative poses; search them for your lookalike, as according to legend, everyone has one.

Both the *henro* walking path up to Unpen-ji and the path down the northern side of the mountain are *henro-korogashi* (pilgrims fall down trails), so walk carefully.

For car *henro*, there are a couple of great options for getting up to the highest temple of the 88. From Temple 65: Sankaku-ji, either drive 32km up the Tokushima (southern) side to the parking lot, a 500m walk from the temple, or drive 30km around to the bottom station of the Unpen-ji Ropeway on the Kagawa side. Opened in 1987, **Unpen-ji Ropeway** (*shikoku-cable. co.jp; return adult/child ¥2200/1100*) changed everything for Unpen-ji, assuring its prosperity. Superb views from the aerial ropeway too.

Entrance gate, Temple 67: Daikō-ji

FROM LEFT: AMEHIME/SHUTTERSTOCK CRAIG MCLACHLAN/LONELY PLANET

**Temple 65:
Sankaku-ji**

21km

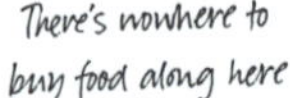

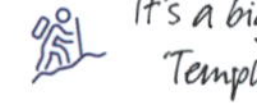

Rakan statues, Temple 66: Unpen-ji

Temple 67: Daikō-ji

Henro are in for a 10km hike from Temple 66, tumbling steeply down the mountains out onto the plains to get to **Temple 67: Daikō-ji** (大興寺; *komatsuoji.com*). In the short walk after getting out onto the flatter land, you'll have noticed a large number of *tame-ike* (water storage ponds). This is an area of high agricultural production, but it needs water. Unlike Kōchi on the wetter, southern side of Shikoku, Kagawa Prefecture is relatively dry and what rain it gets tends to race off in rivers to the sea. *Tame-ike* save the day and there are an astounding number of ponds in the prefecture.

BEST PLACES TO EAT

Tera Cafe, Temple 69 ¥
Lovely little shop and cafe on the temple grounds at Kannon-ji; simple meals and drinks. 寺 *cafe; 10am-4pm Fri-Mon*

Michi-no-eki Fureai Park Mino, Temple 71 ¥
Beneath Temple 71: Iyadani-ji, this *michi-no-eki* (roadside station) is a real find for *henro;* good restaurant and cafe options plus a full-on onsen complex. *park-mino.info; 10am-10pm*

Ikkaku, Marugame ¥¥
Birthplace of Marugame's famous *honetsuki-dori* (chicken-on-the-bone), legendary in Kagawa. *ikkaku.co.jp; 11am-2pm & 5-10pm Mon & Wed-Fri, 11am-10pm Sat & Sun*

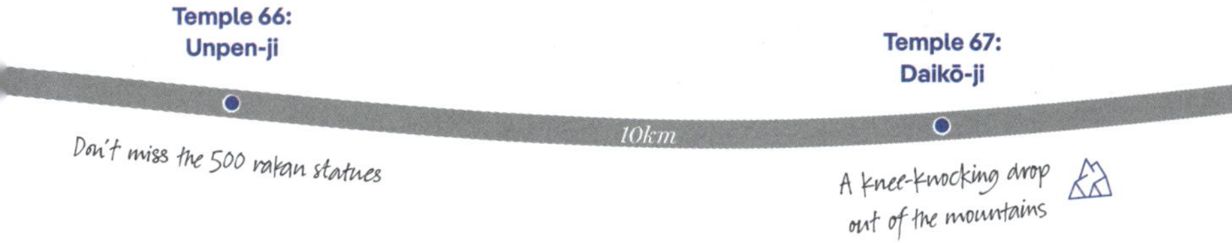

Temple 66:
Unpen-ji

Temple 67:
Daikō-ji

10km

Don't miss the 500 rakan statues

A knee-knocking drop out of the mountains 

HENRO WITH WHEELS

- If you're visiting the Iya Valley (p194), consider driving up to Temple 66: Unpen-ji from Miyoshi on the Tokushima side of the mountains, close to the entrance to the Iya Valley.
- Once you've been to Temple 66: Unpen-ji and are down out of the mountains and onto the flats of Kagawa Prefecture, there's not much distance between temples.
- It's feasible to pick one place to stay, such as in Zentsu-ji, Kotohira, Marugame or even Takamatsu (p210) and visit all 15 temples in this leg over three days.
- By car, it's less than 40km from Zentsu-ji to Takamatsu city.

It's said that the Daishi was here in 822 CE and founded the temple, planting the huge camphor tree that is on its grounds. The temple was burnt by the forces of Chōsokabe Motochika around 1580, during the Tosa warlord's attempts to conquer the island. It was rebuilt, burnt again, rebuilt again, and is now a particularly peaceful and attractive temple.

Temple 68: Jinnein

There's something different coming up as *henro* walk the 9km northwest from Temple 67 to **Temple 68: Jinnein** (神恵院), almost on the Inland Sea coast: two temples at the same place! Only about 100m apart, this is the only place on the pilgrimage where two of the 88 are in such close proximity. Temples 68 and 69 sit together on the eastern side of Kotohiki-san (60m).

It's complicated, but Jinnein (Temple of Divine Grace) was originally built as a branch of the shrine **Kotohiki Hachiman-gū**, at pretty much

Statues of horses, Temple 70: Motoyama-ji

BRESTER IRINA/SHUTTERSTOCK

the same location it is now, a couple of hundred metres to the south. In 1868, as part of the Meiji government's orders to separate Shintō and Buddhist sites, Jinnein was moved slightly north of the shrine, to land that was part of the Buddhist temple next door, Temple 69: Kannon-ji. And there it has stayed, meaning there are two temples at the same place. If you have sore feet, rejoice at small pleasures.

Temple 69: Kannon-ji

Yes, it's only about 100m from Temple 68 to **Temple 69: Kannon-ji** (観音寺). As well as having two temples in the same place, a source of confusion is the name of the city in which the temples are located: it's **Kan'onji,** established in 1878 as a village when the new municipalities system was introduced under the Meiji government. With population growth, Kan'onji went on to become a town in 1890, then a city in 1955. It grew in size, merging with nearby towns in 2005, but kept the name Kan'onji. The local JR railway station is Kan-Onji station. All a bit confusing when you take into account that the temple, city and station all use 観音寺 for the kanji characters of their names. Ask a local though and they'll wonder what you're going on about.

The two temples are so close together that they share plenty, even the same parking lot. Take a break at **Tera Cafe** (p197) in the temple compound, with excellent udon (thick white wheat noodles), tea and sweets options, along with nice outdoor seating.

DETOUR: Zenigata

Zenigata, a massive coin-shaped monument of sand on Ariake Beach, makes for a remarkable view from the observation spot on **Kotohiki Hill**, above Temples 68 and 69. Surrounded by pine trees, the circular coin of sand is 122m in diameter, fully 345m in circumference. The best way to view it is from above, high on the hill, a 15-minute walk up from Temples 68 and 69. Car *henro* can drive up. Legend says that local residents built it in a single night in 1633 to welcome the lord of the Takamatsu domain. Zenigata is illuminated at night.

Temple 70: Motoyama-ji

Things are becoming a lot easier now in Kagawa Prefecture; from Temples 68 and 69, it's only 5km to **Temple 70: Motoyama-ji** (本山寺), at a crossroads by the Saita-gawa. Here you'll find an absolutely stunning **five-storey pagoda** that can be spotted from way back. Originally built in 950 CE, it was reconstructed in 1910 and is arguably the most beautiful pagoda on the pilgrimage.

Motoyama-ji is the only temple with Bato Kannon Bosatsu, with a horses head, as its main image. Suitably, there's a statue of two horses near the *hondō* where the principal image is enshrined; *ema* (small wooden wishing plaques) hanging beside the horses are in the shape of horseshoes.

There are a couple of legends regarding Motoyama-ji escaping being burnt by Chōsokabe Motochika in the 1580s. One says that after his warriors attacked the head priest, they went into the temple to find blood dripping from the hand of a statue of Amida Nyorai and they, to use a modern term, freaked out and ran away. The other legend says a swarm of bees that lived at the temple attacked Motochika's forces, sending them into a hurried retreat. Bees have been revered here ever since.

Temple 67: Daikō-ji

Temple 68: Jinnein

Temple 69: Kannon-ji

Temple 70: Motoyama-ji

9km   100m   5km

Water reservoirs abound in Kagawa

Two pilgrimage temples at the same location

Spot the stunning five-storey pagoda from afar

Temple 71: Iyadani-ji

A 12km walk north of Temple 70 on rural roads just west of busy Rte 11 will bring *henro* to **Temple 71: Iyadani-ji** (弥谷寺; *iyadanizi. xsrv.jp),* up at 200m in altitude on the side of a mountain. You can feel the sacredness here as you climb and descend endless stairs in the temple grounds, 400 of them up to the Daishi-dō (Daishi Hall) from the *niōmon* (main gate). Some of the buildings have been erected directly into rocky cliff faces and caves, though the pilgrims of old never had to contend with gazing out on a buzzing expressway in the valley.

Iyadani-ji is only 7km from Temple 75: Zentsū-ji (p203), the childhood home of Kōbō Daishi, and legend says that the boy Mao, as he was called, came here to meditate and study in **Shishi-no-Iwaya** (Lion Cave) between the ages of nine and 12. It's said that he studied day and night here in the cave, with the opening that looks like a roaring lion.

Temple 71 is where the souls of the dead came for peace. Before the seven temples that are now Temple 77 to Temple 71 (descending) became part of the 88 Temple Pilgrimage, they were an ancient pilgrimage in their own right. Worshippers brought their ancestors' ashes and prayed for their souls at Iyadani-ji, the spirits ascending the mountain to become purified. These days, many worshippers still start at Temple 77 and walk the 16km back to Temple 71, while those who are walking it as part of the 88 Temple Pilgrimage do it in numerical order.

Temple 72: Mandara-ji

Pilgrims are now into a cluster of seven temples in and around the Daishi's childhood home, Zentsu-ji. **Temple 72: Mandara-ji**

BRESTER IRINA/SHUTTERSTOCK

Along the Way We Met...

IRINA I'm a traveller, not a tourist, and have been travelling around the world for the last 11 years. This is my first time in Japan. I love to get out into the countryside, into the small villages and see a side of Japan that most visitors don't see. I can't speak Japanese, but I use Google Translate and the people here are so kind that everything works out. As I'm walking, I try to communicate with everyone I meet.

Irina, from Siberia, is a professional photographer; many of the photographs in this book were taken by Irina.

IRINA'S TIP: *Don't rush. Take a break along the way and try to appreciate this amazing pilgrimage.*

Temple 70:
Motoyama-ji

Temple 71:
Iyadani-ji

12km

Back up onto a
sacred mountain

Temple 71: Iyadani-ji

(曼荼羅寺; *mandaraji.xsrv.jp*) is only 4km from Temple 71. Founded in 596 CE, this is the oldest of the temples on the pilgrimage, built as a family temple of the Saeki family, the lords of Sanuki and ancestors of Kōbō Daishi.

The Daishi was here in 807 CE on his return from China and it's said he took three years to build a temple complex modelled on Seiryū-ji Temple in China. He set up mandalas he'd brought back from China and renamed the temple Mandara-ji. The poet Saigyō Hōshi (1118–90) lived in a hut nearby for seven years; he was known for taking a nap on a large, flat stone at the temple, now known as **Saigyō's Napping Stone**.

🛏️

BEST PLACES TO SLEEP

Minshuku Aozoraya ¥
In a good spot in the remote area below Temple 66, 4.5km before Temple 67: Daikō-ji. There's nothing else around here so book with meals in advance by calling 0875-27-7309.

Temple 75: Zentsū-ji Temple Lodging ¥
As you'd expect at the childhood home of the Daishi, this is the biggest *shukubō* (temple lodging), with 50 rooms and a *daiyokujō* (large public bath). *zentsuji.com*

AZ Hotel Kagawa Utazu ¥
Extremely reasonable rooms in a large chain business hotel within 1km of Temple 78: Gōshō-ji; book online in English. *az-hotel.com/utazu*

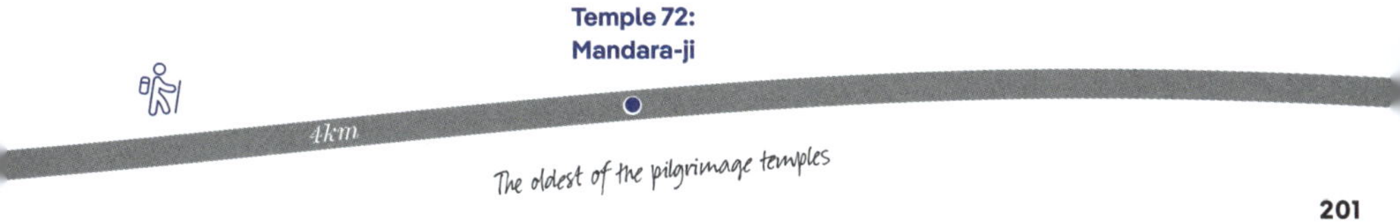

Temple 72: Mandara-ji

4km

The oldest of the pilgrimage temples

BRESTER IRINA/SHUTTERSTOCK

Temple 73: Shusshaka-ji

The temple lost its big drawcard in 2002, when an old pine tree that had been coerced to grow into the conical shape of a pilgrim's hat, 4m high and 18m across, had to be cut down after an attack by pine beetles. Legend says it was planted by the Daishi himself.

Temple 73: Shusshaka-ji

It's only 500m up the road now from Temple 72 to **Temple 73: Shusshaka-ji** (出釈迦寺), virtually surrounded by *tame-ike*, good for fighting fires. Apart from Temples 68 and 69, this is the shortest distance between two temples on the pilgrimage. While you can get your temple stamp here and head on your way with everything you need, take some time to see the *okunoin* (inner sanctuary) up on the mountain **Gahaishi-san**, over 300 vertical metres above you and 1.4km away by a steep concreted road.

The inner sanctuary, **Shashingadake Zenjo** (捨身ヶ嶽禅定), is the essence of this place. This is where, legend says, the seven-year-old boy called Mao, who would go on to become Kōbō Daishi, threw himself off the mountain, crying 'If I am called to save the people, save me, O Buddha! If I am not, let me die!' A company of angels appeared, who caught the boy in their robes, carrying him to safety.

It's said that years later, Kōbō Daishi built the temple on Gahaishi-san, carved a **statue of Shaka Nyorai**, and dedicated it to the temple. What is now the *okunoin* was originally Temple 73, the bell tower still standing on high. Much later, the temple was moved down to the valley to increase its accessibility to worshippers.

Temple 74: Kōyama-ji

There's an easy 3km stroll now from Temple 73 to **Temple 74: Kōyama-ji** (甲山寺), tucked under the far side of a cute mountain known as Kabuto-yama (Helmet Mountain). If it's possible to feel sympathy for a temple, it's this one, because someone has placed a huge gravel quarry next door. In the right (or wrong!) conditions, it's not quite the quiet environment it might well be.

It's said that when the Daishi was thinking of building a temple between what are now Temples 73 and 75, near his childhood home, an old man claiming to be a saint emerged from a cave in the mountain and said 'If you build a temple here, I will protect it forever'. Pleased, the Daishi carved a statue of Bishamonten (god of treasure, wealth, and warriors), enshrined it in the rock cave, prayed and built the temple. Some who have witnessed the quarry next door, might suggest the old man didn't keep his word.

Temple 73:
Shusshaka-ji

Temple 74:
Kōyama-ji

Temple 75:
Zentsū-ji

500m

3km

2km

Temple 72:
Mandara-ji

Head up to the okunoin
if you've got time

The temple sits behind
Helmet Mountain

Kōyama-ji's nickname is 'Rabbit Temple' and there are some 16 rabbit statues around the grounds, the reason being that a statue of Gekko Bosatsu (Bodhisattva of moonlight) shows him holding a moon disk. Japanese see a rabbit in the moon, not a man, so this has become the Rabbit Temple; as well as all the rabbits around the temple, check out the ones on the roof tiles. At the 'parent and child' rabbit statue, cure your ailments by rubbing the corresponding part of the rabbit.

Temple 75: Zentsū-ji

From Temple 74, it's a 2km stroll to **Temple 75: Zentsū-ji** *(善通寺; zentsuji.com),* the biggest, most prosperous and busiest of the 88 temples, and the site of Kōbō Daishi's home when he was the boy called Mao. The temple was called Zentsū-ji after the Daishi's father, Zentsū. Along with Tō-ji in Kyoto and Kōya-san in Wakayama, Zentsū-ji is recognised as one of

CIVIL ENGINEER KŪKAI

The Lord of Sanuki built the first **Mannō-ike**, an artificial water reservoir, in the early 700s. Kagawa has always had a water problem, solved to some extent by its numerous *tame-ike* (water ponds). When the reservoir walls failed in 818 due to flooding, Kūkai was sent to rebuild Mannō-ike. Locals were so eager to work for him that the job was done in only three months. While the walls failed again many times in subsequent centuries, Mannō-ike has kept that association with the Daishi. **Bekkaku 17: Kanno-ji** sits at the western end of the pond, 12km southeast of Temple 75: Zentsu-ji.

Pagoda (p204), Temple 75: Zentsū-ji

SANGA PARK/SHUTTERSTOCK

Statues of Kannon (p206), Temple 77: Dōryū-ji

the three most significant Shingon Buddhist locations in Japan.

There is a lot to see and do here, so *henro* should budget their time accordingly. The temple is naturally split into two large blocks. The Tanjō-in is the western part with most of the important temple buildings, while the Garan, the eastern part, feels more like a wide open park focused around its glorious **five-storey pagoda** made of *keyaki* (zelkova), a tree that symbolises strength and elegance. It's said that the pagoda was constructed over 50 years, completed in 813 CE, to stand 43m in height. It has been renovated four times, but to its original design with the main structure preserved as much as possible.

On the western side, the Daishi-dō is said to have been built on the spot where the Daishi was born. Another highlight is the Kaidan-meguri, a 100m-long path in a tunnel under the main hall, in which pilgrims feel their way in total darkness, trusting the Daishi to get them through. It's well worth the ¥500 fee.

The temple operates a *shukubō* with Japanese-style rooms and a large communal bath; check the temple website.

Temple 76: Konzō-ji

Another flat, easy walk awaits – the 4km stretch north from Temple 75 to **Temple 76: Konzō-ji** (金倉寺). The pilgrim path is well out onto the flats of Kagawa Prefecture now, a mix of agriculture and small-town industry. There is an astounding number of water ponds and plenty of nobbly hills and mountains breaking up the landscape. Only 7km off to the northeast is **Iino-yama** (422m), known as Sanuki-Fuji for its resemblance to Fuji-san.

Konzō-ji is the birthplace of Chishō Daishi (814–91), nephew of Kōbō Daishi and founder of the Tendai Jimon sect of Buddhism. Both men were awarded the title of *Daishi,* which literally means 'great teacher', but is better translated as 'saint'. Statues of both *daishi* are enshrined here in the Daishi-dō. There is little doubt though, as to who is held in higher esteem, as the Japanese have a saying that 'Kōbō stole the title of Daishi', meaning that if anyone speaks of *the* Daishi, everyone knows who they're talking about.

Temple 77: Dōryū-ji

Only 4km northwest towards the coast from Temple 76 will bring pilgrims to **Temple 77: Dōryū-ji** (道隆寺). This is the first of the seven temples in the ancient pilgrimage that ended at Temple 71: Iyadani-ji (p200). With only 16km of walking over the seven temples, it's called the Mairi Path and worshippers carried

Continues on page 206

Enjoy Konpira-san's Steps

Officially Kotohira-gū, but affectionately known as Konpira-san, this Shintō shrine dedicated to the deity of seafarers is nestled on the side of the mountain Zōzu-san, only 7km southeast of Temple 75: Zentsū-ji.

Nearest stop: Temple 75: Zentsū-ji

Getting here: JR Kotohira Station is on the JR Dosan line; Kotoden Kotohira Station is the terminus for trains on the more direct line from Takamatsu (p210; one hour).

Tip: If climbing to the top, take some refreshments with you on the 583-step top leg to the Okusha.

More info: konpira.or.jp

The small touristy town of **Kotohira** is home to one of Shikoku's most famous visitor attractions, **Konpira-san**. Ascending the 1368 stone steps is a rite of passage for many Japanese, with plenty of interesting en-route distractions. Mention to any older Japanese person that you've been to Shikoku and one of the first things they'll ask is if you've climbed Konpira-san.

These days, as Japan's population ages, fewer tour groups come to stay in the town's large *ryokan* and even fewer visitors make it as far as the **Okusha** (inner shrine), the full 1368 steps up the mountain. Many older visitors don't get far past **Omotesandō**, the main street leading to the start of the shrine steps, packed with eateries and souvenir shops.

Allow 45 minutes to climb the 785 steps to the main shrine, **Kotohira-gū**, then another 45 minutes for the 583 steps to the Okusha. Chances are you'll be on your own for the last bit.

On your way down, turn right at step 22 to visit **Kanamaru-za**, Japan's oldest kabuki theatre.

Steps to Konpira-san

Continued from page 204

the ashes of their dead, praying for their souls at the mountain temple, Iyadani-ji, in the hope they would find a state of repose.

Temple 77's walkways are lined with 255 statues of Kannon, goddess of mercy and compassion, many of which have been decorated by worshippers; some wear red cloth bibs, some are draped in prayer beads, some have piles of coins at their base and others hold pinwheels that rotate in the breeze. This is a peaceful temple, even if the location is on a busy local road.

Temple 78: Gōshō-ji

It's 7.5km of walking on busy city roads to get from Temple 77 in Tadotsu to **Temple 78: Gōshō-ji** (郷照寺; *yakuyoke.org*) in Utazu,

passing through the city of Marugame along the way. **Marugame-jō**, famed as one of Japan's 12 original castles, is a short walk from the pilgrim route through the city and is well worth a visit.

Gōshō-ji sits almost exactly where the Seto Ōhashi bridge system hits Shikoku. Opened in 1988 after 10 years of construction, with a total length of 13km, Seto Ōhashi revolutionised travel to Shikoku as it was the first bridge system linking Japan's fourth-largest island to its largest, Honshū. All of a sudden, people could drive or take the train to Shikoku. You can see the bridge from the grounds of Gōshō-ji.

Spectacular here is the **Mantai Kannon-dō**, with 10,000 miniature statues of Kannon, donated from all around Japan, in an underground rectangular corridor.

Along the Way We Met...

EDDY & RUTH One of our sons married a Japanese woman; we're on our fourth trip to Japan. We wanted to get away from the busy parts of the country we've been to before and see a different side of Japan. We have two weeks here, including a one-week self-guided tour of parts of the pilgrimage. We're staying in hotels in cities, then getting out onto the trails each day. We're not doing the whole thing, but it's been a very spiritual experience.

Eddy and Ruth are semi-retired and live on the Gold Coast, Australia.

EDDY & RUTH'S TIP: *You don't have to do the whole pilgrimage to enjoy the experience. Shikoku and its people are like a breath of fresh air.*

Temple 77:
Dōryū-ji

Temple 78:
Gōshō-ji

7.5km

See 255 statues of Kannon, goddess of mercy

Views of the Seto Ōhashi bridge system to Honshu

Miniature statues of Kannon, Temple 78: Gōshō-ji

Temple 79: Tennō-ji

From Temple 78, it's a 6km walk almost directly east across Sakaide city to **Temple 79: Tennō-ji** (天皇寺), the 'Temple of the Emperor'. Emperor Sutoku, banished to Sanuki in a dispute of succession with his younger brother in 1156, was held here before being assassinated in 1164. Though his body was cremated and his ashes taken to Temple 81: Shiromine-ji and buried there, a Shintō shrine was built and dedicated to him at Temple 79, leading to the temple's name, Tennō-ji. That on-site shrine is **Shiramine-gū**, which has an unusual, vermillion **Miwa Torii**, a three-winged shrine gate with a tall centrepiece and smaller gates attached on both sides. Many people come to worship Emperor Sutoku here.

There is a large statue of a horse on the grounds. In Shintō, horses are the sacred mounts of the *kami* (gods), acting as intermediaries between the human world and the realm of the *kami*. While many shrines have statues of horses, some major shrines keep live ones on their grounds.

**Temple 79:
Tennō-ji**

6km

The Temple of
the Emperor

207

Henro motorbike, Shikoku
CRAIG MCLACHLAN/LONELY PLANET

INSIGHT

The Modern Pilgrimage

The Shikoku pilgrimage is said to be 1200 years old, but Kōbō Daishi would no doubt be shocked to see it in its present form. Foreign pilgrims, consulting the Henro Helper app on smartphones, outnumbering Japanese walking *henro*...what is the pilgrimage coming to?

WORDS BY **CRAIG MCLACHLAN**
Craig has walked, driven and written on his pilgrimage experiences.

The Henro of Old

The *henro* of 350 years ago were all walkers and set out on a completely different kind of pilgrimage than the *henro* of today. The first guidebook had not yet been published, the only way to get to Shikoku was by boat, there were no weather forecasts and there was no way to stay in contact with family at home. If they got homesick or lonely, they just had to keep going – or give up. And if they got injured – or worse, died – along the way, they simply disappeared into the wilds of Shikoku, leaving a wondering family at home and, in many cases, an unnamed grave marker alongside the trail.

The Modern Henro

In the mid 2020s, walking *henro* set out under quite different circumstances. They usually have a smartphone, with the Henro Helper app making navigation a breeze, and they know exactly what's coming up from studying guidebooks, websites, Facebook pages, Instagram posts and blogs of other *henro*.

They know if bad weather is on the way and they're fortified against loneliness by being able to video chat with family and friends at home. Modern medical facilities are close at hand if they get injured, and they're wearing comfortable shoes on their feet, not straw sandals.

International *henro,* who, anecdotally, these days make up over half of those walking, don't even need to speak Japanese, thanks to Google Translate and other translation apps.

It's a whole different *henro* world out there.

That said, walking *henro* – and international ones in particular – face a new set of issues. In the 1970s, nearly three-quarters of the 88 temples had *shukubō* (temple lodgings), where solo *henro* could stay the night, with meals included. In 2025, that number had fallen to six of the 88.

In remote regions, such as southern Kōchi and Ehime Prefectures, rural depopulation means that sleeping and eating options for walking *henro* may be few and far between. Japan's famous *konbini* (convenience stores) are incredibly convenient for buying food and drinks...until they aren't there!

For walking *henro,* in more remote parts of the pilgrimage, the question is not 'What delicious Japanese cuisine will I eat each day', but 'Can I find food?' Of course, *henro* with motorised wheels can find what they need in next to no time, as they can quickly get to where there is supply to meet their demand.

> They usually have a smartphone, with the Henro Helper app making navigation a breeze, and they know exactly what's coming up.

An Evolving Pilgrimage

One of the biggest issues for the booming number of international *henro* has been the need to book accommodation a few days ahead of time, usually by phone, in Japanese. This has meant, in many cases, asking a Japanese person to do it for them. But the pilgrimage is continuing to evolve: a number of temples have embraced the internet, running their own websites and Instagram pages. **Henro House** (*henrohouse. jp*) now has over 50 places right around Shikoku on its English-language website that can be booked online. And new accommodation is starting to pop up to meet the international demand: in 2025, **Minshuku Tōnohama** (*m-tounohama.com*) opened accommodation in a former wedding venue in Kōchi Prefecture, with an English-language website and online booking facilities.

Overtourism

The buzzword in Japan for 2024, when 37 million international tourists hit the country's shores, was overtourism. While the government was ecstatic with the economic benefits for Japan, the media was focused on visitors not conforming to Japanese cultural norms.

The pilgrimage is battling with foreign *henro* behaving badly. The biggest bugbear is that foreign *henro* have a bad reputation for cancelling accommodation reservations at the last minute or simply not turning up. This is a major problem for small places, where the owners depend on that income to make a living. Also an issue is wild camping and sleeping in *tsuyado* (places set up as emergency spots for *henro* in trouble).

To help keep everybody happy, foreign *henro* are encouraged to spread the love and contribute appropriately to the pilgrimage and Shikoku while on their journey.

Takamatsu

In Takamatsu (高松), Kagawa's prefectural capital, you'll find both a happening city centre with an array of dining options and lively bars, and one of the country's most spectacular gardens, while the islands of the Inland Sea (Seto-nai-kai) are just a short boat ride away.

WORDS BY
JESSICA KORTEMAN
Jessica is an Australian writer specialising in Japanese travel and culture.

Arriving

By foot For walking pilgrims, it's a 2½-hour jaunt east from Temple 82: Negoro-ji towards Takamatsu city centre.

By bus To utilise public transport, you'll need to walk one hour from Temple 82 to Negoro-guchi bus stop, where you can catch a bus to Takamatsu Station (30 minutes).

By car For *henro* (pilgrims) with wheels the journey between Temple 82 and central Takamatsu is around 25 minutes.

By train If you're starting your pilgrimage here, a train via Okayama and the Seto Ōhashi bridge is the only way to enter Shikoku by rail.

By air Those starting here can fly into Takamatsu Airport (TAK) and then take a limousine bus to Takamatsu Station (45 minutes).

HOW MUCH FOR A

Draught beer ¥600

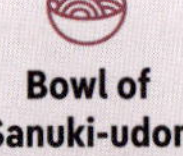

Bowl of Sanuki-udon from ¥400

Entry to Ritsurin-kōen ¥500

Getting Around

Walking The city-centre area has a number of undercover shopping and pedestrian-only streets.

Train Central Takamatsu is well serviced by rail. There's Takamatsu Station for JR lines and next door Takamatsu-Chikkō for the local Kotoden (electric rail) lines. IC cards can be used, but only the local 'Iruca' card can be charged by machines. You can charge a Pasmo or Suica card by asking at the station office of larger stops such as Takamatsu-Chikkō and Kawara-machi, or be prepared to buy paper tickets.

Bus A shuttle bus (¥200) connects JR Yashima and Kotoden-Yashima stations with Shikoku-mura and Yashima-sanjō.

Taxi Supplemental taxi rides can be useful here. There often aren't taxis waiting at the Takamatsu Port, so walk across to Takamatsu Station instead.

For trip planning, go to
Kotoden Route Map:

A DAY IN TAKAMATSU

Head to **Ritsurin-kōen** (p213) early to enjoy a relaxed wander before the crowds arrive. Take in the garden's **South Pond** on a leisurely *wasen* boat ride and from **Kikugetsu-tei** teahouse. Proceed to the city centre by train to Takamatsu-Chikkō Station to explore the castle ruins of **Takamatsu-jō** (p215) at adjoining Tamamo-kōen.

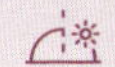

Take a train to Yashima and open-air museum **Shikoku-mura** (p224). Proceed by shuttle bus to Yashima-sanjō, the summit of **Mt Yashima** and location of Temple 84: Yashima-ji (p226), for excellent Inland Sea and city views from **Shishi-no-Reigan Observatory**. Stay for sunset on Fridays and Saturdays when the bus operates late.

Return to the centre to enjoy the lively culinary scene at the many restaurants and bars around **Katahara-machi** and **Kawara-machi.** Either before or after dinner, consider a short side quest to **Busshōzan Onsen**, a sodium bicarbonate spring with indoor-outdoor cypress baths said to improve muscle and joint pain.

Where to Stay

There are lots of options in Takamatsu, including affordable hostels that help keep pilgrimage costs down. For accessibility, staying somewhere convenient to a station on the Kotoden Kotohira line, which includes Ritsurin-kōen, Kawara-machi, Katahara-machi and Takamatsu-Chikkō stations, is a solid plan. Those planning to take an early morning ferry to Naoshima or one of the other Inland Sea Art Islands should stay within the vicinity of Takamatsu Port.

BEST PLACES TO STAY

WeBase ¥ Large city-centre hostel-hotel with a mixed dorm and private rooms. *we-base.jp/ takamatsu*

Guest House Wakabaya ¥ Residential family-run hostel with free parking by reservation. *wakabaya. main.jp*

Kotori ¥ Centrally located hostel. Mixed dorm and private rooms with co-working space. *kotori-japan.com*

Sunny Day Hostel ¥¥ Small boutique hostel with optional in-room picnic breakfast. *sunnydayhostel. com*

Where to Eat

You will find a multitude of options in the vicinity of JR Takamatsu Station and the nearby **Central Takamatsu Shopping Arcades**. This series of eight interconnected and mostly undercover shopping strips is located on the west side of Kotoden stations Katahara-machi and Kawara-machi. The surrounding streets come into their own at nightfall when ample *izakaya* (pub-eateries) start opening their doors.

KAGAWA'S LOCAL SPECIALITIES

Kagawa is known as the *udon-ken* (udon noodle prefecture) with around 400 dedicated udon restaurants serving local dish *Sanuki-udon* (pictured below right). The wheat-based noodles have a firm and chewy texture, and can be enjoyed hot, cold and with a variety of broths and toppings.

Honetsuki-dori (骨付鳥; pictured below left), a kind of bone-in chicken, was invented in the city of Marugame in 1952 by chicken restaurant Ikkaku and is now a popular dish prefecture-wide. Designed to be picked up by the bone and eaten Flintstones style, this grilled chicken, tantalisingly seasoned with salt, pepper and garlic, drips with flavour. Choose between *oya-dori* (a firmer mature chicken) and *hina-dori* (or *waka-dori,* a more tender young chicken).

Also look out for 'olive-fed' beef, chicken, pork and *hamachi* (Japanese amberjack), produced thanks to olive island Shōdoshima. Farmers feed their livestock olive lees (what is left of the olives after pressing), increasing the amount of healthy oleic acid.

FROM LEFT: OKIMO/GETTY IMAGES, BONCHAN/SHUTTERSTOCK

BEST PLACES TO EAT & DRINK

Uehara-ya ¥ *Sanuki-udon* restaurant by Ritsurin-kōen – try its *kake-udon* (sardine broth with green onions). *9.30am-2.30pm Mon-Sat*

Yoridorimidori ¥¥ Top choice for local *honetsuki-dori. 5-10pm Mon, Tue & Thu-Sat*

Mahoroba ¥¥ Friendly cash-only *izakaya* with English menu and great sides. *5-10pm Mon, Tue & Thu-Sat*

Bar Ajisai ¥¥ Classy tatami bar exclusively for women. Solo customers welcome. *5.30pm-4am Tue-Sun*

Explore Takamatsu's Prized Garden

Once the strolling grounds of feudal lords, explore Takamatsu's stunning Edo-era garden, Ritsurin-kōen (栗林公園), awarded the maximum three stars in the Michelin Green Guide for attractions 'worth a special journey'.

Getting here: Ritsurin-kōen is a 10-minute walk from Ritsurin-kōen Station or two minutes from Ritsurin-kōen-mae bus stop.

When to go: Autumn and spring see the most notable foliage changes.

Cost: Garden entry ¥500, South Pond boat ride ¥850

Tip: The garden opens as early as 5.30am depending on the season.

More info: my-kagawa.jp/ritsuringarden/wasen/reserve

The incredible **Ritsurin-kōen** covers 75 hectares of manicured grounds, with six ponds, 13 landscaped hills and over 1000 pine trees, flanked by the ancient burial grounds of towering Mt Shiun. If you're overwhelmed by choice or have limited time, take the South Garden course (one hour) that centres on the **South Pond** (南湖; Nan-ko), the backdrop for just about every tourist brochure for the city.

Featuring **Engetsu-kyō**, the largest bridge in the garden, and three islands, this is undoubtedly the highlight of Ritsurin. Don't miss **Kikugetsu-tei** (掬月亭; ¥), a teahouse on the western side of the South Pond that's as old as the garden itself, where entry is the price of a cup of tea and a sweet. Once you've enjoyed your tea set, you can proceed to **Kikugetsu-no-ma**, a spectacular viewing area that opens out to the water. Another way to enjoy the South Pond is on a leisurely 30-minute *wasen* boat ride, bookable online up to 5pm the day before. Otherwise, try for a same-day ticket at the **boat ticket counter** *(from 8.30am)*.

RICHIE CHAN/SHUTTERSTOCK

Kikugetsu-tei

Revel in Light at an Underground Museum

Located on Naoshima, head underground to explore architect Tadao Andō's most celebrated work among the Inland Sea Art Islands.

Getting here: Catch a ferry from Takamatsu to Naoshima's Miyanoura Port (30 to 50 minutes), then take a 10-minute bike ride or catch the bus.

When to go: Avoid Mondays when the museum (and many of the island's attractions) are closed.

Cost: Online/on-site weekdays ¥2500/2800, weekends and holidays ¥2700/3000, kids 15 and under are free.

Tip: Requires a timed entry ticket; make advance bookings online. Allow one to 1½ hours to explore the building and its artworks.

More info: benesse-artsite.jp/en

Cleverly concealed within the landscape on Naoshima's southern coast, the impressive **Chichū Art Museum** (地中美術館) is a subterranean architectural marvel. While the museum has no exterior, numerous open-air vaults in geometric shapes act like portals to the outside world, allowing changing light and the elements to become part of the viewing experience.

In the Claude Monet Space, admire five original Monet *Water Lily* paintings spectacularly illuminated by indirect natural light. Then ascend the concrete steps in the cathedral-like space of artist and sculptor Walter De Maria's site-specific installation *Time/Timeless/No Time*, featuring a 2.2m-diameter black granite sphere infused with gold crystals and 27 geometric mahogany columns covered in gold leaf. Change positions to appreciate this large sculptural work of light and shadows from varying perspectives. Also on display are three projection and LED light installations by James Turrell. You may need to queue for *Open Field,* an immersive opportunity to 'enter light'.

RAYINTS/SHUTTERSTOCK

Ticket Center, Chichū Art Museum

ART ISLAND NAOSHIMA

A short boat ride off Takamatsu, the rural island of **Naoshima** (直島) is the setting for an innovative (and highly successful) contemporary art experiment aimed at addressing the effects of rapid depopulation. Spearheaded by Japanese company Benesse (then Fukutake Publishing) with a youth campsite in 1989 and later with Benesse House, an art-meets-hotel complex, in 1992, contemporary art would soon become the focus of revitalisation activities across the island-dotted Inland Sea (Seto-nai-kai; 瀬戸内海). Here exquisite nature and modern art combine to create works of art deeply connected to place and community, from underground museums and immersive installations to innovative art houses and seaside sculptures.

Today, **Benesse Art Site Naoshima**, in cooperation with the Fukutake Foundation, encompasses artistic endeavours on Naoshima as well as nearby **Teshima** and **Inujima**. These islands, plus a good number more, make up the multi-island-strong **Setouchi Triennale**, one of Japan's largest contemporary art festivals. Started in 2010, the festival takes place every three years over approximately 100 days and sees even more art installations unveiled across the islands.

Castle boat ride, Takamatsu-jō

Explore the Ruins of Takamatsu-jō

Takamatsu-jō (高松城; *takamatsujyo.com;* ¥200) is considered one of Japan's three best castles on the sea. While the castle keep is no longer, the ruins, spread over present-day Tamamo Park, a short walk from Takamatsu Station, allow visitors to imagine former times. Climb the uneven steps to the observation deck atop the 13m-high stone base that once supported the castle tower, where an astounding view of the port and sluice gate awaits. From the gate, take a 30-minute **castle boat ride** (¥500) on the sea-bream-filled moat, departing half-hourly from 10am to 3.30pm (except noon and 1pm).

Wasanbon sweets

Make Wasanbon Sweets

A short walk from Hanazono Station, make your own *wasanbon* sweets, a Kagawa speciality, at **Mamehana Wasanbon Workshop** (豆花; *mamehana-kasikigata.com;* ¥2000). *Wasanbon*, both the name of the sweet and the finely granulated sugar used to make it, is a type of *wagashi* (traditional Japanese sweet) used in tea ceremony. During this fun, English-language workshop, follow the lead of instructor Uehara Ayumi in a rare opportunity to make *wasanbon* the old-fashioned way using handcrafted wooden moulds called *kashikigata*. The intricate designs are painstakingly etched by Ichihara Yoshihiro, Uehara-san's father, one of the last *kashikigata* artisans in Japan. Reservations required.

215

Tennō-ji

TEMPLE 79

It's amazing how everything looks so flat on a map! With the prefectural capital of Takamatsu enticingly close, the trail heads up once more, only to descend again into the city. Takamatsu may be a nice place, but there are only five temples to go! Two more on mountains – up, down, up, down – then Temple 86 on the coast. You're heading south into the central mountains now for the last climb up to Temple 88: Ōkubo-ji. Don't be fooled, it's not over yet.

Craig McLachlan

Temple 88: Ōkubo-ji (p231)

BRESTER IRINA/SHUTTERSTOCK

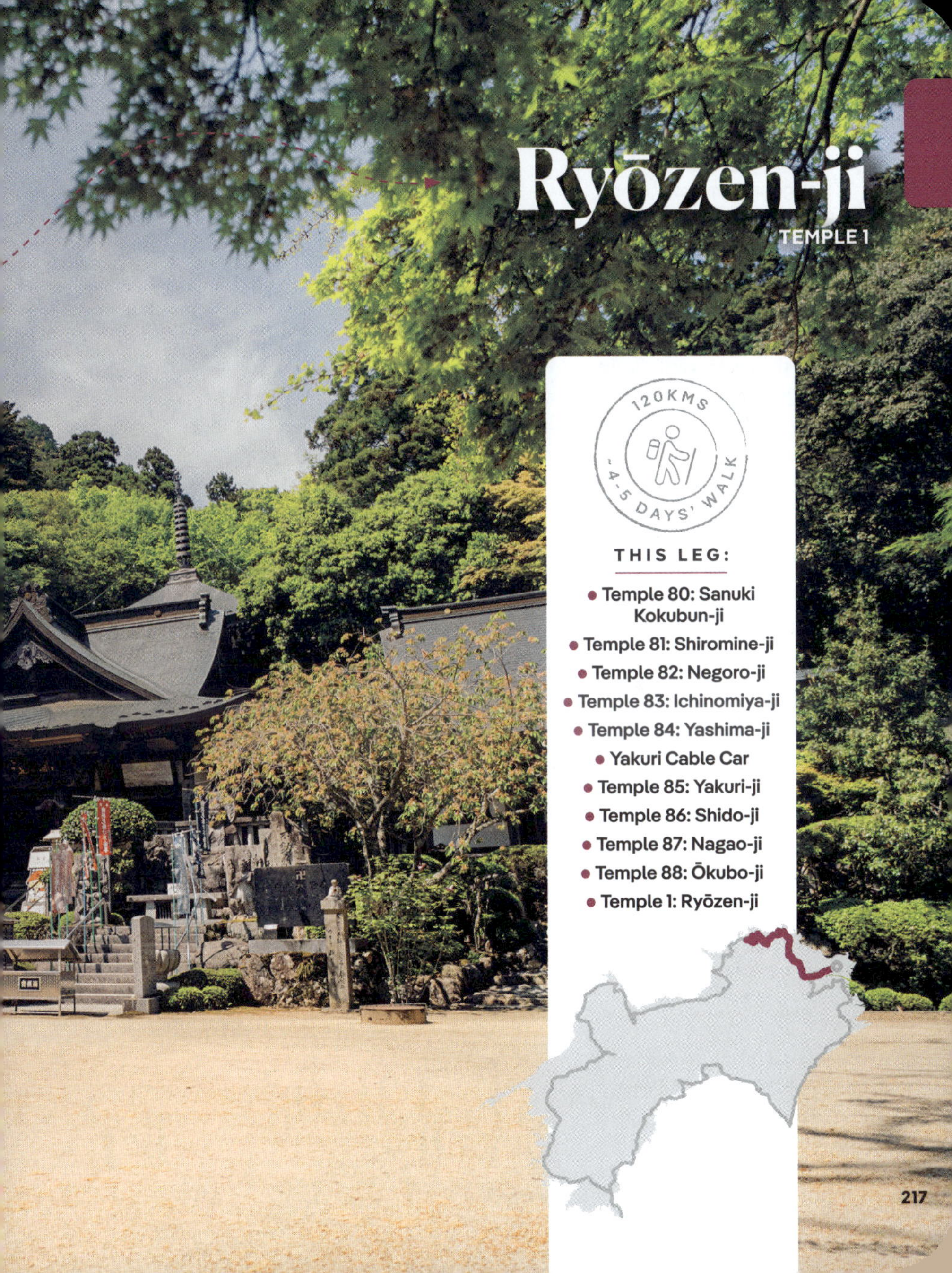

Ryōzen-ji

TEMPLE 1

THIS LEG:

- Temple 80: Sanuki Kokubun-ji
- Temple 81: Shiromine-ji
- Temple 82: Negoro-ji
- Temple 83: Ichinomiya-ji
- Temple 84: Yashima-ji
  - Yakuri Cable Car
- Temple 85: Yakuri-ji
- Temple 86: Shido-ji
- Temple 87: Nagao-ji
- Temple 88: Ōkubo-ji
- Temple 1: Ryōzen-ji

Walking Notes

This stage has some good *henro-michi* (pilgrim tracks) up to and on the Goshikidai plateau, then urban walking on roads through Takamatsu city (p210). It's only appropriate that there should be good climbs up to Temples 84 and 85 and, of course, who wouldn't want to climb another mountain on the way to Temple 88: Ōkubo-ji?

Breaking Your Journey

There are lots of places to stay and eat around Takamatsu city. *Henro* need to think about what do after reaching Temple 88: Ōkubo-ji, though. It's a full 38km back to Temple 1: Ryōzen-ji, so either stay around Temple 88 or aim to get out south into the Yoshino-gawa valley to make the next day a lot easier.

Craig's Tips

MAKE THE EFFORT Take the *henro-michi* over 774m Nyōtai-san to Temple 88: Ōkubo-ji (p231).

FAVOURITE VIEW A glorious panorama awaits from Temple 84: Yashima-ji (p226).

ESSENTIAL STOP It's worth dropping into the Henro Museum (p232).

TOP TIP *Henro* with wheels can ride the Yakuri Cable Car to Temple 85: Yakuri-ji (p229).

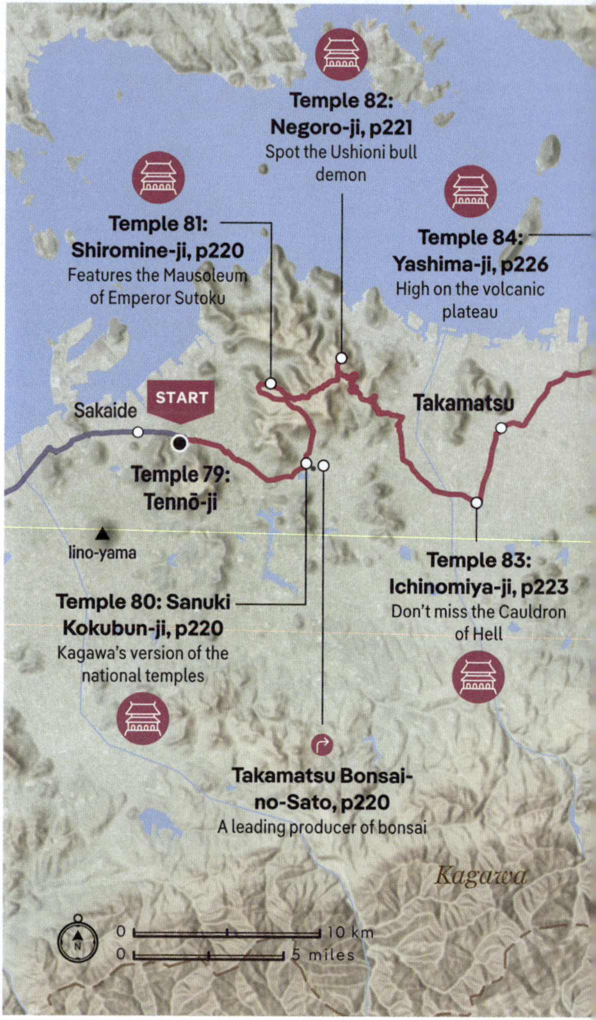

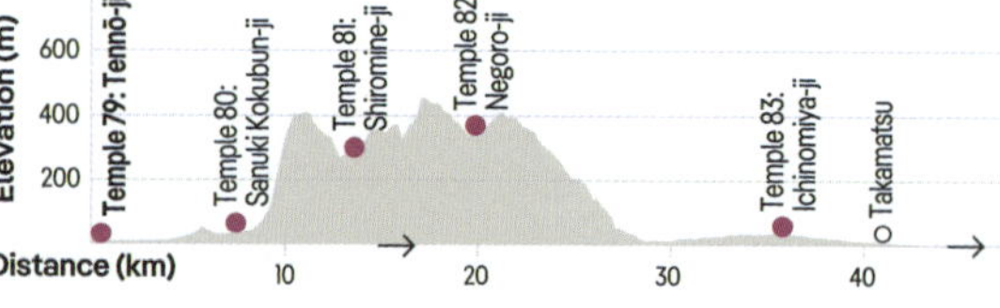

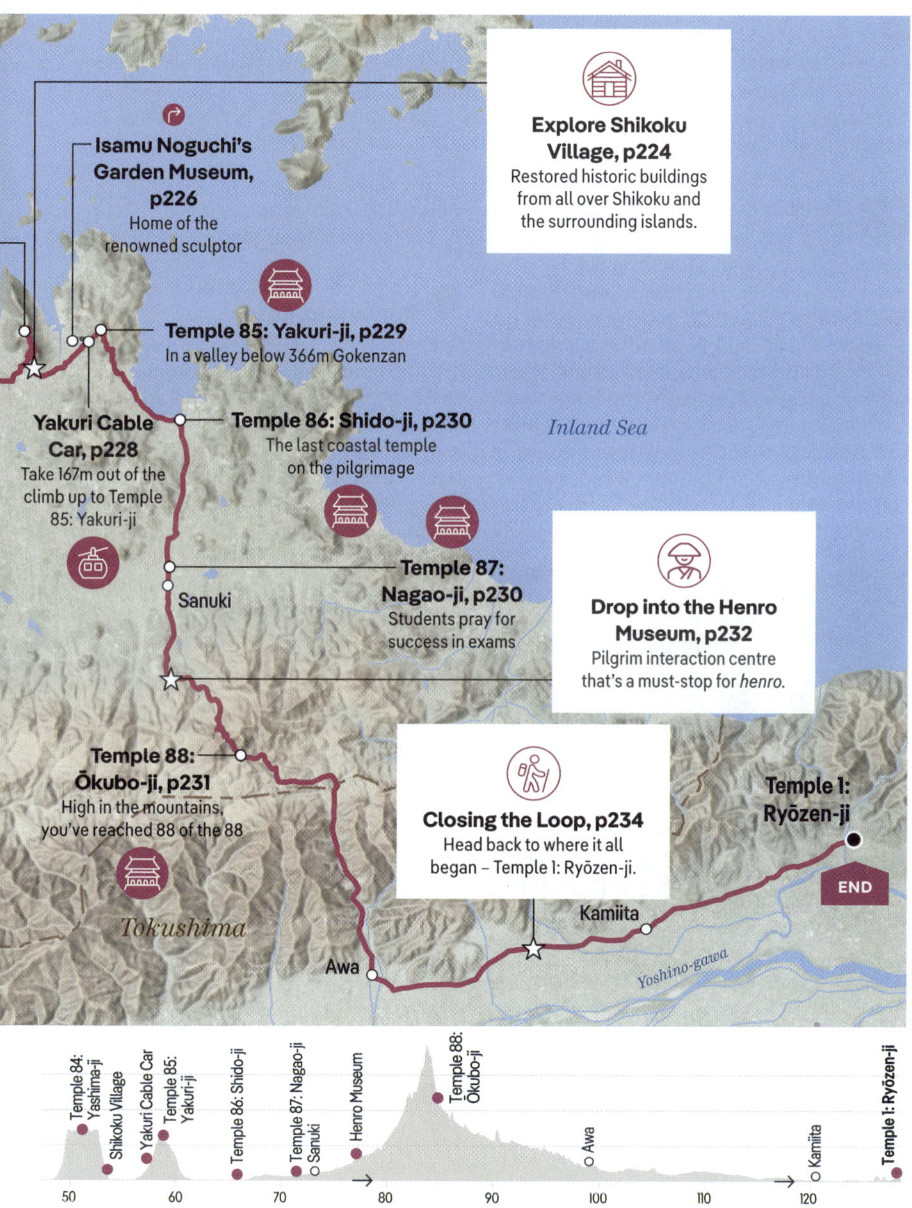
Explore Shikoku Village, p224
Restored historic buildings from all over Shikoku and the surrounding islands.

Isamu Noguchi's Garden Museum, p226
Home of the renowned sculptor

Temple 85: Yakuri-ji, p229
In a valley below 366m Gokenzan

Yakuri Cable Car, p228
Take 167m out of the climb up to Temple 85: Yakuri-ji

Temple 86: Shido-ji, p230
The last coastal temple on the pilgrimage

Inland Sea

Temple 87: Nagao-ji, p230
Students pray for success in exams

Sanuki

Drop into the Henro Museum, p232
Pilgrim interaction centre that's a must-stop for henro.

Temple 88: Ōkubo-ji, p231
High in the mountains, you've reached 88 of the 88

Closing the Loop, p234
Head back to where it all began – Temple 1: Ryōzen-ji.

Temple 1: Ryōzen-ji

END

Kamiita

Tokushima

Awa

Yoshino-gawa

Temple 84: Yashima-ji
Shikoku Village
Yakuri Cable Car
Temple 85: Yakuri-ji
Temple 86: Shido-ji
Temple 87: Nagao-ji
Sanuki
Henro Museum
Temple 88: Ōkubo-ji
Awa
Kamiita
Temple 1: Ryōzen-ji

50   60   70   80   90   100   110   120

 From Temple 79: Tennō-ji head east in the valley, between the hills, for the 7km walk to Temple 80: Sanuki Kokubun-ji. Visiting the temples in numerical order is the standard route, but some pilgrims visit Temples 81 and 82 up in the mountains first, then come back to Temple 80 in the valley below. There's no requirement to visit the temples in a specific order.

Temple 80: Sanuki Kokubun-ji

It's a 7km walk from Temple 79 to the fourth of the national temples on Shikoku that were established in 741 CE, **Temple 80: Sanuki Kokubun-ji** (讃岐国分寺; *sanukikokubunji.jp*).

Sanuki Kokubun-ji is proud of a couple of claims. It is the only pilgrimage temple where the entire original precincts are designated a Special National Historic Site, and the **temple bell** is the oldest on Shikoku. It's also claimed that if the former seven-storey pagoda had survived, it would be larger than the five-storey pagoda of Tō-ji Temple in Kyoto. Unfortunately, only the foundation stones remain. The temple is quite active on Instagram @sanukikokubunji.

DETOUR: Takamatsu Bonsai-no-Sato

Takamatsu city (p210) is known as one of the leading producers of bonsai (miniature trees) in Japan, with some 60 gardens and nurseries in the Kokubun-ji and Kinashi neighbourhoods, growing mainly miniature pine trees. Opened in 2020, **Takamatsu Bonsai-no-Sato** (*Takamatsu Bonsai Centre; takamatsu-bonsai.com*) is only a 10-minute walk from Temple 80. This is a good place to learn about bonsai and its different styles. About 80% of Japan's bonsai pines are grown around here, mainly local Japanese black pine. The centre's market attracts bonsai professionals from throughout the country.

Temple 81: Shiromine-ji

Temple 81: Shiromine-ji (白峯寺; *shiromineji.com*) sits close to 300m in elevation on the sprawling Goshikidai lava plateau that dominates everything between Sakaide city to its west and Takamatsu city to its east. *Goshiki* means 'five colours' and the five high points here are named Aomine (blue), Kiinomine (yellow), Kōnomine (red), Kuromine (black) and Shiramine (white). Shiromine-ji (White Peak Temple) is at the westernmost peak, Shiramine (White Peak). The *henro-michi* to get up here from Temple

Statue, Temple 81: Shiromine-ji

The fourth and last of the national temples

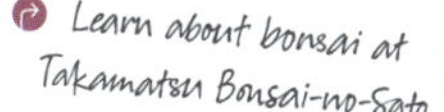

Temple 82: Negoro-ji

80 is recognised as one of the *henro-korogashi* (pilgrims fall down), so watch your step and take your time. It's only an 8km walk, but because of the big climb, allow two to three hours. On the approach to the temple there are spectacular views of the Inland Sea (Seto-nai-kai).

There's a lot to see up here, including lovely temple buildings, statues, tall trees and the Mausoleum of Emperor Sutoku (p207). Temple 81 is active on Instagram @shiromineji81.

Temple 82: Negoro-ji

A 5km walk east from Temple 81 across the Goshikidai plateau, mainly on relatively easy *henro-michi*, will bring pilgrims to **Temple**

BEST PLACES TO EAT

Udon Honjin Yamadaya, below Temple 85 ¥¥
Even in *udon-ken* (udon noodle prefecture; see p195), this place, at the foot of Gokenzan and Temple 85: Yakuri-ji, is considered special; make the effort. *yamada-ya.com; 11am-3pm Mon, Tue, Thu & Fri, 10am-8pm Sat & Sun*

Michi-no-eki Nagao, opposite Henro Museum ¥
Fuel up here for the final climb to Temple 88: Ōkubo-ji; there's a choice of snacks, farm produce, cafe or full set meals. *8am-4pm*

Yasoba-an, Temple 88 ¥¥
Celebrate getting to Temple 88 with *uchikomi-udon* (miso soup udon) at the bottom of the stone steps; ask for a paper bib! 八十八庵; *8am-4pm*

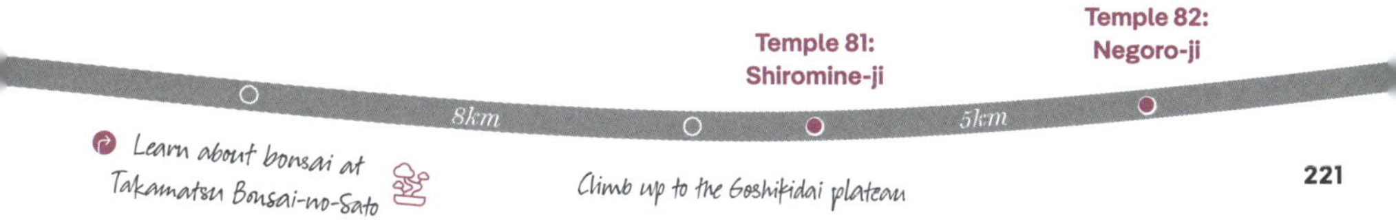

Temple 81:
Shiromine-ji

Temple 82:
Negoro-ji

8km

5km

Learn about bonsai at Takamatsu Bonsai-no-Sato

Climb up to the Goshikidai plateau

BRESTER IRINA/SHUTTERSTOCK

Temple 83: Ichinomiya-ji

GETTING INTO HOT WATER

While Shikoku isn't as blessed with as many natural hot spring onsen as the more volcanic of Japan's islands, it's doubtful you'll have got this far on the pilgrimage without getting into an onsen, or at least a *sento* (public bath). **Kirara Onsen** *(kiraraonsen. com),* only a five-minute walk from Temple 83: Ichinomiya-ji, is embracing the pilgrimage and foreign *henro* with gusto. It has an English-language website and offers the **onsen** *(¥750),* plus its very reasonable restaurant and overnight lodging, to *henro.* Soak away your aches and pains here as you prepare for the last few temples.

82: Negoro-ji (根香寺), at 370m in elevation. It is on Aomine (Blue Peak), the main peak on Goshikidai. Negoro-ji (Fragrant Root Temple) is so-named as after Kōbō Daishi carved a statue of a thousand-armed Kannon, the stump of the tree he carved it from emitted an aromatic fragrance.

You'll encounter lots of steps for climbing and descending here, plus a scary statue of the Ushioni, a bull demon that ate people. Legend says that it was killed by the master archer, Takakiyo, who cut off its horns, dedicating them to the temple, where they are still preserved. Temple amulets featuring the *ushioni* are bought by worshippers to ward off evil. The *hondō* (main

Temple 82: Negoro-ji

13km

Down onto the flatlands of Takamatsu city

hall) features corridors containing an incredible 33,000 metal statues of Kannon that have benn dedicated by worshippers from all over Japan.

Temple 83: Ichinomiya-ji

There's a big descent now from Temple 82, at 370m, out to busy suburban **Temple 83: Ichinomiya-ji** (一宮寺; *sanuki-ichinomiyaji. or.jp, @ichinomiyaji.83*) on the plain in Takamatsu city, but well south of the central business district. It's a 13km walk in all, but flat once out on the plain.

Ichinomiya is a historical term used for the Shintō shrine with the highest rank in each province; below it in rank were *ninomiya* (second) and *sannomiya* (third). **Tamura-jinja**, right next door to Ichinomiya-ji, was the *ichinomiya* for Sanuki Province, so the temple next to the top-ranking shrine has a very Shintō-related name, further evidence of the syncretism of Shintō and Buddhism throughout Japanese history.

At the temple, don't miss the **Cauldron of Hell**, a small building that houses a statue of Yakushi, god of healing. There's a gap in the front that's wide enough for a *henro* to stick their head through to hear the sounds of hell. This is very popular among visiting worshippers, despite the fact that it is also said that if someone who has committed sins sticks their head in, the doors will close and they'll never be able to get their head out again.

Continues on page 226

Along the Way We Met...

KIM, MIKE & LANGLEY We love hiking and we've always wanted to come to Japan. We designed our own trip and are here for two months. Our daughter Langley has joined us for three weeks. We walked Temples 1 to 12, and now from Temple 79 to 87. After that we'll go to the 'art island' of Naoshima (p215). Then we're going to the Kumano Kudō. We love the spiritual aspect of the walk, but didn't want to spend our two months only here on Shikoku.

The Topper family is from San Francisco, visiting Japan to celebrate Mike's recent retirement.

KIM, MIKE & LANGLEY'S TIP: *Shikoku is wonderful. Make the effort to get here, even if you don't walk the whole pilgrimage.*

Temple 83: Ichinomiya-ji

Explore Shikoku Village

At the foot of Yashima and virtually right on the pilgrim trail, Shikoku-mura has 33 restored historic buildings relocated here from all the four prefectures of Shikoku and surrounding islands.

HOW TO

Nearest stop: Temple 84: Yashima-ji

Getting here: Shikoku-mura is a 500m walk north from Yashima Station on the Kotoden Shido line.

When to go: 9am-5pm Wed-Mon

Cost: Adult/child ¥1600/600

Tip: Fuel up with a bowl of udon at Waraya, the thatched-roof noodle shop by the park entrance.

More info: shikokumura.or.jp

Covering a large area in the forested foothills below Yashima, **Shikoku-mura** showcases historic buildings that have been renovated and moved here from all over Shikoku and its neighbouring islands. The buildings include houses, workshops, community buildings, a theatre, rice storehouses, a soy-sauce brewery, lighthouses and more. All were built during a period ranging from 1603 to 1926, and each one was used in real life at its original location before being moved here.

Vine Bridge

Just inside the entrance is a *kazura-bashi,* a vine bridge of the kind you'll have seen if you visited the Iya Valley (p194). It was recreated here by expert artisans, using 3.5 tonnes of vine. Legend says that soldiers of the Heike clan, having lost the battle of Yashima, almost directly above Shikoku-mura, in 1185, hid in the remote Iya Valley

and designed the vine bridges to be easily cut down when pursued.

Lighthouse Precinct

Furthest from the entrance is the lighthouse precinct, with an 1893 stubby white lighthouse of hewn granite blocks that used to stand on Okunoshima in Hiroshima Prefecture. Beside it are the impressive lighthouse keeper's residences from Esaki, Awajishima Island (1871); Nabeshima, an island off Sakaide, Kagawa Prefecture (1873); and Kudakoshima, off Matsuyama city, Ehime Prefecture (1903).

GALLERY & REFRESHMENTS

In a nod to the modern world, visitors will also find the **Shikoku-mura Gallery**, completed in 2002 and designed by renowned Japanese architect Tadao Andō. This modern concrete structure displays works of art from all over the world. Refreshments are readily available at the atmospheric **Waraya udon noodle shop**, in a converted *kominka* (old house), and the **Shikoku-mura Cafe**, housed in an old *ijinkan* (foreign residence) from Kōbe

Left: Shikoku Village
Below: Okunoshima lighthouse

Farmers' Kabuki Theatre

During the Edo period (1603–1868), kabuki stages were built throughout Japan for villagers to perform plays for entertainment. Shikoku-mura's fine kabuki stage came from Shōdoshima in the Inland Sea, famous for its traditional farmers' kabuki performances. The stage is now an outdoor theatre for Shikoku-mura's events, festivals and displays, with audience seating made of tiered stonework. The centre of the kabuki stage features a revolving section 4.7m across; look beneath the stage to view the old mechanisms that make it move.

Continued from page 223

Temple 84: Yashima-ji

There are a few options for walking from Temple 83 to **Temple 84: Yashima-ji** (屋島寺), about 15km all up. One is to take a zig-zagging route on modern urban roads, while the more pleasant, though slightly longer option involves following the Gobo-gawa on its way to the sea.

As its name suggests, Yashima (meaning 'Roof Island') was once separated from the mainland as an island. When the first temple was built around 750 CE, when Kōbō Daishi visited in 815 CE and when the Battle of Yashima took place in 1185, it was an island; however, landfill dating back to the 1600s filled the channel. Nowadays, it's a 293m-high volcanic plateau with Temple 84 on top and a steep final climb to get there. From 1929 to 2005, Yashima Cable Car whisked *henro* up to the temple, but patronage dropped and it closed when the 3.7km-long Yashima Skyway scenic road to the top opened.

The temple is a beauty with soaring views. This is the site of the battle that Minamoto Yoshitsune and legendary warrior Benkei were heading to when they stopped at Temple 3: Konsen-ji (p50) to pray for victory and Benkei showed his strength by lifting the *Benkei-no-chikaraishi*. Check out the **Pond of Blood** at the temple, where victorious warriors are said to have washed the blood from their swords.

Henro with wheels can drive up Yashima Skyway toll-free, with glorious views of the Inland Sea and its islands along the way.

DETOUR: Isamu Noguchi's Garden Museum

Born in Los Angeles to a Japanese poet and an American writer, Isamu Noguchi (1904–88) set up a studio and residence in the town of **Mure**, at the foot of Gokenzan, in 1970. He was seeking a place where he could learn more about stone and dedicate himself to his iconic, large-scale works in granite and basalt. Mure's quiet environment and the beauty of the local landscape provided inspiration for his work and exploration in stone. Noguchi developed a strong working relationship with local stonecutter Masatoshi Izumi, spending about six months of each year in Mure during the last two decades of his life.

The **Garden Museum** (*isamunoguchi.or.jp; admission ¥3300; entry by tour 10am, 1pm & 3pm Tue, Thu & Sat Sep-Jun, 10am & 11.30am Tue, Thu, Sat Jul & Aug)* is filled with hundreds

Temple 84: Yashima-ji

Temple 83: Ichinomiya-ji

Drop into Shikoku Village

15km

Yakuri Cable Car (p228)

of Isamu Noguchi's works, mostly unfinished. Inspiring sculptures are displayed in beautifully restored buildings and in the surrounding landscape. Visitors can also check out the house in which Noguchi lived.

Henro will have to be organised in order to visit: bookings must be made online at least 24 hours in advance. The Garden Museum is only 1.2km on foot from Yakuri Cable Car's bottom station (p228).

HENRO WITH WHEELS

- Allow one to two days for this leg.
- With a car, it's easy to visit Temples 79 to 87 from lively Takamatsu city (p210), where there are lots of accommodation and eating options.
- It's easier to visit Temple 88: Ōkubo-ji, then carry on through the mountains to the Yoshino-gawa valley in Tokushima and continue on to Temple 1: Ryōzen-ji.
- From Takamatsu, it's 35km to Temple 88: Ōkubo-ji and only another 38km on to Temple 1: Ryōzen-ji.

Temple 84:
Yashima-ji

Detour to Isamu Noguchi's
Sculpture Garden

BRESTER IRINA/SHUTTERSTOCK

BEST PLACES TO SLEEP

Fujiya Ryokan, near Temple 86 ¥
This place doubles as a *ryokan* (Japanese-style inn) and a sushi restaurant; sets you up nicely with 20km to walk to Temple 88 the next day. *fujiyaryokan.info*

Minshuku Nagaoji, Temple 87 ¥
Nothing fancy here, but it's right in front of Temple 87: Nagao-ji; a good option for those planning to walk to Temple 88, then carry on the same day towards Temple 1. *nagaozi.com*

Minshuku Yasokubo, Temple 88 ¥
This is the only spot to stay around Temple 88: Ōkubo-ji; go back and enjoy the temple in the evening. Cash only. *yasokubo.com.*

Yakuri Cable Car

First opened in 1931, this cute little retro **cable car** (*shikoku-cable.co.jp; adult/ child one-way ¥600/300, return ¥1000/500; every 15min 7.30am-5.15pm*) takes 167m out of the climb up to Temple 85: Yakuri-ji and is popular with day-trippers and families. Better described as a funicular railway, Yakuri Cable Car is a fun option for those not dedicated to walking and kids especially enjoy it. The autumn colours are particularly admired here, usually from late October, and there's some of the best udon going at Udon Honjin Yamadaya (p221) near the bottom station.

The cable car is only 700m long and takes only four minutes to get to the top station. Many

Temple 84:
Yashima-ji

Yakuri
Cable Car

6km

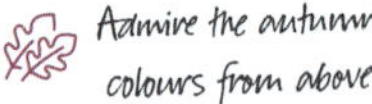
Admire the autumn colours from above

Temple 85: Yakuri-ji

visitors ride the cable car up, explore the temple underneath the soaring cliffs, then walk back down. The cable car can get busy on weekends and during Japanese holiday periods. It is easily accessed by train from Takamatsu city by the Kotoden Shido line (Yakuri Station) and JR Takamatsu line (Yakuri-guchi Station), then by taxi to the lower cable car station.

Temple 85: Yakuri-ji

It may be only 6km from Temple 84 to **Temple 85: Yakuri-ji** (八栗寺; *yakuriji.jp)* but it certainly tests a *henro's* resolve, descending from Yashima-ji at 293m to sea level, then climbing back up to Yakuri-ji at 236m. It's almost

enough to make walkers want to use the Yakuri Cable Car.

Yakuri-ji sits directly below 366m **Gokenzan** (五剣山), meaning 'Five Sword Mountain', and it's said that Kōbō Daishi buried five heavenly swords here in 829 CE and named the mountain accordingly. If you argue that it looks like there are only four peaks, take into account that there was a major earthquake in 1706 and one of them collapsed.

It's also said that before the Daishi went to China, he planted eight roasted chestnuts, and that on his return, the chestnuts had sprouted and grown into trees; the existing temple was renamed Yakuri-ji (Eight Chestnuts Temple).

700m

**Temple 85:
Yakuri-ji**

Down to the last coastal temple

Unlike Temple 84, which stands exposed on the top of the mountain, Yakuri-ji is in a protected valley below the peaks, almost under the steep cliffs. Its remoteness didn't save it from Chōsokabe Motochika's temple burning though, and after he'd been through in the early 1580s, it was rebuilt in 1642. Views out towards Yashima and central Kagawa Prefecture are superb.

Temple 86: Shido-ji

It's a nice easy 7km walk from Temple 85, firstly downhill, then along the coast to **Temple 86: Shido-ji** (志度寺). The temple is almost right on the water at Shido Port, with the *niōmon* (main gate) and its two mammoth straw sandals being designated a National Cultural Property. **Muzentei** (Immaculate Garden) is a stunning landscaped rock and raked-sand garden that shouldn't be missed, while the 33m-tall, **five-storey pagoda** is a reconstruction, completed in 1975. Founded in 625 CE, 2025 saw Shido-ji mark its 1400-year anniversary, making it one of the oldest temples on Shikoku.

Excitement is likely to be building about now as *henro* turn south and inland towards the mountains, with two – make that three – temples to go.

Temple 87: Nagao-ji

It's another easy 7km walk south from Temple 86 to **Temple 87: Nagao-ji** (長尾寺; *nagaoji.com*). At the extensive, sandy grounds here, students and anxious parents come to pray for success in entrance exams. The temple bell hangs inside the main gate, which was built in 1694 and is one of the oldest surviving buildings on the grounds. Like at Temple 86, the gate is flanked by a pair of massive straw sandals, and once you pass through, you're in the shade of a massive *kusunoki* (camphor tree). The East Gate had a previous life at Ritsurin Garden in Takamatsu city and was moved here in 1913.

Temple 87: Nagao-ji

SANGA PARK/SHUTTERSTOCK

Along the Way We Met...

MICHAEL This is my second time walking the Shikoku pilgrimage. I did it in 2023, then did the Camino in 2024 and now I'm back here this year. I did a lot of research after the first time and realised I missed a lot. This time I'm back to do it better. I make sure to allow an hour at each temple to appreciate it and not just rush on through. Everyone's pilgrimage is different, and every pilgrim is out here for their own reasons.

Michael is a retiree from Canada with an endearing sense of humour.

MICHAEL'S TIP: *Read online blogs and the pilgrimage Facebook pages; there's a lot of good advice in these resources.*

On the grounds, there is a **monument to Lady Shizuka** (1165–1211), a tragic figure who was the mistress of Minamoto Yoshitsune (1159–89), the military leader of the Minamoto clan, who along with Benkei, won the Battle of Yashima at the site of Temple 84: Yashima-ji. Later, Yoshitsune became a fugitive and, to avoid capture, the lovers split up. It's said that Shizuka and her mother came to Nagao-ji, deciding to become Buddhist nuns here, and that Shizuka shaved off her hair, which is famously buried under a mound near the monument.

Temple 88: Ōkubo-ji

Only *henro* of stern will are not excited as they head south towards the mountains on the 13km walk to **Temple 88: Ōkubo-ji** (大窪寺). They should keep reminding themselves, however, that there is still a big mountain to climb on the way to Ōkubo-ji and that there's still a 38km walk to get back to Temple 1: Ryōzen-ji to complete the circle of Shikoku. It's not all over at Temple 88.

It's 6km of relatively easy walking to get to the Henro Museum (p232) at elevation 148m, before the tough test begins.

Henro on wheels will follow the roads deep into the mountains, find a large parking lot, and enter Ōkubo-ji through the modern, concrete *niōmon* on the west side. The wooden Niten Gate leads to the temple via stone steps from the small village below on the south side, while walkers, if they hike the *henro-michi,* will come

Continues on page 233

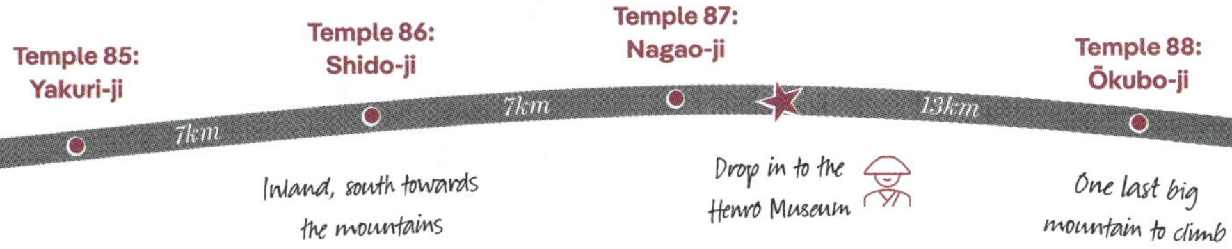

Drop into the Henro Museum

Also known as Maeyama Ohenro Koryū Salon, this place on the route between Temples 87 and 88 is a must-stop for walking *henro*.

HOW TO

Nearest stop: Temple 87: Nagao-ji

Getting here: It's 6km south of Temple 87 on the pilgrimage route.

When to go: 8am-4pm daily

Cost: Free

Help: Sign the guest book to help museum staff track the number of visitors as part of a push to achieve UNESCO World Heritage status.

Tip: Fuel up at the *Michi-no-eki* (roadside rest stop) with restaurants over the road; there's nothing after here until you get to Temple 88: Ōkubo-ji.

Best described as a pilgrim interaction centre, the **Henro Museum** is at 148m in elevation, beside the artificial lake on the Kabe-gawa, some 6km south of Temple 87. It's a popular resting spot for pilgrims before they make their final mountain climb on the way to Temple 88. Opened in 1999, the museum boasts a large collection of his-

torical artefacts and information on the pilgrimage. There's not a lot in English but there's usually an English-speaker on hand. Exhibits include a copy of the oldest *henro* guidebook from 1687 and the oldest stone path marker from 1781.

The highlight though, is a huge three-dimensional map of Shikoku just inside the entrance that illustrates just how mountainous the island is, and shows the temple locations and pilgrimage routes. It's amazing just how much a paper map or smartphone can make a mountainous island look flat.

If you've walked or ridden a bicycle from Temple 1: Ryōzen-ji, pick up an A4-size 'Pilgrim Henro Ambassador' certificate, which certifies that you have completed the pilgrimage (even though you haven't at this stage!).

Henro Museum

CRAIG MCLACHLAN/LONELY PLANET

BRESTER IRINA/SHUTTERSTOCK

Temple 88: Ōkubo-ji (p231)

Continued from page 231
tumbling down into the temple on the trail from the mountains above.

The *henro-michi* up to Nyōtai-san, at 774m, is a *henro-korogashi,* followed by a short, sharp descent into Ōkubo-ji at 450m. Chances are that *henro* will hear the temple before they see it, with the booming of the bell announcing the arrival of countless visitors.

Ōkubo-ji translates to 'Temple of the Big Cave' and it's said that in 815, when Kōbō Daishi returned from China, he was committed to ascetic practice at the cave where the present *okunoin* (inner sanctuary) is located.

The grounds here at Ōkubo-ji are gorgeous and it's definitely a place to take your time. Beneath the Daishi-dō (Daishi Hall) is an underground passage where worshippers can make a symbolic visit to all the 88 temples. Many *henro* leave their *kongō-zue* (staff) here to be burnt at an outdoor fire ritual.

Temple 88:
Ōkubo-ji

Temple 1:
Ryōzen-ji

38km

Head back to the beginning to close the loop

Closing the Circle

While some pilgrims are just happy to get to Temple 88, the essence of the pilgrimage is to close the circle of Shikoku by returning to Temple 1: Ryōzen-ji – for a circle is never-ending, just like the search for enlightenment.

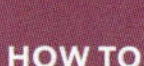

HOW TO

To Temple 1: There are various routes shown on the Henro Helper app for walking back to Temple 1, but the most commonly used for first-time walking *henro* is to carry on east from Temple 88: Ōkubo-ji for 5km, then turn almost directly south on the road following the Higaidani-gawa out to the Yoshino valley, near Temple 10: Kirihata-ji. It's about 38km all up; allow 18km for getting to the Yoshino valley, then 20km walking east to get back to Temple 1.

From Temple 1: Wander down to JR Bandō Station and take an hourly train into Tokushima city (21 minutes).

The Last Leg

Most *henro* have been planning ahead for days as to what to do after they get to Temple 88: Ōkubo-ji.

Arrive late in the day and the best move is to stay near the temple. **Minshuku Yasokubo** (*yasokubo.com; ¥)* is close, friendly and offers meals (cash only). Book the meals as there are not many eateries around Temple 88 and what there is closes early, as soon as the day-trippers leave. The following day, *henro* are facing a 38km walk to get back to Temple 1: Ryōzen-ji.

Arrive early in the day at Temple 88 and – after doing your *mairi* (rituals) and getting a temple stamp – *henro* are looking at an 18km walk south to get out of the mountains and into the Yoshino Valley near Temple 10: Kirihata-ji, where there are some accommodation options (see the Henro Helper app). They are then

faced with a 20km walk to get back to Temple 1: Ryōzen-ji the following day.

Depending on progress, make this decision a few days beforehand and have accommodation booked.

Been There Before!

Back in the Yoshino valley and walking east, drop in for tea and a chat with Asano-san at **Sumotoriya Asano Pilgrim Shop** (p55) as you pass Temple 10: Kirihata-ji. It's a nice easy walk past all those temples that were easily visited in the first

EXPERIENCE ★

VISITING THE DAISHI

A most traditional pilgrimage involves visiting Kōbō Daishi at **Kōya-san** twice, asking for his support before going to Shikoku and thanking him for that support on a safe return. Some *henro* go only after completing the circle of Shikoku, and some don't go at all. The *okunoin* at Kōya-san is arguably the most intensely spiritual place in all of Japan. The Daishi is believed to be in a state of eternal meditation here at his mausoleum at this mountaintop monastery complex where he based his Shingon school of Buddhism.

Temple 1: Ryōzen-ji (p48)

couple of days of your pilgrimage, some 1200km and a lot of experiences ago.

Back at Temple 1: Ryōzen-ji

Back at where it all started (p48), *henro* complete their *mairi*, get their temple stamp and sign out of the logbook for walkers. It's all very low-key; it might be a big moment for the *henro* who has just completed their pilgrimage, but temple staff have seen it all before. If it's you, pat yourself on the back for a job well done.

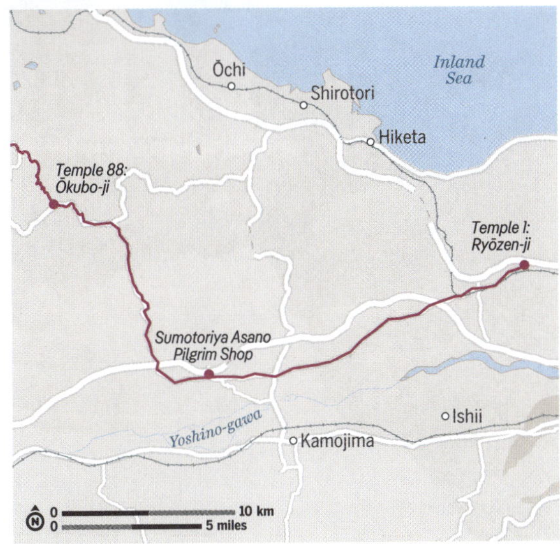

Toolkit

First Time

238

Money

239

Packing

240

Health & Fitness

242

On the Path

243

How to Visit a Temple

246

Where to Stay

247

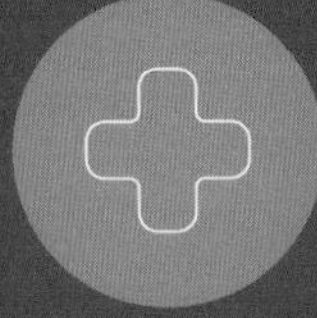

Access, Attitudes & Safety

248

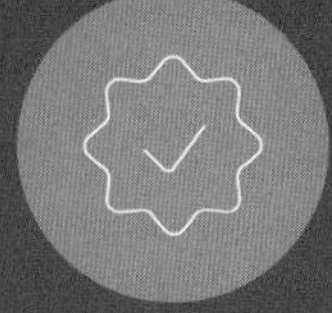

Responsible Travel

249

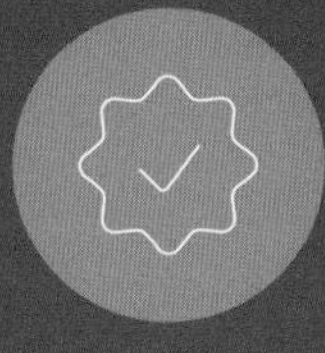

Language

251

Statue, Temple 64: Maegami-ji (p185)

CRAIG MCLACHLAN/LONELY PLANET

First Time

For information on arriving and airports see **Tokushima** (p34).

DRINKING IN JAPAN

The legal drinking age in Japan is 20. You may be asked for ID or to declare you're of legal age at the point of sale by pushing an on-screen button. There are harsh penalties for operating a vehicle under the influence – a blood alcohol limit of 0.03% applies to cars and a breath alcohol concentration below 0.15mg/litre for bicycles. Some pilgrims abstain from alcohol during their pilgrimage as part of their spiritual journey.

Visas & Arrival

Citizens of over 70 countries, including the US, UK, Australia, New Zealand, Canada and most European countries, entering Japan for tourism or other short-stay purposes are eligible for a visa on arrival, typically for a duration of 90 days. To check visa eligibility and requirements, head to the **Ministry of Foreign Affairs Japan website** (*mofa.go.jp/j_info/visit/visa/*). Complete your immigration and customs declarations ahead of time on **Visit Japan Web** (*vjw.digital.go.jp/*).

Travel Insurance

Travel insurance is advised. Note that Japanese clinics and hospitals only accept Japan-issued health insurance. For international claims, you'll need to pay upfront, collect receipts and then apply for reimbursement from your insurance provider. The cost of medical treatment in Japan is low compared to countries like the US, even for emergency care.

SIM Cards & Data

Staying connected is pertinent to safely navigate, check weather updates and contact accommodation. A Japanese phone number is your best bet for bookings, sending SMS, receiving emergency warnings and registering for in-country services. **Mobal eSIMs** (*mobal.com/japan-sim-card*) are a popular choice for pilgrims.

Language

Locals will often converse in regional dialects, but standard Japanese is understood across the country. In rural Shikoku, there is less English-language signage than in major tourist hubs. Language apps (like Google Translate) and a supportive pilgrim culture are there to guide you.

GREETINGS & PERSONAL SPACE

Personal space is highly valued in Japan. Handshakes, hugging and kissing are not part of Japanese greeting culture. Instead, verbal communication and bowing are the way to go. A shallower bow is fine for casual interactions; a deep bow is used to extend great gratitude, respect or apology.

ELECTRICITY 100V/60HZ

Type A: 100V/60Hz   **Type B:** 100V/60Hz

   FUSE/GETTY IMAGES

Money

Budgeting

Costs will vary dramatically depending on how many days you take to complete the pilgrimage, your mode of transportation, your choice of accommodation, the amount of pilgrim gear you buy, and more. That being said, a budget of ¥500,000 (not including airfares, transportation to Shikoku, travel insurance and sightseeing) is a rough estimate for 45 days, the average time for a walking pilgrim. Use **Henro.org's cost calculator** (henro.org/shikoku-pilgrimage/costs) to help determine estimated spending.

HOW MUCH IS
a day on the Shikoku pilgrimage?

Konbini breakfast	¥500
Temple offerings & stamps	¥2000
Lunch	¥800
Snacks & drinks	¥1000
Minshuku bed including dinner	¥7000
Total (per day for one adult)	**¥11,300**

TEMPLE STAMPS

Pilgrims should note that different stamp-collecting methods carry different price tags. Each stamp in a *nōkyō-chō* (stamp book) is ¥500, while for a scroll it's ¥700 (¥1000 at Temple 12: Shōsan-ji) and ¥300 for the white pilgrim vest (*hakui*). Temples may refuse to stamp a *hakui* being worn; you should have a separate one for collecting stamps.

Cash, ATMs & Credit Cards

While Japan is more credit-card-friendly than ever, many small guesthouses on the pilgrimage, along with a good number of businesses and attractions, are still cash-only. Always carry enough cash with you should card payment not be available. You can withdraw cash at ATMs using most internationally recognised cards (Visa, Plus, Mastercard etc) at most post offices and major convenience stores (7-Eleven, FamilyMart and Lawson).

Donations at Temples

It's customary to give a small monetary donation as part of your temple offerings. While you are free to give as much as you'd like, a ¥5 or ¥10 coin is perfectly acceptable. Donations are given a minimum of twice per temple – once at the *hondō* (main hall) and once at the Daishi-dō (Daishi Hall). Temples don't provide a change service, so keep a steady stream of small change on you. A coin purse, easily available at ¥100 stores, is a great idea.

Tipping

There is no tipping culture in Japan. In fact, it may give the impression you believe the business isn't doing well and hence can be perceived as an insult. At Japanese bars and *izakaya* (pub eateries), however, you're likely to encounter the compulsory appetiser known as *otōshi* (お通し). This is a small, unordered dish that arrives shortly after ordering (like edamame) and is automatically added to your bill (typically ¥300 to ¥500 per person). Consider it an edible cover charge.

OHLANLAA/SHUTTERSTOCK

Packing

CLOCKWISE FROM TOP LEFT: GRESEI/SHUTTERSTOCK, TARGET SHOT/SHUTTERSTOCK

Picking a Pack

A 35L backpack is the most common size used on the Shikoku pilgrimage. A larger bag is fine as long as you don't overfill it – remember you'll be carrying it for many hours a day. It's best to keep your pack under 5kg (not including water or snacks). Don't forget to account for any pilgrim gear you'll buy on arrival (p40).

Clothing

Most guesthouses have washing machines and dryers, which are either free for pilgrim use or available for a nominal fee (¥100 to ¥200). Keep it light and wash and wear.

- 1 pair comfortable **walking shoes**
- 3 pairs **T-shirts** – a moisture-wicking fabric is best
- 2 pairs **pants** or knee-length **shorts** – yes, shorts are permitted at temples
- 1 pair **waterproof pull-over pants**
- 3 pairs merino wool hiking **socks**
- 3 pairs **underwear**
- 1 **light fleece** or **jacket**
- 1 heavier **waterproof outer jacket**

FIRST-AID KIT

First-aid supplies are easy to replenish at pharmacies and convenience stores, so carry in small quantities • For blister prevention and management: **Vaseline** • **Plasters** • **Sports tape** • **Pin/needle** for popping blisters • **Antiseptic cream/ spray** to prevent infection • **General pain relief** Bufferin is a commonly available aspirin brand • **Antihistamine cream** for insect bites and stings • **Knee/ankle braces** for added support (if needed)

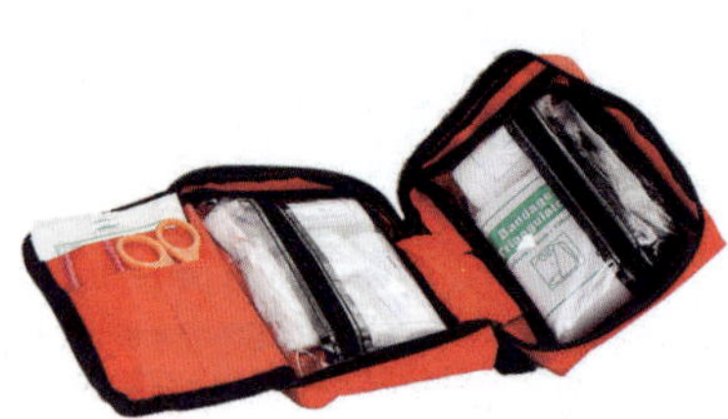

TOILETRIES

Toothbrush & toothpaste • **Hand sanitiser** • **Neutral-smelling deodorant** (perfumes and fragrant deodorants are not considered appropriate in many contexts in Japan) • **Sunscreen** • **Mosquito repellent** • **Lip balm** (stick) • **Essential personal care products** (the bare basics) • Pilgrim accommodation provides **body soap** and **shampoo**, so leave them out unless you have preferred products

CLOCKWISE FROM CAP: LIFESTYLE TRAVEL PHOTO/SHUTTERSTOCK, SKYROSESTUDIO/SHUTTERSTOCK, RUNRUN2/SHUTTERSTOCK, SURADECH PRAPAIRAT/SHUTTERSTOCK, NEW AFRICA/SHUTTERSTOCK, RESUL MUSLU/SHUTTERSTOCK, BOZIDAR ACIMOV/SHUTTERSTOCK., STAS MALYAREVSKIY/SHUTTERSTOCK, DMITRIY KAZITSYN/SHUTTERSTOCK, "CHAINUPONG HIPORN"/SHUTTERSTOCK, WASAN RITTHAWON/SHUTTERSTOCK, HEYMRPATRICK STUDIO/SHUTTERSTOCK, SUMOTORIYA ASANO, REFOX PHOTOS/ SHUTTERSTOCK

Health & Fitness

HYDRATION

Japanese summers are incredibly hot and humid – add in physical exertion and it's a recipe for heatstroke. Avoid June to August for your pilgrimage if you can. Stay hydrated and pace yourself. Electrolyte sports drinks Pocari Sweat (pictured below) and Aquarius are available at any convenience store.

Rest Days

No matter your level of preparation, there are a lot of physical and mental unknowns on a pilgrimage of this length. The best way to fortify yourself against guaranteed roadblocks is to give yourself enough time to work through them. Build rest days into your itinerary to use when you need them, recoup at hot springs, and allow yourself time to explore non-pilgrimage sights in the many interesting cities and towns you'll be passing through.

Temple Time

Minimise physical and mental stress by creating a realistic daily schedule. Temple stamps can only be obtained between 8am and 5pm (until 4.30pm at Temple 12: Shōsan-ji). Factor in a minimum of 20 minutes to visit the *hondō* and Daishi-dō, and get your stamp – more if you're using a scroll, which needs time to dry (hair dryers provided on-site), and if you want to explore the grounds. On some days, several hours may be spent at temples alone.

Caring for Your Feet

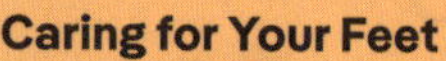

The best blister management is friction prevention. Your shoes should be neither too big nor too tight, and some pilgrims swear by Japan's five-toed socks (五本指ソックス; pictured right) to prevent rubbing between toes. Keep feet supple with Vaseline and if you do get a blister (likely at some point), tend to it quickly and repetitively until it clears.

Preparation

Most pilgrims don't do intense physical training for the Shikoku pilgrimage. That said, going into the pilgrimage with a good general level of fitness will help ease you in. If you aren't used to walking much in your daily life, try steadily increasing your number of steps and heading out on some local trails. Test out your shoes and bring your loaded backpack to see how light you can get it.

CLOCKWISE FROM TOP: CRAIG MCLACHLAN/LONELY PLANET, WILLEECOLE PHOTOGRAPHY/SHUTTERSTOCK, DESINTEGRATOR/SHUTTERSTOCK

On the Path

Pilgrimage Waymarkers

From JR Bandō Station in Tokushima, the closest train station to Temple 1: Ryōzen-ji, start your journey by walking the 'green line'. This literal green line painted on the road leads the way to Temple 1, the most common pilgrimage starting point. Signs assist in directing pilgrims to sacred sites along the pilgrimage route. Look out for red *'henro-michi'* (遍路道; へんろ道) signs with a pictogram of a pilgrim. That said, always use a map for navigation.

Henro Resources

There are many different and intersecting pilgrim paths on Shikoku and not all of them lead to the Shikoku pilgrimage. With numerous possible routes between temples, the free Henro Helper app is an indispensable companion. For paper maps, there's the *Shikoku Japan 88 Route Guide* (¥1980) and the *Pilgrimage Map Made by Everyone*. The latter has more detailed maps for walking pilgrims, but you'll need two volumes (¥2200 each) and a third if doing the *Bekkaku* (20 bonus temples).

The Hard Parts

Along the route are numerous *henro-korogashi* (遍路ころがし). Meaning 'pilgrims fall down,' these are particularly difficult, steep sections of the Shikoku pilgrimage. You may find businesses at the beginning of these trails willing to store your main pack or bicycle for free as a form of *osettai* (pilgrim hospitality). Two *henro-korogashi* have ropeways, namely Temple 21: Tairyū-ji and Temple 66: Unpen-ji, if you want a leg up on the mountain climb.

For a ready-made community and wealth of current information on the trail, join the Facebook group 'Shikoku 88 Ohenro Pilgrimage'. Check out the 'Files' section, which covers many FAQs, and use the search function. For anything you're still unsure about, ask away by making a post of your own.

HOW TO

CYCLE THE SHIKOKU PILGRIMAGE

Rent an e-bike for the duration of your pilgrimage from **Yeti & Ltb** (*yeti-ltb-eng.amebaownd.com*) in Tokushima; discounted rates for long-term rental apply. Free delivery is available within Tokushima city, including to Bandō Station and Temple 1: Ryōzen-ji. For reservations, contact **Ōsugi-san** (*ma-ony@docomo.ne.jp*).

TDUB303/GETTY IMAGES

Temple worker inscribing a *nōkyō-chō*

ACCEPTING OSETTAI

It's believed Kōbō Daishi walks with all pilgrims, so when locals give *osettai* (acts of hospitality) they believe they are giving gifts to Kōbō Daishi himself. Unless the *osettai* inhibits your safety or ability to complete the pilgrimage (eg offering a ride when you intend to walk), you should graciously accept *osettai,* even if you don't really need it. Express thanks by giving them an *osame-fuda* (name slip) in return (p19).

COMPLETION CERTIFICATE

At Temple 88: Ōku-bo-ji, pilgrims can obtain an official certificate called *kechi-gan-shō* (結願証), meaning 'fulfilment of one's wishes', for ¥2000. If you walked or cycled the entire route, you're eligible for an 'ambassador' certificate (free) from Henro Museum (p232). Pilgrims who used any mode of transport can get a free unofficial certificate from Tokushima Welcome Center.

Stamp Books

It is customary for pilgrims to carry a book known as *nōkyō-chō* (納経帳) for collecting temple stamps. In feudal times, when travel was only permitted under certain circumstances (like religious pilgrimage), the *nōkyō* (stamps) served as 'proof' of one's visit. Specifically, they are a record of dedicating sutras to a temple on a Buddhist pilgrimage. Each one features beautiful handwritten calligraphy and is unique to the temple it is received at. Pilgrims must have a stamp book specific to the Shikoku pilgrimage (available at Temple 1: Ryōzen-ji and Buddhist supply stores; ¥2500 to ¥4000); otherwise, temple offices may refuse to stamp it.

Hanging Scrolls

Pilgrims may also collect *nōkyō* on a silk hanging scroll called *nōkyō-jiku* (納経軸). Once completed, the scroll can optionally be mounted onto an ornate backing by a specialist artisan to create an exquisite commemorative piece to hang on your wall at home. Buddhist supply store Sumotoriya Asano (p55), near Temple 10: Kirihata-ji, specialises in high-quality and reasonably priced scrolls (from ¥15,000, including a soft cover), along with scroll mounting (from ¥41,800). The store's proprietor and professional scroll mounter, Asano Satoshi, speaks English and can assist foreign pilgrims with selecting scrolls, arranging mounting, and organising onward international shipping to your home address.

What if I would like more guidance ahead of my pilgrimage? Sign up for the 'Ohenro First Steps' orientation (¥2000; cash only) held almost daily at **Tokushima Welcome Center** *(info@tokushima-tour.jp)*, a two-minute walk from Tokushima Station. Learn what to do at temples, about pilgrim gear, getting around and more. Email for reservations or message via its Facebook page. It can also assist with Tokushima accommodation bookings (¥550 per request, in-person only).

What if I find myself in trouble? Website **Henro Help Desk** *(henrohelpdesk.com)* has a useful list of on-the-ground contacts. If you need in-person assistance, contact the **Henro Patrol Car**, facilitated by Taniguchi Norifumi of **Nojima House** *(facebook.com/groups/530682119240788)*. This network of saintly volunteers can provide support anywhere on the pilgrim trail. If you're able, a ¥2500 donation is appreciated. Message **Taniguchi-san** *(trombird3636@aurora.ocn.ne.jp, Facebook @taniguchi.norifumi)* and he'll organise the rest!

What should I do with my luggage? There's no system for luggage forwarding on the Shikoku pilgrimage. It's often possible to store an extra bag for free at accommodation in Tokushima if you stay with them a night before and after your pilgrimage. Four places near Temple 11: Fujii-dera coordinate free luggage delivery with inn **Sudachi-an** *(sudachian.com/book)* near Temple 12: Shōsan-ji to help pilgrims through this tough section.

JESSICA KORTEMAN/LONELY PLANET

RELAX

Don't be deterred by what seems a complicated process at first. Temple offerings will become second nature as you progress through your pilgrimage. Get acquainted by watching the excellent explanatory videos by **Scattered Blossoms** *(youtube.com/@ scattered-blossoms; scatteredblossoms. com)*. Or pick up an English edition of Temple 4: Dainichi-ji's own book, *Shikoku 88 Temple Pilgrimage Chanting Service*, detailing temple procedures, and translations and transliterations of sutras/mantras (¥1000). Recitations may also be made in any language.

How to Visit a Temple

Temple Etiquette

Visiting temples is core to the Shikoku pilgrimage experience. There are three main locations for a temple visit: the *hondō* (main hall), the Daishi-dō (Daishi Hall) and the *nōkyō-jō* (temple office). Time your visit with office opening hours. Keep noise to a minimum with soft speaking voices and quiet actions, and pay attention to signage on dos and don'ts. Be mindful of other worshippers and respect their privacy when taking photos or videos.

Performing Your Mairi

Main Gate (山門)

Stand to the left and bow once as you enter.

Wash Basin (水屋)

Purify your hands and mouth; water should flow onto the ground, not back into the basin. Put on your neck sash and prayer beads (if using them).

Bell Tower (鐘楼)

Signal your arrival by ringing the bell once. Set ringing hours may apply.

Main Hall (本堂)

Make offerings to the temple's main deity. Start by **lighting a candle** in the metal cabinet, placing it as far back as possible. **Light three sticks of incense** from your candle and place in the communal incense holder (pictured below) as close to the centre as possible. **Ring the bell** once. Place an **osame-fuda** (name slip) into the marked metal box (pictured above) and **shakyō** (handwritten sutra offerings) into the other. Make a **monetary donation** in the main offering box. Place hands together (or refer to a prayer book) and **recite the sutras/mantras**. Conclude with a **silent prayer or wish**, saying *arigatō gozaimashita* (thank you; literally 'it is difficult for such a thing to have existed') and bowing once. You may wish to simplify this by omitting the written sutras and only reciting *Hannya Shingyō* (the Heart Sutra) and the *Gohōgō mantra* (Praise Kōbō Daishi).

Daishi Hall (大師堂)

Repeat offerings at the Daishi-dō, this time to Kōbō Daishi. If you recited any mantras specific to the main deity at the *hondō* (such as the Gohonzon Shingon mantra), omit them here.

Temple Office (納経所)

After visiting both halls, receive your temple stamp (available from 8am to 5pm, to 4.30pm at Temple 12: Shōsan-ji).

Main Gate (山門)

Exit on the left side, turn to face back towards the temple and bow once.

FROM LEFT: JESSICA KORTEMAN/LONELY PLANET, JESSICA KORTEMAN/LONELY PLANET

Where to Stay

What to Expect

Unlike other well-known pilgrimages, it is not always possible to find accommodation on arrival at temples. As a general rule, book your accommodation at least three to four days in advance. It's not advisable to book accommodation for the entire pilgrimage ahead of time as your plans are likely to change. You should, however, plan further ahead for peak periods: March to April, Golden Week (May), Silver Week (September), and October to November. For camping, see (p250).

Main Options

In larger hubs, there's a range of accommodation options from hostel dorms to chain hotels. On the trail between, expect mostly *minshuku* (small family-run inns) and other simple guesthouses geared towards a pilgrim crowd. The proprietors of these establishments are predominantly older and typically only accept reservations by phone (in Japanese). Dinner and breakfast are usually provided, unless you opt for *sudomari* (素泊まり), a 'stay without meals'. Special dietary requirements often can't be accommodated.

Temple Lodgings

Some temples provide *shukubō* (temple lodgings; pictured below), where you can stay overnight and participate in religious rituals. At the time of research, six of the 88 temples offered *shukubō*: Temple 6: Anraku-ji, Temple 7: Jūraku-ji, Temple 19: Tatsue-ji, Temple 37: Iwamoto-ji, Temple 58: Senyū-ji and Temple 75: Zentsū-ji. Along with two of the *Bekkaku* (additional 20) temples: Bekkaku 7: Shusseki-ji (no meals) and Bekkaku 18: Kaigan-ji. Circumstances change regularly around *shukubō;* be sure to book ahead.

HOW MUCH FOR...

Guesthouse with/no meals from ¥7000/4000

Shukubō with/ no meals from ¥8000/5000

City hotel from ¥10,000

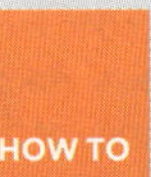

HOW TO · **MAKE BOOKINGS**

Regular booking sites aside, **Henro House** (*henrohouse.jp*) and **Henro Yado** (*henroyado.com*) are useful websites connecting foreign pilgrims with accommodation. Facebook group 'Shikoku 88 Ohenro Pilgrimage' also maintains a list of budget accommodation. For phone-only reservations, ask your current lodging to assist you.

TIPWAM/SHUTTERSTOCK

GOOD TO KNOW

Fire/Ambulance 119

Police 110

Non-emergency Police Consultation (English & several other foreign languages) 03-3503-8484

Japan Visitor Hotline (24/7) English, Chinese, Korean 050-3816-2787

Access, Attitudes & Safety

Weather & Disaster Management

An important safety consideration for all pilgrims is extreme weather and natural events. Always check forecasts and heed local warnings and safety advice. Seek shelter during typhoons, and steer clear of the coast and head to higher ground in the case of a tsunami warning. Mountain trails can become incredibly dangerous during heavy rains and in the days following. There are often a variety of ways to get between temples, so a road route may be available even if a mountain trail isn't. Stay updated by downloading the **NERV Disaster Prevention app** (nerv. app/en), which provides real-time disaster and emergency weather alerts.

Wheelchair Accessibility

Many temples have steps, gravel and other uneven surfaces that make them largely inaccessible to pilgrims using wheelchairs, other mobility aids and strollers. That said, accessibility varies across temples and some have ramps to the side or back that can be accessed upon request. Sporadically, there are more deliberate accessibility features. For instance, Temple 31: Chikurin-ji has a manual 4WD wheelchair for on-site use and Temple 75: Zentsū-ji's temple lodgings have two wheelchair-accessible rooms. A self-guided Kōchi itinerary for wheelchair users with sights both on and near the pilgrim trail is found on **Accessible Japan** (accessible-japan.com/an-accessible-tour-of-kochi).

Theft

Although not very common, incidences of theft on the pilgrimage are increasing. Pilgrims carrying scrolls, in particular, have become targets for opportunistic thieves, especially towards the end of the pilgrimage when most temple stamps have already been obtained; a completed scroll is worth more than ¥60,000 in temple stamps alone. It's common for pilgrims to put their pack down at temples to complete offerings. Be mindful of where you leave your belongings and ensure valuables are packed away or, better yet, on you. Guesthouses often don't have locks on room doors.

Solo Travel & Women

The vast majority of pilgrims embark on the Shikoku pilgrimage as a solo venture and fortunately most don't encounter issues related to personal safety. There have, however, been isolated reports of physical assault and sexual misconduct towards women along the pilgrimage route. Female pilgrims are advised to remain vigilant about their surroundings, inform someone of their whereabouts each day, and stay in formal, paid lodgings. Some carry personal safety beacons and whistles. It's often possible to find other women to walk with for parts of the journey. Connect with fellow female pilgrims in the 'Shikoku 88 Pilgrimage Women's Group' on Facebook.

Responsible Travel

Climate Change & Travel

While it's impossible not to leave any carbon footprint when we travel, there are plenty of ways we can reduce our impact. Consider the number of flights you take and use public transport when possible. Fortunately, the Shikoku pilgrimage's walking-pilgrim culture is as ecofriendly as movement gets. Others cycle or take buses or trains, or even skateboard. If driving, opt for a compact, more fuel-efficient vehicle – you'll be grateful for the small size on narrow mountain roads too!

The **UN Carbon Offset Calculator** shows how flying impacts a household's emissions:

The **ICAO's carbon emissions calculator** allows visitors to analyse the CO_2 generated by point-to-point journeys:

Mind Your Rubbish

Japan has very few public means for disposing of rubbish. It's also notorious for excessive packaging. Eating in when possible is a good way to minimise unnecessary waste. Walking pilgrims will encounter sections where convenience stores and vending machines are the only option. Both will typically have bins for customer use.

AMEHIME/SHUTTERSTOCK

Henro's *kongō-zue*, hat and backpack

Respect Your Hosts

Pilgrims are supported along lengthy and remote stretches of trail between major hubs by the good graces of residents willing to provide essential services. This includes opening their homes as guesthouses and providing meals. Many of these lodgings are reservable by phone only and work on the trust that guests will show up as agreed. In some locations, there are only a handful of beds available across two or three inns. To keep these establishments in business (and to encourage the possibility of more opening), be mindful of the time, energy and income of innkeepers, and communicate any changes to your plans as early as possible.

Camping

Wild camping is not permitted along the pilgrimage. Pilgrims pitching tents outside official campgrounds or sleeping rough is one of the largest social and legally contentious issues on the Shikoku pilgrimage. It's important to observe the legal rights of landowners, as well as community wishes, from a safety and cultural perspective. If intent on camping, you may use official campgrounds – they are inexpensive or donation-based. Most pilgrims, however, find there are too few to make carrying camping supplies worthwhile. Whatever you decide, plan to pay for accommodation on every night of your pilgrimage.

CRAIG MCLACHLAN/LONELY PLANET

Henro in the *hondō*, Temple 11: Fujii-dera (p56)

HOW TO

HAVE A POSITIVE IMPACT ON THE SHIKOKU PILGRIMAGE

Forget wild camping Don't be swayed by online content encouraging wild camping. It is not welcomed along the pilgrimage trail. Only use pilgrim huts, known as *henro-goya (henrogoya.com/koya.html),* for their intended purpose of daytime rest use, not overnight stays.

Stay and pay local Frequenting paid accommodation allows the economic benefits of pilgrimage tourism to filter to local communities who make the modern-day pilgrimage possible. Without their willingness to continue to support pilgrims, there is no pilgrim economy. Less formal temple and private stays known as *tsuya-dō* and *zenkon-yado* are at a small number of locations, but should only be used as a last resort and with a donation.

Be a good representative How foreign pilgrims behave on the trail has a direct impact on local residents' perceptions of international tourism. Never no-show on your accommodation, call ahead if running late and always conduct yourself in a respectful manner.

Visit the salon Around 10km before Temple 88: Ōkubo-ji, sign the guestbook at the Henro Museum (also known as the Henro Salon). This data provides valuable feedback about pilgrim numbers and, in turn, how best to sustain the pilgrimage and its surrounding economy.

Language

There are lots of great language apps to help decipher Japanese (日本語; *nihon-go*) that will get the point across most of the time. You can minimise misunderstanding from sometimes clunky translations by using short, simple sentences. Learning a few basic phrases, however, is a great way to deepen connections.

HANDY WORDS TO KNOW

Hello *kon-ni-chi-wa*

Yes *hai* / **No** *ii-e*

Please (when requesting) *o-ne-gai-shi-masu*

Thank you *a-ri-ga-tō*

Excuse me *su-mi-ma-sen*

5 Phrases to Know Before You Go

Do you speak English? *eigo ga ha-na-se-masu ka*

May I use the toilet? *toi-re o ka-ri-te mo ii desu ka*

A temple stamp, please *nō-kyō o o-ne-gai-shi-masu*

Could you call a (guesthouse) for me? *(min-shu-ku) ni ren-ra-ku shi-te ku-re-ma-sen ka*

I don't understand *wa-ka-ri-ma-sen*

Getting to know people

What's your name? *o-na-ma-e wa nan desu ka*

My name is... *wa-ta-shi no na-ma-e wa...desu*

Nice to meet you *yo-ro-shi-ku o-ne-gai-shi-masu*

Sleeping

I'd like to make a reservation *yo-yaku shi-tai-n desu ga*

I would like breakfast/dinner *chō-sho-ku/yū-sho-ku o-ne-gai-shi-masu*

Without meals *su-do-ma-ri desu*

How much is it? *i-ku-ra desu ka*

I'm going to be late *o-so-ku na-ri-masu*

I am at...now *ima...ni imasu*

I will arrive at (six) o'clock *(roku) ji ni tsu-ki-masu*

Directions & Navigation

Where is...? *...wa doko desu ka*

How far is it to...? *...ma-de do-no ku-rai ka-ka-ri-masu ka*

Left *hi-da-ri*

Right *mi-gi*

What's the address? *jū-sho wa nan desu ka*

Can you show me (on the map)? *(chi-zu de) o-shi-e-te ku-re-ma-sen ka*

Could you please write it down? *kai-te ku-re-ma-sen ka*

Eating & Drinking

'I will receive' (said before a meal) *i-ta-da-ki-masu*

Thank you for the meal (said after completion) *go-chi-sō-sa-ma*

What would you recommend? *o-su-su-me wa nan desu ka?*

Delicious! *oi-shii*

I'm vegetarian *wa-ta-shi wa be-ji-ta-ri-an desu*

I'm allergic to... *wa-ta-shi wa...a-re-ru-gii desu*

Emergencies & Illness

Help! *tasu-ke-te*

I'm ill *wa-ta-shi wa byō-ki desu*

I'm injured *ke-ga o shi-te i-masu*

I'm lost *mi-chi ni ma-yoi ma-shi-ta*

Please call an ambulance *kyū-kyū-sha o yon-de ku-da-sai*

Please call the police *kei-sa-tsu o yonde ku-da-sai*

Please contact... *...ni ren-ra-ku shi-te ku-da-sai*

Index

Jizō-ji 52
Jōdo-ji 164-5
Jōraku-ji 68
Jōruri-ji 144-5
Jōshinan 66
Jūraku-ji 52

K

kabuki theatres 142, 225
Kagawa Prefecture 11, 22, 188-235
kakejiku 61, 244
Kakurin-ji 73
Kamikatsu 72
Kamojima 56
kana writing system 25
Kangiten 165
Kanjizai-ji 136
Kannon 68
Kannon-ji (Temple 16) 68
Kannon-ji (Temple 69) 199
Kan'onji 199
Kasuga-jinja 180-1
katsuo-tataki 21
Katsurahama 97, 107, 110-11
Katsuura 73
Kichijō-ji 185
Kiragawa 89-90
Kirihata-ji 55
Kiyotaki-ji 113
Kōbō Daishi 12, 15, 19, 24-6, 92-3
    ascetic practices 24-5, 57, 75
    birthplace 200-2
    burial site 16, 235
    carvings 66, 68, 88, 91, 108
    childhood home 203-4
    China sojourn 113
    Emon Saburō 162-3
    enlightenment 17, 86-7, 89
    folklore 50, 57, 73, 139, 145, 178, 179-80, 184, 187, 202, 229
    hot springs, springs & wells 16, 52, 68-9, 113, 163-4, 179, 203
    mother 70
Kōchi city 96-101, **97**
    accommodation 98
    festivals 101
    food 21, 98
    gardens 100

Journey legs 000
Map pages **000**

itineraries 97
markets 101
museums 100, 101
transport 96
Kōchi Prefecture 9-10, 21-2, 79-127
Kokubu-gawa 106
konbini 67
Kongōchō-ji 88-9
Kongōfuku-ji 122-3, 126
kongō-zue 19, 40, 60, 139, 233, 249
Kōnomine-ji 90-1
Konpira-san 205
Konsen-ji 50-1
Konzō-ji 204
Kōon-ji 184-5
Kotohira 205
Kotohira-gū 205
Kōyama-ji 202-3
Kōya-san 235
Kūkai, *see* Kōbō Daishi
Kuma Ski Land 145
Kumadani-ji 52-4
Kuma-kōgen 141
Kuwano-gawa 76

L

Lady Shizuka 231
language 238, 251
legal matters 238
Longevity Cedar 50
luck 76-7
luggage storage 245

M

Maegami-ji 185-6
Maeyama Ohenro Koryū Salon 232
mairi 12, 246
Makino Botanical Garden 100
Mandara-ji 200-2
Manjirō, John 125
Mantora Cave 166
maps 243
Matsuyama 146-51, **147**
    accommodation 148, 151
    castles 150
    cycling 151
    food 21, 148
    foot baths & onsen 149, 151
    gardens 150
    itineraries 147
    temples 165-9

transport 146
    walking paths 150
Median Tectonic Line 186
medical services 248
Meiji Restoration 9, 26, 93, 106-7, 110, 112, 137, 140
    shinbutsu-bunri 14, 15, 26, 93, 199
Meiseki-ji 139
Mihara 127
Mikurodō Cave 86-7
Mitsubishi 91
mobile phones 238
Monet, Claude 214
money 239
Monju-in 145, 162-3
Motochika, Chōsokabe 14, 111, 112, 185
    temple burning 54-5, 66-7, 71, 169, 180, 198, 199, 230
motorcycle travel 28, 141
Motoyama-ji 199
mountain climbing 182-3, 195
Mugi 84
Mure 226
Muroto Unesco Global Geopark Center 86
Muroto-misaki 17, 27, 86-7
    temples 85, 88-9

N

Nagao-ji 230-1
Nagare, Masayuki 75-6
Nagoro village 195
Naka-gawa valley 73
name slips 43, 165, 244
Nankōbō 176
Naoshima 215, 223
Naruto Whirlpools 38
National Historic Sites 106, 220
National Places of Scenic Beauty 68, 108
national temples
    Temple 15: Awa Kokubun-ji 68
    Temple 29: Tosa Kokubun-ji 106
    Temple 59: Iyo Kokubun-ji 179-80
    Temple 80: Sanuki Kokubun-ji 220
neck sashes 40
Negoro-ji 221-3
ningyō jōruri 39
niō 154
niōmon 154
nōkyō 85, 152, 239, 242, 244
nōkyō-chō 48, 93, 152, 239, 244

Journey legs 000
Map pages **000**

THIS BOOK

Destination Editor
Selena Hoy

Production Editor
Lauren O'Connell

Assisting Editor
Anne Mulvaney

Image Researcher
Virginia Moreno

Cartographer
Daniela Machová

Cover Illustration
Matt Saunders

Map Illustration
James Gulliver Hancock

Product Development
Anne Mason, James Smart,
Marc Backwell, Katerina Pavkova

Series Development Leadership
Darren O'Connell, Piers Pickard, Chris Zeiher

Thanks
Sofie Foldager Andersen, Jessica Boland,
Melanie Dankel, Kellie Langdon

All rights reserved. No part of this publication may be copied, stored in a retrieval system, or transmitted in any form by any means, electronic, mechanical, recording or otherwise, except brief extracts for the purpose of review, and no part of this publication may be sold or hired, without the written permission of the publisher. Lonely Planet and the Lonely Planet logo are trademarks of Lonely Planet and are registered in the US Patent and Trademark Office and in other countries. Lonely Planet does not allow its name or logo to be appropriated by commercial establishments, such as retailers, restaurants or hotels. Please let us know of any misuses: lonelyplanet.com/legal/intellectual-property.

Mapping data sources:
©Lonely Planet, ©OpenStreetMap, ©Natural Earth, ©GEBCO, ©Esri, ©NASA Earth Observatory, ©USGS-ASTER and the GIS User Community